Anonymous

How we Cook in Los Angeles

A Practical Handbook

Anonymous

How we Cook in Los Angeles
A Practical Handbook

ISBN/EAN: 9783744670647

Printed in Europe, USA, Canada, Australia, Japan

Cover: Foto ©Andreas Hilbeck / pixelio.de

More available books at **www.hansebooks.com**

HOW WE COOK

IN

LOS ANGELES

A Practical Cook-Book Containing Six Hundred or
More Recipes Selected and Tested by
over Two Hundred Well
known Hostesses

Including a French, German and Spanish Department

With MENUS,

Suggestions for Artistic Table Decorations,
and Souvenirs

BY THE

Ladies' Social Circle, Simpson M. E. Church

LOS ANGELES, CAL.

"Some ha'e meat that canna' eat,
And some wad eat that want it,
But we ha'e meat and we can eat,
And sae the Lord be thankit."

LOS ANGELES, CAL
COMMERCIAL PRINTING HOUSE
mdcccxciv.

Good cooks always use the best
materials in preparing food.
It is of still greater importance
that your medicines should consist
of the purest drugs.

We devote ourselves mainly to the prescription trade, and in this department are used
only chemicals and parmaceutical preparations
from the best manufacturers, both foreign and
American.   It is with confidence that I invite
the public to have their prescriptions prepared
at my store.   Purity and accuracy is my motto.

Yours very respectfully, '

ADOLF EKSTEIN,

BRADBURY BLOCK   Prescription Druggist

Watches. Diamonds. Sterling Silver
Wares, Cut Glass. Silver Plated
Goods. Leather Goods
Silver Mounted. and
Silver Novelties
of all kinds

Los Angeles Angel Spoon

Sold only by Montgomery Bros

The
Largest
... Stock,
the Finest Goods.
the very lowest Prices

Montgomery Bros.

Jewelers and Silversmiths

120 and 122 N. Spring St.,   LOS ANGELES, CAL.

PREFACE

THE PUBLISHERS of this book, firmly believing that it is no more expensive to furnish a table with food which is well and appetizingly prepared, than it is to furnish it with food which is poorly prepared, have earnestly endeavored to provide a cook-book so superior that if the general directions and recipes are faithfully followed, failures with the consequent discomforts may be avoided. To accomplish this, scores of ladies have been communicated with, and asked to furnish two, three or more of what they considered their choicest recipes. Thus have the recipes for the various departments been secured with the names of the donors attached.

A reference to the list of contributors we feel is a guarantee of the worth and popularity of this book. We have presented American, Spanish, German and French departments — a thing unusual.

Great care has been taken to give concise general directions for each chapter ; indeed, to make this book so valuable that no lady, whether rich or poor, can afford to be without it.

Mrs. R. M. WIDNEY   Mrs. CARRIE SCHUTZE
" W. J. BROWN   " W. B. ABERNETHY
" W. G. WHORTON   " E. R. SMITH
" W. F. MARSHALL   " J. E. MURRAY

Committee on Publication

...... LIST OF CONTRIBUTORS ......

Mrs W B Abernethy
" A S Allen
" W H Anderson
" G L Arnold
" H C Austin
" A S Averill
" J J Ayers
" A S Baldwin
" Anna Bancroft
" Hancock Banning
" W H Barnard
Miss Martha Bashor
Mrs A S Baxter
" Mary Bear
" John Beckwith
" S E Bennett
" J W Bessey, Orange, Calif
Miss Bertha Bessey, Orange, Calif
Mrs Vida A Bixby, Orange, Calif
" Jotham Bixby, Long Beach
" Anna Bixby
" C W Blaisdell
" M M Bovard
" L A Bradish
" T W Brotherton
" F W B
" W J Brown
" Charles Capen
" C C Carpenter
" T J Carran
" W T Carter
" S B Caswell
" Burdette Chandler
" Emeline Childs
Miss Ruth Childs
Mrs J S Chapman
Dr Chase
Mrs Cheever
" E W Clark
Miss Delia Clemons
Mrs G I Cochran
" C W Congdon
" J F Conroy
" C C Converse, Boston
" Homer Cooke, Waukegan, Ill
Mr Elwood Cooper, Santa Barbara
Mrs Alice M Cooper
Miss Juliet Corson
Mrs Kenyon Cox, Long Beach
" Alice Curtain
" Jennie Curtin
" E J Curson
" Mrs M J Danison
" D S Dickson, Petaluma

Mrs W M Dickson, Petaluma
Miss Lois Dickson, Petaluma
" Mary Dickson, Petaluma
Mrs Elizabeth Dickey
" A C Doan
" C G Du Bois
" Geo B Dunham
" I R Dunkleberger
" W J Elderkin
" C J Ellis
" J F Ellis
" E P Ewing
" Adolf Ekstein
" J A Fairchild
" S H Fairchild
Miss Farmer, Boston
Mrs Alex Faucett
" Mary E Flanders
" Flanders
" H J Fleishman
Miss Honora Fogarty
Mrs Charles Forman
Miss Eloise Forman
Mrs James Foord
" S C Foy
" Jessie Benton Fremont
Miss E Benton Fremont
" H B Freeman
Mrs G W Garcelon, Riverside, Calif
" M A Gibson
" J A Gilchrist
" J W Gillette
" A J Glassell
" R R Glassell
Mr. L. C. Goodwin
Mrs A C Goodrich
Mr J A Graves
Capt F Edward Gray, Alhambra
Mrs T C Griswold
" C H Haas
" M Hagan
" A M Hall
" Orr Haralson
" A D Hall
" Marian Harland
" Henry T Hazard
" Frank S Hicks
" J W Hendricks
" J A Henderson
" Susie G Hill
" W B Holcomb
" E Hollenbeck
" W J Horner
" F M Hotchkiss

Mrs C H Howland, Centinella
Mr J L Howland, Pomona
Mrs S C Hubbell
" R C Hunt
" Gerard Irvine
Mr H Jevne
Miss Mina Jevne
Mrs Hancock M Johnston
" J M Johnston
" J H Jones
" A C Jones
" J C Joplin, Orange Co., Calif.
Miss Josie Kaiser
Mrs M E Kerr, Orange, Calif.
Miss Ella Kerr, " "
Mrs Flora Kimball, San Diego
Miss Nellie King
Mrs E F C Klokke
" H T Lee
" Geo Lerrigo
" Katherine Duncan Lewis
" W W Lord
" E W Lucas
Mr Charles F Lummis
Mrs C D Major
" W F Marshall
" T Masac
" Mary Mathison
Miss Ida A Maynard
Mrs E Verona May
" T M McCamant
" J W McKinley
" W J McKloskey
" R L McKnight
" C C McLean
Miss M E McLellan
Mrs H McLellan
" Harriet J Meakin, San Diego, Cal
" J J Mellus
" J J Meyler, Bowling Green, Ky
" E B Millar
" Frank A Miller, Riverside
" M G Moore
" Morrell
" M Mudge
" J E Murray
" J H Norton
" G G O'Brien, Riverside, Cal
" Anna Ogier
" Anna O'Melveny
" H G Otis
" Owens
" H Z Osborne
" Elwood Packard, Pomona
" Z L Parmelee

Mrs H L Parlee
Miss K R Paxton
Mrs J H F Peck
" Mrs S J Peck
" W H Pendleton
" C W Pendleton
" W H Perry
" Frank E Phillips
" M Pickering
" F H Pieper
" J E Plater
" H S Powell
" E A Pruess
" I H Preston
" A C Radford
" J C M Rainbow, San Diego
" W J Robinson, New Brunswick
" Augusta Robinson
" S T Rorer
" L J Rose
" Erskine M Ross
" W W Ross
" S S Salisbury
" E H Sanderson
" Carl Schutze
" Fannie H Shoemaker
" George Segar, Riverside, Cal
" C M Severance
" M C Severance
" Ella Sherrard
" Charles Silent
" Edward Silent
" H Sinsabaugh
" J C Slaughter
" Converse Smith, Boston
" Henry Smith
Mrs E R Smith
" H E Smith
" I Smith
" S E Smith, St Johns, N B
" Guy Smith, Tustin, Calif
" S Speedy
" E F Spence
" J S Stanway
" George Steckel
" J M Stewart
" D G Stephens
Miss Kate Stevens
Mrs A C St John
" T D Stimson
" Willard Stimson
" Ezra Stimson
" E P S
"'76"
Mrs Cameron Thom

Mrs C C Thomas
Mr P C Tomson, Philadelphia
Mrs John Truslow
  " A T Tuttle
  " Hugh W Vail
  " I N Van Nuys
  " F M Van Doren
  " Vaughn
  " Carrie G Waddilove
  " Charles Walton
  " Helen Widney Watson
  " Weiside
  " Mary B Welch
  " G Wiley Wells
  " A M Whaley
  " S W Wheeler

Mrs D L Whipple
  " B C Whiting
  " G W White
  " W G Whorton
  " J P Widney
  " W W Widney
  " R J Widney
  " R M Widney
Miss Frances Widney
Mrs John Wigmore
  " Charlotte L Wills
  " M H Williams
Miss Eva E Williams
Mrs Modini-Wood
  " C B Woodhead
  " W H Workman

SPANISH DEPARTMENT

Mrs Vida A Bixby
Señorito Epitosia Bustamente
Mrs A F Coronel
  " J G Downey
  " Don Juan Foster
Marie de la Domingues de Francis

Sister Immanuel
Mrs Walter Moore
A Sepulveda de Mott
Mrs E A Preuss
  " Carrie Schumacher
  " Dolores Sepulveda
M Bandino de Winston

Mrs. Isabel del Valle   Camulos.

GERMAN DEPARTMENT

Mrs W W Holt
  " J Johansen
  " G Kerckhoff
  " W G Kerckhoff
  " A Knoch

Mrs E F C Klokke
  " John G Mossin
  " E A Preuss
  " Rutz
  " Carrie Schumacher

FRENCH DEPARTMENT

Mme V Chevallier
Mrs C C Ducommun

Mrs E A Preuss
  " Carrie Schumacher

RUSSIAN DEPARTMENT

Mrs P A Demens

Mrs E R Smith

THE LADIES' SOCIAL CIRCLE

THE LADIES' SOCIAL CIRCLE of Simpson Tabernacle are responsible for the publication of this book. The proceeds are for the benefit of the church. We are very grateful, and we wish here, publicly, to express our gratitude to the many contributors for their kindness, interest and generosity in furnishing recipes, menus, general directions, suggestions for table decorations, and souvenirs, as well as for all help given in any way, in either department of this book. The book will be for sale by all members of the Social Circle.

OFFICERS AND MEMBERS

President, MRS R M WIDNEY   *2d Vice Pres.*, MRS F H PIEPER
1st V-Pres., MRS ALICE L CURTAIN   *Fin. Sec. and Treas.*, MRS W J BROWN
Recording Secretary, MRS E W LUCAS

Mrs W B Abernethy
" O L Allen
" D B Alexander
" H L Banks
" A S Baxter
" J W Bear
" J N Beecher
" W W Beckett
" L A Bradish
" N J Brown
" W T Carter
" G I Cochran
" J T Conley
" Alice L Curtain
" E J Curson
" E Dickey
" A C Doan
" A M Dunsmore
" S H Fairchild
" A R Frasher
Miss Lulu Gibson
Mrs J A Gilchrist
" C H Haas
" A M Hall
" W J Horner
" W B Holcomb
" R C Hunt
" E J Keihl
" George Lerrigo
" W W Lord
" S W Little
" S J Linn

Mrs E W Lucas
" W F Marshall
" S A Mattison
Miss Kate Mertz
Mrs C C McLean
" T F McCamant
" H G Miller
" J E Murray
" Z L Parmelee
" C B Patterson
" S J Peck
" M Pickering
" F H Pieper
" I H Preston
" A C Badford
" A L Robinson
" M L Sampson
" L C Schutze
" C H Shaffner
" E R Smith
" E Robinson Smith
" H E Smith
" H Y Stanley
Miss Eliza Stoughton
" Olive Storm
Mrs A T Tuttle
" W J Warneke
" M L Webster
" A M Whaley
" W G Wharton
" M H Williams
" W W Widney

Mrs R M Widney

FOOD COMBINATIONS

Miss R. R. Paxton

If only two vegetables are used with lean meat, use one starchy and one green. The object of eating is to repair the body which is constantly throwing off used up material, and during the period of growth to form new tissue.

The nutritive supply must be adapted to the requirements of the system, nitrogen must be replaced by nitrogen, carbon by carbon. We therefore need a mixed diet, which must be varied according to individual peculiarities, age, occupation, climate, etc.   As a general thing, five or six times as much carbonaceous as nitrogenous food is required --the nitrogen forming tissue, the carbon producing heat.

SOUP

Crackers, croutons, breadsticks.

FISH

Potatoes, bread, cucumbers.   Potatoes prepared in various ways.   Garnish fish prettily.

BEEF-ROAST

White and sweet potatoes, corn, peas, asparagus, cauliflower, tomatoes.

BEEF-BOILED

Potatoes, carrots, turnips, parsnips, cauliflower, cabbage, spinach.

VEAL

As for beef.

MUTTON

Potatoes, peas, spinach, asparagus, cauliflower, rice, cold slaw.

LAMB

Same as mutton.

PORK

This in a carbonaceous food, and should be combined with food containing nitrogen, as beans, peas, lentils, cabbage.   With ham, which is very oily, we use eggs (which are highly nitrogenous) apple sauce, horse radish, turnips, tomatoes.

TURKEY

Potatoes, onions, turnips, cold slaw, in fact any vegetable, cranberry sauce, currant jelly.

CHICKEN

Boiled rice, rice croquettes, tomatoes, potatoes, cauliflower, cold slaw.

DUCKS

Potatoes, peas, turnips, onions, parsnips, macaroni.

SMALL BIRDS

These are nice roasted with a strip of bacon pinned around them.   Pin with a sharp wooden tooth pick.

LIVER

Onions, bacon, potatoes.

BRAINS

Peas.

SWEETBREADS

Peas, tomatoes.

VENISON

Potatoes, tomatoes, spinach, rice, currant or wild plum jelly.

OLD TIME HOSPITALITY

Jessie Benton Fremont

Washington was my chief home although we had two others equally ours, for one was my father's house in St. Louis and the other my mother's — and our birthplace in Virginia, a colonial grant to my great grandfather a Scotch officer, whose wife came over reluctantly. (I do not blame her, it is weary work to leave home and old civilization for a new country), but as this is altogether a paper on domestic and social habits, I only refer to her as having stamped her Virginia home with the comfort and decorum and much of the elegance of French housekeeping. For Scotland and France were in close relations through the past century, and to this day we find the good traces in their gardens and housekeeping, and I feel its life-long benefits in health, for there, as well as in St. Louis, which was completely a French town in my early day, we were saved from the over-use of meats, and were used to fowls and vegetables carefully prepared and served as a course. Soups, from the "gumbo" to clear bouillons were the rule in all households. The whole health is influenced by this predominance of lighter food, fruits and vegetables; with breads of all kind and soups, these make not only better health but better tempers and promote temperance in eating by maintaining a calm stomach. This is a fad with me. From both sides, my father as well as my mother, we were trained to nicety and giving as well as receiving pleasure from the family table. The best education in all things comes from unconscious imitation and influence of environment, when later, the reasons are given one is fortified against less refined influences.

We were four little sisters and it was the law to be fresh and tidy, and in the parlor a quarter of an hour before dinner

—in Washington this was at five to meet the daily hours of the Senate.

My father, who was certainly one of the most largely useful and busy men in Government affairs *never* omitted his care for the family.   He was our chief teacher, with masters coming at fixed hours to add their teachings in languages and general studies, for we were homebred.   And my mother, who overlooked her household as only a Southern woman with slaves *had* to do, filled her social position also, fully, while by her example we were trained to "pretty manners."

One invariable inflexible law was maintained, and I kept to it in my young household, and wherever I could have instilled it into young families.   Not only were we to be quite tidy in person but we were to keep, for that hour of family reunion whatever we had seen or known through the day—of things or from books — which would give pleasure to all.   And if any opposite state of mind cropped out, any crossness or temper, or small rudeness, nothing was said ; but the next day that child ate by itself at a side table with its face turned from us : all education my father held should be on the lines we must follow more fully as we grew older.   This "sending to Coventry" of a social offender was what would surely overtake us when we were grown if we made ourselves unwelcome, it was the law of "Doing to others as we would be done by," not preached but acted on.

This I write to show the family atmosphere that made dinners a charming time of social exchange of one's best, and not exclusively a function of necessity, or for empty show.

Washington had always exceptional advantages in people to meet in that way.   From all over the country great lawyers brought cases before the Supreme Court — these met on common ground at my father's, where the ruinous hospitality of (the past) South had full sway.   Many men have told me since, that never had they sat at such real feasts of brilliant minds, and delicate excellence of food as at that table round. Not only lawyers, but the great interests, from the shoes of Lynn to the sugars of Louisiana — the military men of the day fresh from Indian wars—on into the Mexican war, for my father was for twenty-eight years chairman of the Senate Military Committee and understood their needs and was their powerful ally—the many interesting, travelled, diplomats with all of whom there were international interests and with some close personal relations— these made a constantly recurring yet varying set of agreeable guests who might well say they looked forward to their business visits to Washington as bringing them again to that delightful table.

We grew up from babyhood, most of our children were born there too—in that dear home. Then it was burned in 1855. In 1856 the South excommunicated me—to go against my people was hard, but there was no choice possible, and in 1858 my father died. Often I ran down from New York to stay a day or so with him—but my mother was gone and only my father turned the old look of welcome—the younger people looked, and felt me, gone from their ideas, and it was more pain than pleasure, but I kept my children as much as I could with their grandfather. Except for brief stays in California, and longer in Europe, I lived in that uncommon atmosphere for nearly thirty years.

Your request brought up so much of the past I just *had* to tell you why I was from a very early age a practised critic and comprehending person at ceremonious dinners— invited, and not entirely misplaced either as a guest at splendid dinners in New Orleans, and in Washington at the Presidents and the best houses of foreign ministers as well as our own people of high position. From my twelfth year on I was on dinner lists, for I was tall for my age, and spoke French and Spanish so well I was constantly put by some Minister whose English was elementary, and who had no shyness in asking *me* to interpret — nor had my good home training left me any false shyness, for usages, people and all I was familiar with in my own home.

And now I will tell you of some dinners of my young time:

Mr. Van Buren had been our minister to England and liked elegance.   He found the President's house rather shabby, and though he and his three sons made a family of men only, yet men can have nice and pretty ideas as well as women.   Congress was slow in voting new furniture, and the old satins and velvets below had to go on. But the smaller dining-room, and the library and sitting-rooms above were all made fresh and cheerful at the President's expense by English chintzes.   Lots of books, pictures, china things, such as are usual now, gave another effect to these rooms which were not open to the public, and the dreadfully open windy hall below he had protected by a glass screen—later a Tiffany art glass screen divided the long enclosure.   Mr. Van Buren also used his own beautiful table furnishings.   When he was asked if it was true as a certain Senator had said in a speech against him, that he was "an aristocrat wasting the people's money on gold spoons."   "I do own gold tableware", he said—"and the Senator knows it is mine, for he has had the spoons in his mouth, often, at my table."

Smith Van Buren was just eighteen, and his father invited a birthday company of suitable ages—the youngest attachés and young Americans, and the girls were all under sixteen — I was just thirteen.   The President came in for dessert.   The dinner was like all other dinners which never seem to get away from the soup, fish, entrées, filet de boeuf and salad and game—served quickly and quietly in courses, but one innovation was the fresh flowers in place of the great table decoration brought from Paris long before—that venerable long mirror, with its ormolu balustrade and its groups of statuettes upholding baskets of artificial flowers.   Those flowers were still on duty in President Polk's time when I had reached the mature age of twenty-three.   But for us, in our early spring time, the President had ordered tulips and hyacinths, and for the first time I saw them used naturally, in old-time champagne glasses at each plate. The ices too, were moulded and colored to imitate fruits, and there were the unfailing tall pyramids of oranges in quarters, and grapes, all covered and hung with a network of spun sugar. And each girl had a lovely and large bon-bon box from Paris with the finest candies and fruit glacés.

The next year the whole house had been made over fresh; and I was again there at a great dinner, this time in the State dining-room, for I was one of eight bridesmaids, (all under sixteen, as the bride was that age), though the bridegroom who was the Russian minister was over sixty, and the groomsmen matched *his* age : Mr. Buchanan, the English minister, the Belgian and so on. Artificial flowers and marble cupids were good enough for this December and May business, and we nearly fell asleep over the length of the dinner, for our groomsmen took advantage of our youth to be at their ease and talked to each other and dined seriously. Everything was very much as it is now — only more prolonged, but Washington has always had its liberal foreign infusion and is exceptional in having had always a fixed order of society and usages. So it was in advance of other localities in breaking the shell of provincialism.

Both in our Virginia and St. Louis homes, and always in Washington, I was only among the sort of people who had neither wish nor temptations to coarse feeding or any habits of intemperance in food or drink. My father's well known contempt and avoidance of any form of self-indulgence naturally brought him like companionship. I was almost thirty before I ever saw *a gentleman* stupefied by drink. Perhaps I had an exceptional life, but since my earlier days I have seen many people, and I am constantly pleased and cheered to see how right prevails over wrong; and good outnumbers bad, and generally I feel it *is* a fairly good world, and we can each make it the better and more beautiful by doing our very best just around us —which is my moral from our family dinner table.

The Sunday dinner was, always, an especial pleasure to all of us. It had been, in my father's unmarried time, the day when he and his more intimate friends could dine at leisure as they were free from business. But my mother, with her Scotch-Presbyterian training, felt differently. I have heard my father laughingly explain how she "weaned him"—being a womanly as well as a clear-headed woman she made no opposition to old habits, (for my father was nearly forty when he married), but she made the family luncheon on Sundays so attractive, so flattering to all his preferences, that any friend he wished to have he would ask home from church—and so it came that we grew up to it as a special pleasure to have my father at that one o'clock meal—the wholesome hour. Mr. Sumner coming in by chance once, begged to be invited other Sundays, and for seven years he was always when in Washington, expected and nearly always in his favorite place facing the flower-stand—in a broad south window.

STEAMED TURKEY OR CHICKENS

A HAM (SMALL, CURED FOR AT LEAST FOUR YEARS IN THE SMOKE-HOUSE)

BUFFALO TONGUE

A SALAD OF LETTUCE, OR TOMATOES, OR CUCUMBERS

(WITH MAYONNAISE DRESSING)

ROASTED POTATOES.   HOME-MADE BREAD, <u>ALWAYS</u> COLD

ALL PLACED UPON THE TABLE AT ONCE

FOR DESSERT

WINE JELLY   FRESH FRUITS   CAKE

CLARET   PRESERVED GINGER

DRY PINE-APPLE CHEESE

It was always a cold dinner, for my mother felt the servants should have the day of leisure also. She had grown up among slaves who could object to nothing—and though our own servants were free-born, and some had been set free by my parents, yet the idea of claiming equal rights to rest, or religion, did not occur to them — but it did to my mother to give them. For this everything was prepared on Saturday.

But our cook "Aunt Betsey" who lived twenty-three years with us had been not only "a born cook" but "made" by training under a French chèf (and practice under a Virginia housekeeper) and each thing was as completely delicately good, and handsome to see too, as for a fine supper of to-day. Only claret on the table: my father was really temperate in food and almost wholly so in drink — abstemious is a better word, for his tastes were refined. For example, the turkey was never roasted for he thought that "coarse", but steamed, with a stuffing of oysters, and a white sauce of cream and herbs. This was Mr. Sumner's delight, for he greatly enjoyed nice food (as Longfellow's letters show) also the delicate flavor of the buffalo tongues, a luxury not easily had, but sent through the Fur Company to my Father. He had said in a speech on the future Railways of the West that the buffalos were the natural engineers who had found the best passes across the Rocky Mountains. For this Mr. Sumner called them "Engineers' tongues". The only hot thing was the potato, which could be left in the hot ashes of the covered fire — for cooking ranges were unknown at first and then despised by both epicures and cooks. With the natural hunger-hour, the pleasant people, the unusual freedom from work-a-day obligations no wonder the food seems so good, and it was as good and attractive as it was satisfying. It was a favor to be asked—verbally—to our Sunday early dinner. There was always provision made for more people though it was if possible confined to very few. Years later when I had a sea-side home at Nahant, near Longfellow's, Mr. Sumner, who always made his friend long visits there, came regularly in the old intimate way to my house—"I get tired of fish-dinners", he would say, and "you keep house like your mother — I never feel I intrude or disturb any one".

It was my "well-done" as one of that centre of wit, of large ideas, of large hospitality, represented at our home table.

Los Angeles, May 14, 1894.

MRS. ALCOTT'S TABLE

Mrs. C. M. Severance

Through the infectious enthusiasm of a friend I was beguiled into a pledge which I find must now be redeemed, despite its evident lack of fitness to the matter in hand. For of all imaginable rôles, that of catering to the public taste in the way of *menus*, or in recipes for popular dishes, is for me, a most grievous "misfit." But, as a compromise, and perhaps as a novelty, I have been kindly permitted to give as my contribution, what will be a mere outline or hint of my own ideal menu and cooking, as illustrated practically at the table of Mrs. Bronson Alcott, the sturdy and capable mother of our famous Louisa and her sisters.

In later years the family purse was well filled by the results of Louisa's profitable literary work. But when I was first a guest, the luxury of a hired cook was not to be indulged; and the brave housemother put before her visitors the work of her own hands and brain, the latter a factor not to be had for the asking, nor for any given number of dollars per week, from our untrained maidens of our time.

The element of brains and the charming home atmosphere no doubt counted for much in the relish of the food. Certainly to me those meals were "fit to set before a king," so dainty were they in their getting up, so delicate in their flavors, so perfect in kind and color, "so done to a turn," after the best fashion of our grandmothers.

No odor of frying fat, or of crude, pungent vegetables polluted the pure, fresh air of the house. The usual "cuts and joints" being replaced by deliciously-cooked breads, by "crushed wheat" moulded into the appetizing and artistic forms of corn, melons, and other pretty fruits, and smothered in genuine cream; or by pears and apples baked to a luscious tenderness and a rich brown: so that these special dishes came to stand with me, for the veritable plain living which is the poetic accompainment of high thinking, *"the feast of reason"* which begets, or at least does not hinder, the flowing together over it, of noble souls. And those meals gave us not "roasted Lady," but a useful, sweet, gracious hostess, generous of herself as well as of her stores, with no smell of the kitchen upon her garments, nor worry of it on her placid face. For nearly all these dishes were prepared in the early morning hours, and cooled by the Concord breezes for the summer days delight and refreshment. And of such meals the bluff old Abernethy would not have needed to utter his strong statement that "we dig our graves with our teeth;" for by such diet; which discards the unnecessary stimulus of condiments, of high flavors, and harmful, because too tempting a variety at any one meal; a normal appetite is cultivated and satisfied, which keeps instinctively to "the golden mean of not too much."

But for such meals it is evident that no special recipes are needed, beyond the suggestion of the skillful use of the cook's good brains, a scrupulous exactness of measure, and of time, and the use of only the best material. I may add, however, directions for one item of this simple *menu*, and that somewhat modified by later experiment, the "Graham biscuit or roll," now called the whole wheat gem.

Take of this modern meal (which includes all the nutritious elements of the grain, leaving out only the harsh outer husk,) 1 cupful, 1½ cups of fresh milk, or of cold water a trifle more or less, the former making the gem moister within and crisper and browner of crust. Beat the meal and milk together smartly, then pour the mixture into *very hot, iron* gem-pans and put these into a very hot oven. Twenty minutes, or less, will take to give an even nut-brown color, and eaten with fresh butter they will give the full sweetness of the grain and of the well-baked crust. To a natural, healthy appetite no item of the gourmand's feast can be more tempting nor eaten with keener relish.

Saying this I will no doubt find myself justified in the eyes of "the world's people" in my opening statement of being a misfit in a 19th century cook-book, and must appeal from this to the verdict of the better time coming in the 20th century, where I am confident of winning my case.

TABLE DECORATIONS

Mrs. Anna Bancroft

[The following charming letters were kindly contributed by Mrs.
Anna Bancroft, who has spent six months in Chicago, at the World's
Fair as assistant to Mrs. Candace Wheeler, the latter being Director
of the Women's Building. Mrs. Wheeler is President of the Associated
Artists of New York City—indeed was the founder of that society.]

My Dear M.:—I have lately had the pleasure of accept-
ing several very pleasant invitations to breakfasts, luncheons,
etc., and as you said in your letter, that you wanted to do
some entertaining, I thought you might like to know how
they do that sort of thing here.

Last Wednesday, I went to a breakfast which will long
linger in my memory, the decorations being so charming.
It was given by a young couple, both artists, who are famed
for their informal entertainments.   One leaves with the
thought that here, at least, they have rested in an oasis in
the dreary desert of most social functions.   Formality began
and ended with the written invitations.   One felt perfectly
certain when greeted by the host, in white flannels, and the
hostess, in an airy, white, lace-trimmed "confection", that
a good time was coming.   Nothing was formal, nothing stiff.
And, although eighteen people of different tastes and char-
acters, sat down together, each felt the atmosphere of the
house at once; and long before the table was reached, was
in a frame of mind to be delighted with everything, and to
add his or her share to the general entertainment.

The breakfast room was the perfection of brightness.
The shades and hangings had been taken away from the
windows to allow the sun to pour through a lattice-work
of green vines so cleverly woven back and forth that

Nature seemed the handmaiden. Vines were trailed from the sides of the room to the chandelier, hiding the fixtures, and forming a bower over the dainty table; in the center of which was a large bowl filled with white sweet peas, whose delicate fragrance could not interfere with the most fastidious appetite, as a heavier odor might have done. The dainty green of the asparagus vine trailed o'er the blossoms and along the table in every direction. Before each guest were individual flower-holders filled with the same blossoms; the vine running around each plate formed a refreshing nest for the good things to come. The center bowl and holders were of the dainty rainbow ware that reflects the many shades of pinks, purples and blues; and here, together with the sunlight, furnished just enough color to add character to the whole. Almost no silver was used. The linen was embroidered in light and airy designs; everything was simple and refreshing. And the eyes and brains of all, feeling the effect, the conversation partook of the brightness and crispness of the hour.

Well might the hostess sit smiling and unconcerned. If the cook had not been "on time", nor the menu all that it should have been, every one, by this time, was too agreeably impressed to be affected by such trifles.

As I looked at the table, I thought how the scheme might be varied from green and white by using forget-me-nots, pink sweet peas, mignonette, or the pink and white Lady Washington geraniums.

The menu was—well it would take too long to tell of its delights, so I will leave that for another letter.

Yours, A.

MY DEAR M.:—As in your last, you seemed pleased with what I wrote you about the breakfast decorations, and expressed your willingness "to sit at the feet of the scribe," I will tell you something about some lovely luncheons it has lately been my good fortune to attend.

Luncheons are the pride, and alas! often the downfall
of many a hostess. In the hands of some women, they are
dreams of fairy land—everything that is beautiful, artistic,
and satisfactory. While another poor mortal with a wild
desire to outshine her dearest friend, will take the greatest
liberties with the materials on hand. Colors run riot. The
drawn work and embroidery and other art (?) works are
trotted out—the more the merrier. Gossip has its fling; it
always does when things are at sixes and sevens; and one
goes home with the feeling that she has been looking
through a kaleidescope. The brain is weary, the eyes are
tired, and the digestion upset. In spite of the wild craze
for over-decorating, however, the best-dressed tables are
becoming more simple each year, and consequently, more
refined. Fancy work is used in moderation, and flowers
in less profusion. But pardon my preaching, as I have
just come from such a lovely luncheon which I will not
describe; but tell you about two or three I attended lately
which were really soul, or perhaps I might say mind, satisfying.

At the first one, given by a bride in return for some
luncheons given by her school friends, the decorations were
pink azalias. The table was covered with drawn work and
would have looked very much over-trimmed but for the
beautiful color scheme which was so perfect that I was
tempted to forgive the hostess for spoiling her eyesight.
By the way, more handwork is put on the linen, nowadays,
than ever before. An artistic hostess finds she must exer-
cise great judgment in order to have everything embroidered
and befuddled just enough. But to return to my table.
The cloth of very fine linen was bordered with fifteen
inches of drawn work, and lined with delicate pink silk
fringed, and hanging about an inch below the fringe of the
cloth. An oblong runner, almost entirely drawn, beautifully
worked and lined with the same pink, reached to the edge
of the plates.

An oblong cut glass dish filled with azalias, white with

pink edges, and maiden hair fern graced the center. At every plate was placed a little white spoon made of twisted tissue paper with a bunch of tiny pink blossoms tied on the handle with white ribbon. These served a double purpose; the salted almonds being in the bowl of the spoon and the name of each guest in gilt lettering on the handle; as dainty a name card as one would wish to see. The sherbet glasses were hidden in beautiful tissue paper tulips, white with deep edges and dashes of pink color. A small lace doyley lined with pink set off these pretty flowers. Larger doilies with the same lining were under the finger bowls of cut glass; a single azalia and spray of maiden hair fern floating on the water. Potted azalias and ferns were in effective positions about the room. The china service was in white and gold.

Last week, Mrs. S. gave a luncheon to her sister. She, Mrs. S., is a beautiful brunette who goes in for style (with a capital S) and stunning effects that startle rather than soothe. The decorations of the room were in yellow and black. The runner and napkins were embroidered in deep yellow ribbons, bowknots and ends. In the center, a low, flat dish was filled with yellow and black pansies (pulled up by the roots instead of picked) giving the impression of a bed of growing flowers which was made more real by the bunches being raised in the center of the bed. From this glowing wealth of colors, rose a brass standard lamp, the base, and part of the standard completely hidden by the pansies. The shade, which was immense, almost a canopy for the table, was made of light yellow silk with a very full and deep flounce. Perched all over the top of this were stuff-ed black-birds in every conceivable position, and looking as if a flock had settled there for the afternoon. A few birds with out-stretched wings hovered over the table and about the room. These were suspended from the ceiling by invisible wires. Bunches of yellow pansies alternated with black ones at the plates. Great dishes of the pansies were placed on sideboard and dresser; and a round table in the

bay window was simply a bed of yellow and black flowers.
On the name cards, which were painted in water colors,
were pretty girls, who on some were in yellow tulle, and
on others, in black tulle; those in yellow being placed with
the yellow pansies, and those in black with the black
flowers.

Mrs. G. gave a dainty forget-me-not lunch to the M's
who were just starting for Europe. This was a great
contrast to the yellow and black affair of Mrs. S. The
linen was all embroidered in forget-me-nots and white
ribbon. A pot of tall maiden hair fern spread its feathery
sprays high and far over the table. Banked so as to
completely hide the pot, and reaching almost to the plates
was a garden of the forget-me-nots apparently growing in
their own foliage. At each cover was a bunch of the same
flowers; and a little pin tray in the center of which was
painted a wreath of forget-me-nots, the name of the guest,
and the date of the luncheon. They were souvenirs as well
as name cards and were too pretty to be lost on the way
home. The ices were served in paper ice-cups twined
with sprays of the same dainty blue flowers; and a spray
was also dropped into each finger bowl. Four silver
standard lamps were placed about the room; the shades
of white silk completely covered with artificial forget-me-
nots. As a background to the whole, potted plants were
placed in all the corners and around the room. The china
service at this lunch was delicate blue and silver.

But this letter is unconscionable long so I must close.

Yours ever, A.

- - - - -

My Dear M.:—What of dinners? Don't I go to any or
don't they give dinners now? Yes to . both questions,
although I think luncheons predominate. There is very
little difference between the luncheon and dinner decorations. There is so much attempted for the luncheon that
little new is left for the heavier meal, and people are

satisfied to decorate in much the same manner. At one or two places, they have used the bare table; but I think, and have good authority for thinking, that that is only suitable for informal luncheons, late teas, and theatre suppers; or when the repast is Bohemian in its nature. At a dinner where many courses are served and where silver, glass, and china are used in abundance, the bare boards are cold and do not show off the elegance and daintiness of the necessary decorations. .Crumbs, bits of fat, etc., that are always dropped upon a table do not brush easily from the wood but leave greasy little roads running from corner to corner, that are anything but appetizing. This is not so at an informal lunch or supper, as the crumbs are allowed to remain unmolested during the meal. There is a freshness and a cleanliness to a white-dressed table that is very appetizing, and the flowers with other decorations show to the very best advantage.

At a dinner I attended lately, the decorations were quite unique; being made of the new crepè paper. In the center of the table was a large, round, flat dish of maiden hair fern; with lavender and deep purple orchids of the butterfly variety made of the paper. The tall central lamp of brass had an immense square shade of the white crepe paper with deep purple fringe tinted in water color. A scroll work in purple was painted above this edge. Large bows of the paper wired, and pasted in two opposite corners gave a light and butterfly effect. Fifteen large orchids, each four inches across, made of paper and beautifully painted to represent the natural flowers were scattered over the entire top and side. A big bow and a bunch of the orchids were tied about half way up the standard of the lamp. The table was round and seated twelve. At regular distances from the center, and from each other, were tall candle sticks covered with white paper. The candles were white, and had quite good sized shades all bordered with the same purple-tinted edges and trimmed with small orchids. As the shades were furnished with mica chimneys and spreaders, there was no blaze to flame up and startle all, just when the guest of honor had reached the point of his story. At the covers of the ladies were beautiful white baskets made of twisted paper, tinted and trimmed to match the shades, and each filled with a pound of delicious candy. The name of each lady was painted in gold on a white ribbon tied to the handle. Alternating with these beautiful souvenirs were penwipers for the gentlemen. Two cunning little brownies of opposite sexes, one dressed in white, the other in deep purple, stood on a mat of crocheted paper and held in their tiny hands the name cards of the gentlemen who were to carry them home. The ice-cups were white, buried in a wreath of orchids. Nothing daintier or less expensive could be devised for an effective decoration.

At another dinner, the table was trimmed with white pond lilies; the leaves and long, rubber-like stems adding much to the grace and elegance of arrangement. From the chandelier hung an immense bunch of the white blossoms and leaves which had been pulled from the bottom of the lake instead of being picked. The long stems hung quite to, in fact touched, a round mirror which formed a good sized lake in the middle of the large round table. Around the edge and trailing over the glass were the blooms and leaves. At intervals, the bunches of flowers were raised like a mound to hide a small fairy lamp with a pink shade that shed a faint glow over the glass and flowers. As the entire lighting was shaded in faint pink the same effect was produced all over the room. At each cover was a fairy lamp completely hidden with a bunch of flowers and leaves. A card painted and cut out to represent the real flower bore the name and served as a souvenir. The patties were served in pond lilies made of paper, and the large natural leaves were pinned together with little sharp twigs to make pretty cups for the ices. The whole effect was charming.

But for the present, adieu, A.

MENUS AND DECORATIONS .

MENU

Raspberries on small branches

Lobster a la Newberg	Toasted Crackers
Sweetbreads in Scollop Shells	Biscuit
Broiled Spring Chicken	Saratoga Chips
Cucumbers (served in hollows of ice)	French Dressing
Orange Sherbet in Orange Baskets	Cake, etc.

BREAKFAST — (Mrs. Hugh W. Vail)

MENU

Sliced Figs with Cream

Germea

Baked Eggs   Parisienne Potatoes

Corn Cakes   Whole Wheat Gems

Coffee with Whipped Cream

A ROSE BREAKFAST — (Mrs. Ezra Stimson)

DECORATION

Cloth, white; service, dainty as possible; center piece, candelabra with pink shades; careless arrangement of pink roses at either end of the table. At each cover, a half open bud of same rose; the name card, a single satin rose petal. On side table, banquet lamp with pink shade; and scattered about the room, baskets or bowls of roses. The strawberry ice served in real roses, the centers removed and filled. The fragrance and beauty of a "rose screen" is its own reward. Cover a screen with coarse green or pink net; and by use of florists' wire, cover it with roses; unfold and place across one corner of the room.

MENU

Strawberries

Timbale of Shrimps   Cream Sauce

Rolls

Fried Spring Chicken   Peas

Potato Balls Parsley

Tomatoes

(Stuffed with chopped cucumbers, served on cress and capped with Mayonnaise)

Cheese Straws

Strawberry Ice   Lady-fingers

Coffee

BREAKFAST — (Miss K. R. Paxton)

MENU

Fruit   Oranges

Germea   Cream

Chops French Rolls

Coffee

BREAKFAST — (Miss K. R. Paxton)

MENU

Cherries

Oatmeal   Cream

Tomato Omelet

Toast Coffee

JULY BREAKFAST — (Mrs. Ezra Stimson)

MENU

Omelet with Herbs
Finger Rolls   Fried Frogs Legs
Olives
Veal Cutlets   Tomato   Sauce
Potato Croquettes
Coffee Cakes   Coffee
Strawberries and Cream

OCTOBER BREAKFAST — (Mrs. Ezra Stimson)

MENU

Deviled Oysters in Scollop Shells
Broiled Chicken   French Peas
Vienna Rolls   Coffee
Mayonnaise of Tomatoes
Cheese Fingers   Wafers
Ices   Cakes
Fruits

BREAKFAST — (Miss K. R. Paxton)

MENU

Bananas
Wheatena   Cream
Broiled Steak   Creamed Potatoes
Cornmeal Gems
Coffee

A MAGENTA LUNCHEON — (Mrs. G. Wiley Wells)

DECORATIONS

This may not be æsthetic, but it is *"fin de siecle"*. As many flowers take on this glowing shade called "nature's red", it will not be difficult to decorate the table with brilliant magenta which is most effective with cut glass, and the satin damask of the cloth.

At each plate, place quite a broad bow of magenta ribbon with a spray of pretty white flowers tied in it. On one loop, painted in silver, the name of the guest and date of luncheon. Have white candles with little magenta shades. Fill bonbon dishes with magenta and white candies. Place around the edge of a cut glass olive dish a circle of magenta pickled beets. Decorate pickle dishes in the same fashion. Another dish with small magenta radishes will add another touch of color.

MENU

Raspberries or Strawberries

Bouillon

Deviled Crabs in Shells

(In serving, surround with Magenta petals)

Turkey   Mashed Potatoes

(Use the white meat only—garnish with pickled beets)

Sweetbread Patties   Green Peas

Raspberry Ice

Celery Salad   Cheese Cakes

(Garnish the salad with slices of egg — the whites dyed magenta with beet vinegar)

Charlotte Russe

(Served in small white paper cases tied with narrow magenta ribbon the top decorated with a few candied cherries)

Ices

A brick of Vanilla and Raspberry Ice

Fruit   Bonbons

Coffee

A JANUARY LUNCHEON — (Mrs. I. N. Van Nuys)

MENU

Raw Oysters
Bouillon
Deviled Crab   Olives
Broiled Quail   Spiced Currants
Potatoes Parisienne   Green Peas
Celery Salad Garnished with Shrimps   Cheese Straws
Individual Charlotte Russes
Fruit Salad   Angel Food
Confectionery
Black Coffee

⁒

LUNCHEON — (Mrs. Hugh W. Vail)

MENU

Shaddocks
Broiled Shad with Tartan Sauce
Saratoga Potatoes
Chicken Patties   Olives in Cracked Ice
Lamb Chops   Chestnut Sauce   Green Peas
Chocolate with Whipped Cream
Cheese Straws   Orange Salad
Lemon Jelly with Almonds
Bonbons ·   Salted Almonds

LUNCHEON — (Miss K. R. Paxton)

MENU

Thinly-Sliced Cold Meats
Fried Tomatoes
Bread   Coffee
Lemon Sponge

LUNCHEON — (Mrs. W. W. Ross)
MENU
Sugared Pomegranates
Bouillon
Creamed Oysters on Toast
Veal Cutlets with Mushrooms
Fried Bananas with Sweet Sauce
Apricot Sherbet

Potted Quail   Potatoes   Green Peas
Welsh Rabbit   Stuffed Olives
Sweetbread Patties
Lettuce Salad   Cheese Sticks
Tutti Frutti Cream   Asssorted Cake   Confections
Tea   Coffee

LUNCHEON — (Mrs. Willard H. Stimson)
DECORATIONS

Use plain white damask table cloth; let the embroidery of center piece be also in white. In center of table, place a large rose bowl filled with carnations and ferns. Before each lady, place a long-stemmed bouquet of delicate pink carnations and ferns, tied with pink satin streamers. On each ribbon, fasten the dinner card. Arrange the bouquets so as to form the chief decoration of the table.

MENU
Oysters on the Half Shell
Bouillon   Toasted Crackers
Deviled Crabs   Sauce Tartare
Sweetbread Croquetts   Parker House Rolls
Pine Apple Sherbet
Broiled Squabs   Potato Bouletts
Water-cresses
Tomatoes Stuffed with Celery Mayonnaise
Cheese Straws
Nesselrode Pudding
Coffee

MAY DAY LUNCHEON — (Mrs. M. M. Bovard)

TABLE DECORATIONS

From chandelier over table was suspended a large basket of grasses and brilliant May flowers. Dinner cards of dainty little May baskets with salted almonds.

MENU

Amber Soup	Olives
Turbot a la Creme	
Lamb Chops	Green Peas
Spring Chicken—Maryland Style	
New Potatoes	
Luncheon Muffins	Green Apple Fritters
Lettuce and Tomatoes	Mayonaise Dressing
Strawberry Short Cake	Strawberry Sauce
Candied Rose Leaves	May Baskets
Iced Tea	

LUNCHEON — (Miss. K. R. Paxton)

MENU

Raw Oysters in Ice Form

Bouillon

Shad Roe   Croquettes   Bechamel Sauce

Rolls

Creamed Chicken with Mushrooms

Pine Apple Ice

Mayonnaise of Sweetbreads

Cheese Straws

Cream and Ices in Individual Molds

Meringue   Fancy Cakes

Coffee

LUNCHEON — (Miss K. R. Paxton)

MENU

Beef Stew   Dumplings
Lettuce   French Dressing
Rolls   Tea

LUNCHEON — (Miss K. R. Paxton)

MENU

Baked Halibut   Fish Sauce
Cold Slaw
Hot Biscuit   Chocolate
Baked Apples

A JUNE DINNER — (Mrs. I. N. Van Nuys)

MENU

Pine Apple Sherbet   Consommé Royale
Halibut   Sauce Tartare   Potato Croquette
French Artichokes   Mayonnaise
Boiled Turkey   Oyster Sauce
Peas   Mashed Potatoes   Spiced Peaches
Lettuce Salad   French Dressing
Strawberry Meringue
Individual Ices   Fancy Cakes
Coffee

A SPRING DINNER IN GREEN AND WHITE – (Mrs. Charles Forman)

DECORATIONS

Lay the table with pure white napery; placing in the center a large low bowl of Paris daisies with their own foliage. For the ladies, have corsage bouquets of long-stemmed daisies tied with No. 4 green satin ribbon in loops and flowing ends; across one of which write the name in gold to match the daisy's center. For the men's places, write the name on a plain white card, through one end of which pass the green stem of a white carnation with a bit of feathery green, for a boutonaire.

MENU

Oysters in a block of Ice encircled with Smilax

Salt   Pepper   Lemon   Crackers

Green Asparagus Soup

Baked Barracuda   New Potatoes with Cream Sauce

Sliced Cucumbers

Boiled Calf's Tongue   Spinach and Pickles

Artichokes with Melted Butter

Roast Lamb   Mint Sauce   Green Peas

Lettuce with French Dressing   Cheese Straws

Snow Pudding

Pistache Ice Cream   Lady Cake

Black Coffee

SIGMA CHI GREEK DINNER – (Mrs. M. M. Bovard)

DECORATIONS

The Daneburg Cross of white enamel with gold letters, Σ.Χ., the badge of the fraternity; white carnations, the flower; blue and gold, the colors. The tables were formed in the shape of the cross; around the border of the cloth was marked a Greek border of laurel leaves. The center piece was a Greek cross formed with mirrors imbeded in white carnations and lace ferns.   Suspended from the chandelier, a cross of the new white centaurea margaretta; the beauty of which was twice told in the mirror below.   Dinner cards of white celluloid Daneburg cross, with names and dates painted in blue and gold.   Table talk: Greek quotations given while a tiny bundle of pine fagots were tossed by each guest into an earthen bowl painted in blue and gold, containing burning alchohol and salt.

MENU

Almond Soup   Olives
Salted Almonds
Boiled Salmon   Hollandaise Sauce
Pine Apple Ice
Roast Turkey   Oyster Dressing
Scalloped Asparagus   New Potatoes
French Rolls
Lobster en Mayonnaise
Russian Cream
Moussee   Angel Food Cake
French Nongat
Coffee

DINNER —(Mrs. E. B. Millar)

MENU

Raw Oysters   Consommé
Crabs en Coquille
Fillet of Beef
Green Peas   Duchesse Potatoes
Lemon Sherbet
Salmi of Duck
Lettuce Salad   Cheese Straws
Nesselrode Pudding
Coffee

DINNER —(Mrs. J. E. Plater)

MENU

Oysters—Half Shell
White Soup
Baked Shad White Sauce
Boiled Potatoes
Mushroom Patties
Lemon Ice
Fillet of Beef with Mushrooms
Mashed Potatoes Baked Tomatoes
Asparagus cold Sauce Mayonnaise
Strawberries Ice Cream
Black Coffee

DINNER —(Mrs. C. E. Thom)

MENU

Raw Oysters
Green Turtle Soup
Trout Tartare Sauce
Duchesse Potatoes
Sweetbread Patties
Turkey Stuffed with Chestnuts
Cranberry Jelly Green Peas
Haunch of Venison Currant Jelly
Salad
Lettuce with Paté de Foie Gras
Orange Sherbet Cakes
Black Coffee

DINNER FOR OCTOBER OR NOVEMBER — (Mrs. J. H. F. Peck)

DECORATIONS

In the center of the table, place a large cut glass dish filled with purple and white grapes. Tie a bow of lavender ribbon (of generous width) and place on the grapes; drawing the ends of ribbon to the corners of the table, or up over the chandelier. Take small bunches of grapes, crystallized with sugar; tie with ribbons. and place at each plate.

MENU

Oysters (raw)

Amber Soup

Creamed Sweetbreads browned in Shells

Olives   Salted Almonds

Orange Sherbet

Fried Chicken a la Jersey

Peas   Glazed Sweet Potatoes

Potato Croquettes

Salad   Romain Lettuce   French Dressing

Raspberries in Form

Served with whipped cream and white pound cake

Cheese and Coffee

DINNER — (Miss K. R. Paxton)

MENU

Mock Bisque Soup

Roast Beef   Brown Sauce

Baked Sweet Potatoes   Mashed Potatoes

Onions

Water Cress   French Dressing

Wafers   Cheese

Preserved Ginger

Coffee

DINNER — (Mrs. Hugh W. Vail)

MENU

Oysters in block of Ice

Mushroom Soup

Crab Creole

Saddle of Lamb with Stuffed Potato

Green Peas   Stuffed Peppers

Asparagus

Cucumber Salad

Pickles   Currant Jelly

Fruit Pudding

Black Coffee   Cheese

DINNER — (Miss K. R. Paxton)

MENU

Raw Oysters

Consommé

Salmon   Sauce Hollandaise

Larded Fillet of Beef   Mushroom Sauce

French Peas

Broiled Quail   Jeslimne Potatoes

Lettuce

Cheese   Wafers

Charlotte Russe

Coffee

DINNER —(Miss K. R. Paxton)

MENU

Clear Soup

Roast Chicken   Giblet Sauce

Rice Croquetts   Baked Stuffed Tomatoes

Mashed Potato

Mayonnaise of Celery

Brie   Wafers

Hamburg Cream

Coffee

SALADS

In salad making, the best success is obtainable only by a close observance of three very important rules, viz.:

I. The ingredients composing the salad and dressing must be suitably chosen.

II. They must be introduced into the mixture in a certain specific order.

III. The method of mixing must be suited to the nature of the ingredients.

A dressing should not be the prominent feature of a salad. It should be a dressing *only;* an adjunct to tone down too sharp an acid, or a flavor too pungent; or to render more distinctive the individuality of the fruits, vegetables, etc., composing the salad. This is the true mission of the dressing.

There are four distinct classes of salad dressing:

1. Transparent dressing.   2. French dressing.
3. Cream dressing.   4. Mayonnaise dressing.

TRANSPARENT ORANGE DRESSING

Three oranges (juice only); 4 ounces of sugar; 1 lemon (juice only); 1 egg.

Beat together, using the white and shell of the egg. Heat to boiling point. Simmer five minutes. Strain. If liked, a little of the grated peel of both orange and lemon may be added.

JELLIED TRANSPARENT ORANGE DRESSING

Add to the above mixture before heating a half ounce of gelatine soaked in half a gill of water.

TRANSPARENT TOMATO DRESSING

One pint of tomato, stewed and strained; 1 tablespoon arrowroot mixed in cold water; 1 ounce butter; ½ teaspoon each of sugar and salt; a little pepper.

Boil tomato and arrowroot two minutes. Add butter, salt, pepper, and sugar. Nice either hot or cold with any kind of meat salad.

FRENCH DRESSING

Four teaspoons of vinegar; ½ teaspoon of salt; ⅛ teaspoon of pepper. Mix, and pour over salad, then add Howland's olive oil to taste.

CREAM DRESSING

One pint of boiling cream; 2 ounces of flour; 2 ounces of butter. Stir the flour and butter to a smooth paste, add the boiling cream and cook two minutes. Remove from the saucepan, and add the butter, stirring until cool and perfectly mixed; then season to taste with lemon juice, vinegar, salt, pepper, mustard, capers, minced onion, parsley, chopped pickled cucumbers; any or all of these.

SOUR CREAM DRESSING

One cup of sour cream; ¼ cup of vinegar or lemon juice; season with salt and cayenne pepper. Use on vegetable or fish salads.

HOT CREAM DRESSING

One ounce of flour; 1 ounce of butter; 1 pint sweet cream; salt, and pepper. Cook flour and butter together two minutes; add cream, and season to taste. Use on cauliflower, beets, potatoes, or any vegetable.

MAYONNAISE DRESSING

One teaspoon of mustard; 1 teaspoon of salt; 1½ teaspoons of vinegar; 1 yolk of egg; ½ pint Howland's olive oil.

Use a two quart bowl to allow room for beating. Mix the mustard, salt and vinegar; add the yolk, beat well, add the oil, pouring it in, in a fine, thread-like stream, beating rapidly all the time. Vinegar or lemon juice may be added if required to make it of the proper consistency.

COOKED MAYONNAISE DRESSING

Five yolks of eggs, 5 tablespoons vinegar; 4 ounces of butter; ½ pint sweet cream; salt, pepper and mustard.

Beat in the yolks, cook in boiling vinegar until stiff, being careful to stir clean from the sides of the bowl while cooking. Remove from the fire, add the butter; stirring until cool and smooth. Season to taste, and thin with cream. Oil may be used in place of cream if preferred.

MAYONNAISE SAUCE

Mrs Henderson's Cook Book

Yolk of 1 egg; 2 saltspoons salt; 1 saltspoon mustard powder; oil (Howland's); vinegar; lemon juice; cayenne pepper.

Beat yolk of egg well, in cold bowl, with silver fork; then add salt and mustard worked well together. Mix in last, a little good oil, slowly, a few drops at a time, alternated with a few drops of vinegar. In proportion as the oil is used, the sauce should gain consistency. When it begins to have the appearance of jelly, alternate a few drops of lemon juice with the oil. When the egg has absorbed a gill of oil, finish the sauce by adding a very little pinch of cayenne pepper, and one and a half teaspoons of good vinegar. These proportions will suit most tastes, yet some may prefer more oil and mustard. Be cautious in the use of cayenne.

By beating the egg a minute before adding the oil, there is little danger of the sauce curdling; yet if by adding too much oil at first it should curdle, interrupt the operation immediately. Beat the yolks of one or two eggs on another plate, add the curdled mayonnaise by degrees and finish by adding oil, lemon juice, salt, pepper, and cayenne according to taste.

SALAD DRESSING

Mrs. E. Hollenbeck.

Eight eggs, yolks; 1 cup sugar; ½ cup cream; 1 cup of butter; 1 tablespoon salt; 1 tablespoon mustard; 1 tablespoon black pepper; 1 pinch of cayenne; 1½ pints of vinegar.

Beat the yolks, add cream, sugar, salt, mustard, pepper, and cayenne. Mix thoroughly. Bring the vinegar to the boiling point, add the butter and boil again. Pour this on the other ingredients, and mix well.

This dressing, if bottled when cold, and stored in a cool place, will keep good for weeks.

MAYONNAISE DRESSING

Mrs. H. Z. Osborne.

Yolks of two eggs; 1 tablespoon soft butter; ½ teaspoon dry mustard; 3 tablespoons Howland's olive oil; the juice of one lemon; ½ teaspoon salt; a dash of cayenne pepper and also of sugar.

Free the yolks entirely from the whites of the egg, stir briskly with silver fork one or two minutes, add the softened butter, then the mustard, and the oil, a teaspoonful at a time. Stir constantly for two minutes, and add the sugar and cayenne pepper, and lastly, the lemon juice, and salt. Stir all a minute or two, or until very smooth and well blended.

If you follow directions carefully, you will have a dressing that has not " curdled " and will not curdle, and can easily be made in ten minutes.

MAYONNAISE DRESSING
Mrs. A. J. Glassell.

Three tablespoons of oil; 1 tablespoon salt; ¾ tablespoon mustard; ¾ tablespoon sugar; ½ tablespoon pepper; 2 eggs; 1 teacup vinegar; 1 teacup milk.

Beat together until thick, the oil, salt, sugar, mustard and pepper. Add the eggs well beaten, then the vinegar, little by little, lastly the milk. Place the bowl containing mixture in boiling water, stir it constantly until cooked to a thick cream, (this will require from ten to fifteen minutes). If bottled and kept cool, it will keep two weeks.

Good for lettuce or potato salad.

ENGLISH SALAD DRESSING
Mrs. Anna O'Melveny.

Three eggs; 1 teaspoon salt; 1 teaspoon dry mustard; ½ teaspoon pepper; 6 tablespoons Howland's olive oil; 10 tablespoons vinegar; 4 tablespoons sweet cream.

Rub together until very smooth, the yolks of two hard boiled eggs, and one raw egg. Add the salt, pepper and mustard; and by degrees the oil and vinegar. Beat thoroughly, adding the cream last.

BOILED SALAD DRESSING
Mrs. Emmeline Childs.

One pint of vinegar; and 2 teaspoons salt — heated. One tablespoon butter; 2 tablespoons white sugar; 2 teaspoons of dry mustard; 6 tablespoons cream; and 6 eggs—mixed.

When these are well beaten, pour on the hot vinegar, slowly; carefully beating all the time. Then boil until it becomes thick like boiled custard. Thin with cream, if desired.

SALAD DRESSING
Mrs. J. G. Gilchrist.

Half cup of vinegar; ¼ cup water; ¼ cup sugar; 1 teaspoon mustard; ½ teaspoon salt; 1 egg; a pinch of cayenne pepper; butter the size of an English walnut.

Heat together the vinegar, water, sugar and butter, then add the other ingredients.

PARKER HOUSE SALAD DRESSING
Mrs. J. E. Packard, Pomona.

One level teaspoon dry mustard; 1 egg; ⅓ teaspoon salt; 3 tablespoons Howland's olive oil; 1 tablespoon vinegar; ⅙ teaspoon black pepper.

Mix the mustard and the yolk of the egg smoothly together, then add the oil drop by drop, then the vinegar, then the salt and pepper. Last of all add the white of the egg beaten to a stiff froth, stir this into the mixture and your dressing is complete.

CREAM SALAD DRESSING
Mrs. Anna O'Melveny.

Four eggs; 1 tablespoon melted butter; ½ cup thick cream : 2 tablespoons strong vinegar; pepper, salt.

Rub until smooth the yolks of three hard-boiled eggs. Beat in the yolk of one raw egg. Add butter, salt and pepper. Beat the cream, mix, and last add the vinegar.

LETTUCE SALAD
Mrs. Mary Bean.

Dressing. Half cup vinegar; ½ cup sweet cream; 2 tablespoons sugar; a pinch each of salt and pepper.

Wash the lettuce, dry with a towel : place in salad bowl, and pour the dressing over it.

CELERY SALAD.
Mrs. Parker.

Six heads celery; 1 egg yolk; 1 teaspoon mustard; a little salt and pepper; three tablespoons water; juice of one lemon; 4 ounces Howland's olive oil.

Wash and dry the celery, cut it in pieces in a salad bowl; mix the yolk, mustard, salt, pepper, lemon juice, and two tablespoons of water. Beat all together; pour the olive oil in drop by drop, then add a tablespoon of hot water. Pour over the celery.

GREEN PEPPER SALAD.
Mrs. L. J. Rose.

Bell peppers, tomatoes, onions, salt.

Cut the peppers in halves, remove the seeds; chop the tomatoes very fine; add half the pepper seeds, with a little onion and salt. Mix all together. Fill the peppers and pour Mayonnaise Dressing over them.

DELICIOUS TOMATO SALAD
Mrs. Anna O'Melveny.

Cut a circle from the stem end of large, ripe tomatoes, remove the pulp with a sharp knife, being careful not to break the skin. Chop the pulp with one fresh cucumber (peeled) and a slice of onion. Season with pepper, salt, and a little of Howland's olive oil. Place in the ice box with the skins. Prepare a thick mayonnaise which should be put on ice also. Just before serving, drain off the superfluous liquid, fill the skins with the chopped mixture, placing a large spoonful of mayonnaise on top of each. Set the stuffed tomatoes in the center of a platter, with a border of crisp lettuce leaves. Serve as a course, with delicate crackers and cheese, or cheese straws.

TOMATO SALAD
Mrs. J. J. Mellus.

Use tomatoes the size of an egg. Remove the skins and a little pulp, from the stem end; turn them to drain, and keep them on ice one hour, then fill with mayonnaise. Serve with lettuce and garnish with hard-boiled eggs and green peppers; cut as fine as possible.

The lettuce should be washed, and kept on ice several hours, being careful to shake out all the water.

POTATO SALAD
Mrs. Helen Widney Watson.

One pint of sour cream, (very thick); 1 tablespoon of vinegar, (generous measure); 1 tablespoon of Durkee's salad-dressing, (generous measure); 3 yolks of eggs.

If these proportions do not suit all tastes, the quantity of vinegar and salad dressing can be added to or diminished. The potatoes should be cold but freshly-cooked. Fill a three-pint salad dish within an inch of the top with layers of thinly-sliced potatoes ; each layer to be salted, peppered and strewed with tiny bits of onion, then pour the dressing over it.

POTATO SALAD
Mrs. Alice Curtain.

For the salad : Six large potatoes; 1 coffee cup chopped celery, (using only white stalks.)

For the salad dressing: Three eggs; 1 cup milk; one tablespoon each of sugar; Howland's olive oil; salt; 1 scant tablespoon mustard; 1 cup vinegar.

Boil the potatoes till done, when cold slice thin. Put in the salad bowl a layer of potatoes, then a layer of the celery, then a layer of the dressing, until potatoes and celery are used. Prepare the dressing as follows : Rub the salt, mustard and sugar in a bowl till smooth, work in well the oil and the eggs, beat well, then add the vinegar slowly, and lastly the milk. Set the bowl in a basin of boiling water, and cook until it thickens, stirring constantly.

CUCUMBER SALAD
Mrs. Hugh W. Vail.

Large green cucumber; tomato; celery; parsley; onion; mayonnaise.

Peel and cut the cucumbers in two, lengthwise, remove the seeds, mix with the pulp of the tomato, chopped celery and parsley, (a little onion if preferred,) cover with mayonnaise, and fill the cucumber with the mixture, and serve in a large bowl of cracked ice.

BEET SALAD

Beets boiled and sliced thin, with an equal quantity of sliced potatoes. Served with cream dressing, either hot or cold.

CABBAGE SALAD
Mrs. M. J. Danison.

One half head of cabbage; 4 slices of boiled ham; 1 cooked beet; 2 hard-boiled eggs; 1 tablespoon of dry mustard; ½ cup of sugar; 1 cup of vinegar.

The pieces of ham, fat and all chopped fine ; cabbage and beet chopped separately, and fine ; eggs chopped mediumly fine. Season with salt and pepper to taste. Mix all together, pouring the vinegar on last.

Corned beef may be used instead of ham.

CABBAGE SALAD
Mrs. J. M. Stewart.

One salad bowl cabbage (cut fine); ½ pint rich cream; ¾ pint vinegar; butter size of a walnut; 1 teaspoon sugar; ½ teaspoon salt; ½ teaspoon corn starch; 1 teaspoon grated horseradish, (dry); 2 pinches black pepper; 1 egg; (2 if cabbage is watery.)

Put all ingredients; except cream, cabbage and egg; in a double boiler. Bring to a boil, then stir in slowly the egg—well beaten; then the cream. Pour over the cabbage while hot.

CHEESE SALAD

Sprinkle grated cheese over crisp lettuce, and serve with either French or cooked mayonnaise dressing.

MIXED SALAD
Mrs. J. J. Mellus.

Slice ripe tomatoes, cucumbers, and tiny young onions.

Arrange them in layers in a salad bowl, garnish with young lettuce, and the moment before serving, cover with French dressing. The cucumbers should be peeled and soaked in ice water for two hours before using.

OYSTER MAYONNAISE
Mrs. E. P. Ewing.

Heat medium-sized oysters to the boiling point, in their own liquor. Drain them well, when cold, dress with Mayonnaise, highly seasoned with salt, pepper and mustard, sprinkle finely cut celery on top of the salad.

SALMON SALAD
Mrs. E. P. Ewing.

Salmon; cabbage; cream dressing.

Pick cooked salmon into small pieces, have white crisp cabbage finely shaved; sprinkle a layer of cabbage in the bowl, cover it with bits of salmon; repeat until the desired quantity is obtained; pour over it a cold cream dressing, and garnish by sprinkling on the top some shavings of cabbage.

SHRIMP SALAD
Mrs. S. C. Hubbell.

One can of shrimps; 1 good-sized lemon; 1 cup sour cream —thick; 1 yolk of egg; 3 tablespoons Durkee's salad dressing; celery; cayenne pepper.

Break the shrimps in two or three pieces, squeeze the juice of the lemon over them, and add half the quantity, of celery. For the dressing, add the well-beaten yolk to the cream and Durkee's dressing, using very little cayenne.

SHRIMP SALAD
Mrs. M. S. Mathison.

Soak canned shrimps in ice water several hours, and serve them with boiled mayonnaise dressing.

Dressing.—Three eggs; 1 teaspoon mustard; 2 teaspoons salt; ¼ saltspoon cayenne pepper; 2 tablespoons sugar; 2 tablespoons melted butter; or Howland's olive oil; ½ cup of hot vinegar; cream, lettuce, English walnuts.

Beat the yolks with the mustard, salt, cayenne, sugar, butter and vinegar. Froth the whites and cook all in a double boiler until thick. Thin with cream. Garnish with English walnuts, and lettuce.

SHRIMP AND CUCUMBER SALAD
Mrs. W. G. Whorton.

One can of shrimps; 3 large cucumbers.

Soak the shrimps in ice water one hour. Pare the cucumbers; lay them in ice until very cold and crisp; cut in cubes. Cut the shrimps in two or three pieces; mix with the cucumbers. Serve with mayonnaise or lettuce.

LOBSTER SALAD
Miss Wister.

Select small, heavy lobsters; put them in warm water and boil half an hour. Take from the shells and claws all the edible meat. Cut it in blocks, and cool it thoroughly. Use Mayonnaise dressing, very cold. When ready to serve make a nest of lettuce on the dish; mix about three-fourths of the Mayonnaise with the prepared lobster; place it in the dish; cover with the rest of the dressing : garnish with small tufts of lettuce, and the smaller claws.

COVE OYSTER SALAD
Mrs. M. R. Sinsabaugh.

Two cans of cove oysters: ½ teacup cream; ½ teacup of vinegar; 3 eggs; 1 tablespoon butter (heaping); 1 tablespoon celery seed, or celery, cut fine; 1 teaspoon sugar; 1 teaspoon salt; 1 teaspoon mustard; ¼ teaspoon cayenne; handful of rolled crackers.

Beat the eggs. Add to them the cream, vinegar, butter, sugar, salt, mustard and cayenne. Cook in a steam boiler until it thickens; add the celery. Drain the liquor from the oysters; chop them, add the cracker crumbs; pour the dressing over them when cold.

MAYONNAISE OF SWEETBREADS
Mrs. George Steckel.

One pair of sweetbreads ; 1 teaspoon salt ; 1 pint mayonnaise ; lettuce, onions.

After the sweetbreads are cleaned and parboiled, let them lay in cold water half an hour, then remove the skin and fat;

and cover with boiling water. Salt and simmer gently twenty minutes, then set aside to cool. Wash and dry, tender leaves of lettuce. Rub the bottom of a bowl with onion, and in it make one pint of mayonnaise. Place in the center of the salad dish a thin slice of onion and arrange lettuce leaves around it. Cut the cold sweetbreads in thin slices; mix carefully with mayonnaise, and add to the dish.

This is a delicious salad, and if prepared as directed will have only the faintest suspicion of onion.

CHICKEN SALAD
Mrs. Henderson's Cook Book.

One chicken; white celery stalks; 3 tablespoons vinegar; 1 tablespoon Howland's olive oil; salt, pepper, mustard.

Boil chicken till tender, when cold, separate the meat from the bones. Cut into small bits; do not mince it. Cut some white, tender stalks of celery into three-quarters inch lengths. Mix chicken and celery together; stir into them a mixture in the proportion of three tablespoons of vinegar to one of oil; pepper, salt, mustard to taste. Set this aside for an hour or two. When ready to serve mix the chicken and celery with a mayonnaise dressing, reserving a portion of the mayonnaise to mark the top. Garnish with fresh celery leaves, stick a bunch of these in the center of the salad and from the center to each of the four sides, sprinkle rows of capers.

Chicken salad is often made of lettuce instead of celery. Marinate the chicken alone a moment before serving, add the small, tender, sweet lettuce leaves, then pour mayonnaise dressing over the top. Garnish with the center heads of lettuce, capers, cold chopped red beets, or sliced hard-boiled eggs. Sometimes little slips of anchovy are added for a garnish. When on the table it should all be mixed together.

Many may profit by this recipe for chicken salad, for it is astonishing how few understand making so common a a dish. It is often minced and mixed with hard-boiled eggs for a dressing.

CHICKEN SALAD
Mrs. E. A. Otis.

In mixing chicken salad allow one yolk of an egg to each chicken, and to four chickens one and a half pints of olive oil. Pick the chickens apart with fingers, removing carefully all fat and skin. Then take celery, pick likewise into small pieces and add it to the chicken until there is an equal quantity of each. If celery cannot be obtained, use lettuce prepared in the same manner.

For the dressing one level teaspoon of salt to each yolk of an egg; pepper to taste, one teaspoon of dry mustard, and juice of one lemon, more if the lemon is not very juicy. The oil should be added a few drops at a time, stirring constantly. While stirring, add an occasional drop of vinegar. To this mixture add the last thing one-half cup of rich cream, and when thoroughly mixed, pour over the salad just before it is served. The object of the lemon is to cut the oil, and make the dressing of a cream-like consistency.

SALAD OF STUFFED EGGS
Mrs. L. J Rose.

One dozen eggs; 2 tablespoons Howland's olive oil; onions, salt, red pepper.

Peel and cut in halves the hard-boiled eggs; remove the yolks, mash and add the oil. Use a little onion, salt and pepper to taste; when thoroughly mixed, fill the white cups. Press them together and serve on lettuce leaves.

EGG SALAD
Mrs. J. A. Fairchild.

Six hard-boiled eggs; 3 medium-sized pickles; 1 teaspoon mustard; 2 teaspoons sugar; 1 teaspoon salt; 1 tablespoon Howland's olive oil; 2 tablespoons vinegar; a little parsley, a little pepper.

Cut the eggs in halves; take out the yolks, powder them, and mix with the chopped pickles, parsley, and other seasoning. Cut a small piece from the round end of the eggs; fill with the mixture, and garnish with parsley.

EGG SALAD
Mrs. Orr Haralson.

Eight eggs, hard-boiled; 4 tablespoons Howland's olive oil; 2 tablespoons vinegar: 1 small teaspoon salt; ½ teaspoon pepper; ½ clove garlic; ¼ teaspoon mustard; 1 sprig parsley—chopped fine.

After the eggs are boiled and thoroughly cold, cut them in halves; take out the yolks, mash, and mix them with the other ingredients. Fill the whites with the mixture. Tie two halves together with a dainty ribbon, and place on crisp lettuce and cover with mayonnaise.

FRUIT SALAD
Mrs. L. J. Rose.

This delicious dish is made of several kinds of fruit. Leave the small fruits whole, and slice the larger kinds. Sweeten to taste, and serve with ice cream.

SHADDOCKS
Mrs. Hugh W. Vail.

Cut the shaddocks in halves; remove the pith and seeds; fill with sugar and cracked ice.

ORANGE SALAD
Mrs. Hugh W. Vail.

Quarter the oranges and serve with lettuce and mayonnaise.

FRUIT SALAD
Mrs. John A. Henderson.

Three oranges; 1 lemon; 1 can pineapple; ½ box gelatine; 1 coffee cup granulated sugar; candied cherries, white grapes.

The juice of three oranges; if not very juicy use four; the juice of the lemon and juice from the pineapple. Cut the slices of pineapple in small pieces. Soak the gelatine for one hour in just enough water to cover it. Then pour over it half a cup of boiling water to dissolve it. Add the pieces of pineapple to the juices and gelatine with the sugar and set away to harden. Add candied cherries as the salad begins to harden; white grapes may also be then added. Bananas may be used instead of pineapple.

FRUIT SALAD

Mrs. A. M Hall.

One box of gelatine; 1 cup cold water; 1½ pints boiling water; 2 or 3 lemons; 2 cups sugar; oranges, bananas, strawberries and pineapple.

Pour the cold water over the gelatine and soak one hour. Pour over this the boiling water and strain. Add the juice of the lemons and the sugar. When almost cool stir in sliced oranges, bananas, strawberries and pineapple.

SOUPS

M. B. W.

Broth, or stock, may be made by boiling the cracked joints of beef, veal, or mutton in water; in the proportion of two and one half pints to each pound of bones and meat. The bones and meat should be of about equal weight. Chicken and veal added to beef make a more delicate soup.

Put the meat in the pot, cover with cold water, and let it come to a boil, then skim. Next set the pot where it will simmer slowly four or five hours, when it should be done.

The next day, when the broth is cold, and and the fat which has hardened on the top has been removed, a nice jelly will be formed, which, if kept in a cold place, should keep one week. When vegetables are used, they should be added only in time to become well cooked. If onions are used, they should be fried in a little hot butter, before they are added to the soup. Potatoes and cabbage should be boiled in separate water, before they are added to a soup.

Just before dinner each day, if soup is to be served, it is only necessary to cut off some of the jelly, heat it, serve it alone or add any flavoring desired, as onion, tomato, asparagus, green peas, macaroni, vermicelli, tapioca, or any other flavoring.

Stock should be kept in a stone jar, and is valuable aside from making soups, for gravies, sauces, and stews.

TO CLEAR SOUP STOCK

Allow the white and shell of one egg for every quart of stock. Set it on the fire and stir till hot, let simmer ten minutes, then add a cup of cold water, and strain through a fine strainer or napkin.

SOUP
MRS. B. C. WHITING.

All flavoring should be added to the soup after the stock is made and when cold; no vegetables should be boiled with stock, as it gives it a bad flavor. Boil the vegetables first and press them through a colander, then add them to the stock, and boil two minutes; otherwise soups disagree with some people.

CARAMEL FOR COLORING SOUPS
MRS. LINCOLN.

Melt one cup sugar with one tablespoon of water in a frying pan. Stir until it becomes a dark brown color. Add one cup of boiling water; simmer ten minutes and bottle when cool. This should be always kept on hand, as it is useful for many purposes. It gives a rich, dark color to soups, coffee, and jelly; is more wholesome than browned butter in sauces, and is delicious as a flavoring in custards and pudding sauces.

PROFITEROLES FOR SOUP
MRS. FRANK E. PHILLIPS.

One fourth cup boiling water; 2 eggs; ½ scant cup flour; ¼ cup butter.

Put the water and butter in a sauce pan and place on the fire. When it boils rapidly add the flour all at once. Beat well with a strong spoon for two minutes. Turn into a bowl and put away to cool. When cool add the eggs one at a time and beat 15 minutes. Roll the size of peas and drop on buttered tins, and bake ten minutes.

TO MAKE FORCE MEAT BALLS
MRS. J F. CONROY.

Chop cooked meat until fine; add chopped parsley, a little fine onion, salt, pepper, and bread crumbs; dip in egg and fry. Before serving put balls in soup and boil once, then add two lemons sliced, with tomato catsup, and a little vinegar—say 1 tablespoonful—just before serving.

MARROW-FAT BALLS FOR SOUP

MRS. M. G. MORE.

One cup of marrow; 2 eggs (well beaten); 1 cup dry bread crumbs; a little salt.

Remove the marrow from soup bones.   Soak or wash free from blood, chop fine.

Mix the ingredients together, form into balls and cook in soup one half hour.

BOUILLON

Juliet Corson.

This is the most elaborate, and at the same time the most delicate, and nutritious soup that can be made.

Four quarts of cold water; 4 pounds soup beef and bone; 1 chicken or fowl weighing from 3 to 4 pounds; the small end of a leg of veal, (the knuckle).   One large carrot; 1 small onion; 1 large turnip; 3 roots parsley; 1 blade of mace; 1 dozen whole cloves; 1 stalk celery; 1 dozen pepper corns; 1 bay leaf; a sprig of any dried herb, (sage excepted); 1 tablespoon of salt.

Carefully pluck, singe, draw, and truss the fowl for boiling. Cut the beef in a large piece from the bone.   Break the bones in small pieces, removing the marrow; put them in the bottom of the soup kettle; lay on them the beef and fowl; pour in the water and let it gradually heat and boil, removing all scum as it rises.   Peel the onion, carrot and turnip, leaving them whole; stick the cloves in the onions.   Wash the parsley with stalk and leaves attached; in the midst of it put the mace, bay leaf, celery, pepper corns, etc.   Wrap the roots and leaves of the parsley about these and tie in a compact little bundle. (This makes a bouquet or fagot of herbs).   After the soup is skimmed clear, add the bouquet, the vegetables, and the level tablespoon of salt.   Cover the kettle, and place it where its contents will boil slowly from one side, for three hours at least.   When the chicken is tender take it up.   It can be used for any of the dishes made of cooked chicken.

Strain the bouillon through a *clean* towel laid double in a colander set over an earthen bowl. When cold, remove every particle of fat. Mix for each quart, the white and shell of an egg, with one tablespoon of cold water in a sauce pan; pour in the bouillon, set it over the fire, stirring occasionally to keep the egg loosened from the pan until it begins to boil; then place where it will boil gently until the soup looks clear as wine, under the thick scum of egg. Strain again through folded towel and colander, allowing it to run through without squeezing the towel, as that might force through some tiny particle of the egg. It should be perfectly clear and sparkling, and of the color of amber.

The bouillon after it is clarified will keep from three to ten days, according to the weather. Sealed in jars it will keep indefinitely.

AMBER OR CONSOMME
Mrs. Rorer

Four pounds beef; 1 ounce suet; 1 small onion; 3 quarts cold water; 4 cloves; 1 small carrot; piece of celery; 1 egg, (white).

Cut into dice four pounds of lean beef from the round. Put about one ounce of suet and one small onion, sliced, into the soup kettle, and cook until a good brown; then add the meat. Cook without covering thirty minutes; add the cold water; cover the kettle and simmer gently for about three hours; at the end of this time add the cloves, carrot, piece of celery, and simmer one hour longer. Strain and stand away to cool. When cold, remove all grease from the surface. Turn the consommé into a kettle; beat the white of egg with a half cup of cold water; add it to the boiling consommé; boil one minute and strain through cheese cloth. Season, and it is ready to serve. If not dark add a teaspoonful of caramel.

CONSOMME ROYALE
Mrs. Edward Silent

Three eggs; ½ cup of stock; ⅓ teaspoon salt.
Beat the eggs well, then add the stock and salt. Butter a

small pan; pour the custard in and set it in a large pan of hot water and cook in a slow oven until the custard is firm. When cold cut into squares and add to any soup.

MULLAGATAWNY SOUP
Mrs. A. C. Jones.

One chicken weighing 3 pounds, 3 pounds veal, two large onions, 2 large slices carrot, 4 stalks celery, 3 tablespoons butter, 1 tablespoon curry powder, 4 tablespoons flour, salt and pepper to taste; 5 pints water.

Take two tablespoons of the fat from the opening of the chicken and put in the soup pot. As soon as melted, put in the vegetables, which have been cut fine. Let all cook together for twenty minutes, stirring frequently, then add the veal cut into small pieces. Cook fifteen minutes longer, then add the whole chicken and the water. Cover and let it come to a boil, skim and set back, where it will simmer for four hours, (in the meantime taking out the chicken when tender.) Now put the butter into a small frying pan, and when hot, add the dry flour; stir until a rich brown; then take from the fire, and add the curry powder; stir this mixture into the soup and let it cook half an hour longer, then strain through a seive Rinse out the soup pot and return the strained soup to it. Add salt, pepper and the chicken, (which has been freed from the bones and skin, and cut into small pieces,) Simmer very gently thirty minutes. Skim off any fat that may rise to the top, and serve with small squares of toasted bread.

PLAIN BEEF SOUP
"76"

One shank bone; 1 cup pearl barley; 3 or 4 good-sized potatoes.

Take a shank bone, wash nicely, and after breaking it in several places, put it into a pot of cold water, without salt. Let it boil slowly half an hour, taking off the scum as it rises; add the barley and let it boil two and one half or three hours. Half an hour before taking it up, have the potatoes pared and sliced an eighth of an inch thick, and put them in to boil. Add salt and pepper to taste. If the soup is too rich, skim off the fat from the top before putting on the table.

OX-TAIL SOUP
Mrs. E. Hollenbeck.

One joint beef, (well filled with marrow); 2 ox tails; ½ pound okra; salt; a little red pepper; handful rice; 1 soup bunch.

Let beef and ox-tails come to a boil, then skim well. Let boil 1½ hours; then add okra cut up small, rice and vegetables. Remove vegetables when done, add salt and pepper. This soup should cook five or six hours.

BROWN SOUP (Southern Soup)
Mrs. J. F. Conroy.

Soup beef; 12 whole cloves; soup bunch; water; 3 tablespoons brown flour; force meat balls.

Put beef into cold water, allowing 1 pound to 1 quart of cold water, add cloves. Boil until the meat is tender; take up the meat, put in soup bunch, boil 1 hour. Take from fire and strain, return the clear soup to the pot, set on the fire. Take two tablespoons brown flour, moisten with cold water until smooth like cream, stir into soup before putting in force-meat balls.

WHITE SOUP
Mrs. Owens.

Six tomatoes; 4 onions; 4 tablespoons crushed tapioca; 1½ pints milk, butter, pepper and salt; 2 quarts water.

Boil the vegetables in the water till soft, rub through a sieve, return the paste to the water, add the tapioca and boil fifteen minutes; season, add the milk, and as soon as hot, serve.

SCOTCH SOUP
Training School of Glasgow.

One bone; 1 pound lean beef; 1 teacup of oatmeal; 2 onions

or leeks; a bit of carrot; turnip and celery; 10 coffee cups of water, salt and pepper.

Take the fat from the bone and put it on to boil with the water; add the onion, carrot, turnip and celery. Set it to boil three hours, and strain. (This makes stock and may be made a day or two before it is used.) Then put a little beef drippings in the soup pot; cut the meat in small squares, also chop the onion finely, and fry them all in the drippings; add the stock and allow it to boil, then add gradually the oatmeal, one dessertspoon of salt, and a little pepper. Let all boil for three quarters of an hour and serve.

KENTUCKY CHICKEN SOUP
Mrs. G. Wiley Wells.

One chicken; 1½ gallons cold water; 1 tablespoon finely chopped onion; 1 potato—size of an egg; ½ teacup rice: 1 quart fresh milk; 1 teaspoon flour; salt; pepper; lump butter.

Cut chicken into pieces, put into a gallon and a half of cold water. Boil slowly two hours, then put into it the onion and potato cut up fine, and half cup of uncooked rice. Let all boil until the water is reduced to a quart, then put in a quart or more of fresh, rich milk. Thicken with a teaspoon of flour, mixed in a little cold water. Boil again; season with salt, pepper and a lump of butter, size of a pigeon's egg.

Boil this soup five or six hours.

CHICKEN SOUP
Mrs. J. F. Couroy.

One full-grown chicken; 3 pints water; 1 teacup cream; ½ teacup pearl barley or rice: pepper and salt.

Cover and let cook slowly one hour, skim, and add teacup of cream just before serving.

The chicken may be eaten with mashed potatoes, or used for salads or croquettes.

GUMBO SOUP
Mrs. G. L. Arnold.

Two pounds of beef and bone; ½ pound of ham or salt

pork; 1 quart of tomatoes—sliced; 2 quarts of gumbo—sliced; 4 tablespoons of butter.

Put the meat and gumbo in a pot, with one quart of cold water; stew for one hour, then add the tomatoes, and two quarts of boiling water, more if needed. When the contents of the pot are boiled to pieces, put in the butter and pepper. Strain and serve with croutons.

GUMBO SOUP
Mrs. W. J. Elderkin.

One spring chicken; 1 small slice ham; 1 heaping table-spoon lard; okra; 1 or two large tomatoes; 1 spoon of flour; a little boiled rice.

Cut up the chicken in small pieces, also the ham. Put into a pot with the tablespoon of hot lard; when fried, add okra, cut into small pieces, the tomatoes and flour. Cover the whole with water, and let it simmer over a slow fire. If crabs or shrimps are obtainable add them, and season the whole highly. Salt to the taste.

Place a little boiled rice in the center of a soup plate, add some gumbo. Serve very hot.

Many persons in New Orleans add Chili pepper.

OKRA SOUP
Mrs. J. F. Conroy.

One can of okra; (if you cannot procure fresh okra); 1 tablespoon minced onion; 1 tablespoon butter; 1½ pints boil-ing water; salt and cayenne pepper to taste.

Put can of okra in pot, with the onion and butter, when boiling hot add the boiling water; salt and cayenne pepper to taste.

MUSHROOM SOUP
Mrs. Hugh W. Vail.

One tablespoon flour; 1 tablespoon butter; 1 quart milk; 1 pint mushrooms.

Melt flour and butter until very smooth, (do not brown),

add the milk slightly heated to the flour and butter. Stir constantly in a double sauce pan until it becomes thick like cream.

To prepare the mushrooms. Peel and boil for two hours; when cold, press through a fine colander, and stir into the previously prepared soup until well heated through. Serve.

CORN SOUP
Miss M. E. McLellan.

One pint grated green corn; 1 quart milk; 1 pint hot water; 1 heaping tablespoon flour; 2 tablespoons butter; 1 slice of onion; salt and pepper to taste.

Boil the corn cobs in the water half an hour; take them out and put the grated corn in, and the onion. Let them boil about half an hour, then strain and add the flour and butter —mixed smooth in a little milk. Cook a few minutes, add the milk boiling hot. Season and serve.

CORN SOUP
Mrs. W. J. Elderkin.

One quart of corn, fresh or canned; 3 pints fresh milk; pepper; salt; butter size of an egg; 1 teaspoon corn starch; 4 tablespoons cream.

Place over the fire, in just enough water to cover it, 1 quart of corn. When well stewed, press through a colander into a fresh sauce pan, then add pepper, salt and butter. Let this stand while you place over the fire three pints of fresh milk, when this has come to a boil, (be careful not to scorch), stir in slowly the corn. Let all cook together very slowly for ten minutes, or until it has boiled well five minutes; then add the corn starch which has been dissolved in cold milk and also the cream. Serve immediately very hot.

POTATO SOUP
Mrs. Charles Silent.

Three potatoes; 1 pint of stock; 1 teaspoon chopped onion; 1 stalk of celery; 1 teaspoon salt; ½ teaspoon celery salt; ½ saltspoon white pepper; ¼ saltspoon cayenne pepper; ½ tablespoon flour; 1 tablespoon butter.

Wash and pare potatoes; let soak in cold water half an hour. Put into boiling water and cook until very soft. Cook the onion and celery with the milk in a double boiler. When the potatoes are soft, drain off the water and mash them. Add the boiling milk and seasoning. Rub through a strainer, and put it on to boil again. Put the butter in a small sauce pan, and, when melted and bubbling, add the flour, and when well mixed stir into the boiling soup; let it all boil five minutes, and serve very hot. If the soup is too thick, add more hot milk. The celery salt may be omitted if you have fresh celery—if you like, add 1 tablespoon of fine chopped parsley just before serving.

SPINACH SOUP
Mrs. Edward Silent.

One peck of spinach; 3 tablespoons of melted butter; 3 tablespoons of flour; 1 tablespoon of sugar; 1 teaspoon of salt, and a little pepper; 1 quart of stock or milk.

Wash the spinach and cook in a little water until tender, drain, chop and pound the spinach to a paste, then add the butter, flour, sugar, salt and pepper. Cook ten minutes, then add the stock or milk, when hot rub through a sieve. Serve.

POTATO SOUP
Mrs. W. B. Holcomb.

Six potatoes; 1 quart of milk; ½ cup of butter; 1 egg; pepper and salt.

Boil and mash the potatoes, while mashing, add the butter and pour in gradually the boiling milk. Stir well and strain. Heat once more. Beat up the egg, put in the tureen and pour over it the soup when ready to serve.

POTATO SOUP
" 76."

Three good-sized potatoes; 1 teacup sweet milk; 2 quarts of water; 1 cup sweet cream; pepper, salt and butter to taste.

Peel and slice potatoes, boil in the water till nearly done, then add the milk, pepper, salt and butter to taste. Just before removing from the fire, pour in the sweet cream.

MOCK BISQUE SOUP
Mrs. C. H. Walton.

One half can tomatoes; 1 quart milk; 1/3 cup butter; 1 tablespoonful corn starch; 1 teaspoonful salt; 1/2 saltspoonful white pepper.

Stew the tomatoes until soft enough to strain easily. Boil the milk in a double boiler. Cook one tablespoonful of the butter and the corn starch together in a small saucepan, adding enough of the hot milk to make it pour easily. Stir it carefully into the boiling milk and boil ten minutes. Add salt, and pepper and the strained tomatoes. If the tomatoes be very acid, add half a saltspoonful of soda before straining. Serve very hot.

TOMATO SOUP
Mrs. C. C. McLean.

One quart soup stock; 1 quart tomatoes—canned or fresh; parsley and small onion, for flavor.

Boil 15 minutes; strain and thicken with flour. Add butter, pepper and salt. Serve very hot.

TOMATO CREAM SOUP
Mrs. J. J. Ayers.

Boil till soft four large tomatoes; strain through a sieve, and then add one teaspoon of soda; a quart of milk; 4 rolled crackers; butter; pepper, and salt.

TOMATO SOUP
Mrs. D. G. Stephens.

One quart stock; 1 quart can tomatoes; 1 teaspoon soda; 1 quart milk; 2 tablespoons butter; 2 tablespoons corn starch.

Heat together the stock and milk. Put the tomatoes through a colander, place on stove, when hot add soda. Melt the butter and stir into it the corn starch. Add this to the tomatoes. Stir the milk and tomatoes into stock. Season to taste.

TOMATO CREAM SOUP
Miss M. E. McLellan.

Six tomatoes; 1 small salt spoon soda; 1 pint of milk; 2 large teaspoons flour; 1 dessertspoon butter.

Stew the tomatoes, add the soda, then strain through a fine strainer. Boil the milk and thicken it with the flour; add the butter, then the tomato. Season to taste and serve.

TOMATO SOUP
Mrs. A. C. St. John.

One pint cooked tomatoes; 1 teaspoon salt; pinch of soda; 3 rolled crackers; ¼ teaspoon pepper; 1 heaping tablespoon butter; 1 quart sweet milk.

Put the tomatoes through a sieve, add the soda and boil for five minutes; then add the milk, butter, salt and pepper; when this boils add the rolled crackers; let just boil and serve at once.

Instead of the quart of milk, a pint of water and a pint of milk may be used, and still make an excellent soup.

[GREEN PEA SOUP
Mrs. J. Wigmore.

Three pints green peas; ¼ pound of butter; 2 slices ham; 3 onions, sliced; 4 heads lettuce, (shredded); 2 French rolls, (crumbs of); 2 handfuls spinach; 1 lump sugar; 2 quarts medium stock.

Put the butter, ham, 1 quart peas, onions and lettuce to a pint of stock; simmer one hour; add the rest of the stock and the rolled crumbs; boil for another hour. Boil the spinach and squeeze dry. Rub the soup through a sieve, and spinach with it to color it. Then have ready 1 pint of young peas boiled, add them to the soup. Put in sugar, give one boil and serve.

GREEN PEA SOUP.
Mrs. Edward Silent.

One quart green peas; 1 quart water; 1 pint milk; ½ teaspoon salt; ¼ saltspoon pepper; ½ teaspoon sugar; 1 table spoon butter; 1 tablespoon flour.

Put the peas into 1 pint of boiling water and cook until soft.   Mash them in the water in which they boiled, and rub through a strainer, gradually adding a pint of water.   Put on to boil again   Cook the butter and flour in a small sauce pan, being careful not to brown it.   Stir into the boiling soup. Add salt, pepper, sugar and the milk, which should be hot.

This is a good way to use cold peas, or peas that are old and hard.   When the pods are fresh, wash them thoroughly, allow more water, and cook them with the peas.

BEAN SOUP

"76."

One quart small white beans; 1 quart cold water, (to be thrown away after five minutes boiling); 1 scant teaspoon soda; 2 quarts rich milk; 2 quarts cold water; salt and butter to taste.

Boil beans in 1 quart of water with the soda five minutes; take out, throw away water, and rub skins off in cold water; then put beans into 2 quarts of cold water and boil until very soft; this will require 2 or 3 hours.   Add the milk, pepper, salt and butter to taste; boil up once, and it is ready to serve. This is a superior soup.

CELERY SOUP

Mrs. A S. Averill.

Bones of a roasted turkey or chicken; 3 good heads celery; butter and milk.

Take the bones of a roasted turkey or chicken with the bits not suitable for reappearance upon the table, cover with cold water, and boil thoroughly two or three hours.   Strain out the bones and set aside for stock.

Cut up the celery, using all not fit for table.   Cover with hot water, and boil until soft.   Strain through colander.   Add stock and season.   Add butter and sufficient good rich milk. Serve hot.

CELERY SOUP
Mrs. J. F. Conroy.

One bunch celery; 1 pint salted water; 1 tablespoon chopped onion; 1 pint milk; 1 tablespoonful butter; ½ tablespoon flour; salt and pepper.

Cut celery into inch pieces, and boil until very soft in salted water, mash in the water left from boiling. Boil the onion in the milk ten minutes, and add it to the celery. Press all through a fine sieve and boil again, adding the butter and flour, (cooked together); salt and pepper to taste. Boil five minutes and strain.

CREAM OF CELERY SOUP
Mrs. F. W. King.

One quart milk; ½ cup rice; 1 quart soup stock; 1 large head of celery; lump of butter; salt and pepper; 1 cup of whipped cream.

Boil the rice in the milk, with a shade of mace, until soft enough to rub through a colander. Boil celery in soup stock twenty minutes; add lump of butter, salt and pepper to taste; strain this into the milk, cook together a few minutes. Add cup of whipped cream after pouring soup in the tureen.

CREAM OF ASPARAGUS
Mrs. S. C. Hubbell.

Two bunches asparagus; 1 pint stock; 1 tablespoon butter; 2 tablespoons flour; salt and pepper; 1 pint hot milk.

Cut off the hard parts of the asparagus; boil in the stock half an hour, then rub through a sieve and put on to boil again. Melt the butter and stir into it the flour; add it the stock and season with salt and pepper. When the soup is boiling add the milk and the asparagus tops which have been previously cooked tender in salted water.

ASPARAGUS SOUP
Mrs. C. H. Walton.

Two bunches asparagus; 1 pint white stock; 1 pint cream or milk; 3 tablespoons butter; 1 tablespoon chopped onion; 2

tablespoons of flour; 1 teaspoon sugar: 1½ teaspoon salt; one-eighth teaspoon pepper.

Cut off heads of asparagus and stew the rest with stock. Cook butter and onion ten minutes; add flour and stir until smooth.   Add this with seasoning and simmer quarter of an hour.   Rub through a sieve, return to stew pan, add cream and asparagus heads, boil once and serve.

ALMOND SOUP
Mrs. M. M. Bovard.

One quart milk; browned flour; 2 eggs, (whites only); 1 tablespoon butter; ½ teaspoon extract of almond.

To the milk add the butter and enough browned flour to make the thickness of cream.   (Cook in a double boiler). Add the almond extract, and just before serving beat in the whites of eggs beaten stiff, and some blanched almonds chopped finely.

NEW ORLEANS CRAB GUMBO
Mrs. A. J. Glassell.

Two tablespoons flour; 2 tablespoons lard; 2 onions; 1 teaspoon gumbo, fillet.

Fry the flour in the lard with the onions, cut up fine, until a nice brown.   After the crab is cut up and picked out, add it and stir until all is brown; then put this into ordinary soup stock, and boil until well done.   When ready to dish up stir in 1 teaspoon of gumbo fillet, and pour out as soon as it thickens, as the fillet will get gritty if boiled over a minute.

N. B.   This is not okra but fillet, a powder ground from leaves by the Indians.

This recipe will answer for Oyster Gumbo also.   But the oysters must be added when the soup is nearly done.

CRAB SOUP
Mrs. C. C. Thomas.

One crab, chopped fine; 2 quarts milk; ½ cup butter; 1 large spoonful flour: ½ cup sweet cream.

Cook butter and flour together, do not brown; add milk

and cook until smooth as cream. Season with cayenne pepper, and salt. Add crab, which scald, but do not boil after adding to the milk. Pour into the tureen ½ cup sweet cream; and then add soup.

CRAB SOUP
Mrs. J. W. Hendricks.

One quart milk; 2 medium-sized or 1 large crab; 6 eggs, (yolks); salt, cayenne or tobasco sauce.

Pick the meat of the crab into fine shreds, and let it soak in the milk for one hour: then put it on the stove, and let it come *just* to a boil, stirring constantly. When at boiling point, add the beaten yolks of six eggs: stir quickly for a minute or so, and serve immediately. Season well with salt, and cayenne pepper or tobasco sauce. I prefer the sauce, using about six or seven drops.

GREEN TURTLE SOUP
Mrs. Lincoln.

One can green turtle : 1 quart brown stock : 2 tablespoons each of butter and flour; one lemon.

Cut the green fat into dice and lay it aside. Simmer the remainder of the turtle meat in the stock for half an hour. Brown the flour in the browned butter, add it to the soup. Season highly with salt and pepper. Serve with thin slices of lemon, egg balls, and the reserved green fat.

MOCK TURTLE SOUP
Mrs. J. H. F. Peck.

One pint black beans; 4 or 5 quarts of water: ½ pound of beef, or ½ calf's head: 1½ pound salt pork: 1 onion; 1 grated carrot; 1 turnip: 1 teaspoon whole cloves; 1 lemon; 1 hard-boiled egg.

Soak the beans over night in cold water. The day following, boil them in four or five quarts of fresh water with the beef, (or half of calf's head,) salt pork, onion, carrot, turnip and cloves, for from three to six hours. Strain through a colander and skim off the fat. Place lemon sliced and hard-boiled egg in tureen, and pour the soup over.

OYSTER SOUP
Mrs. W. J. Brown.

One quart of hot water; 1 pint of milk; ½ teacup of butter; 1 quart oysters; 2 teaspoons salt; ¼ teaspoon pepper; 4 crackers, rolled fine.

Put the hot water in a granite stew pan, add the other ingredients in the order they come; boil as soon as possible, then add the oysters; let the whole come to a boiling heat quickly, remove from the fire and serve hot.

BISQUE OF OYSTERS
Mrs. Frank E. Phillips.

One quart of oysters; 1 quart of sweet cream; 1 pint of chicken stock; 1 pint stale bread crumbs, scant; 2 tablespoons of butter; 1 tablespoon of flour; ¼ teaspoon of white pepper; 1-10 teaspoon of cayenne pepper; 1 bay leaf; 1 sprig parsley; 1 stalk of celery; 1 small slice of onion; 1 bit of mace; 4 eggs—yolks only.

Put the chopped oysters with their own liquor, half the stock and seasoning, into a stew pan, and cook slowly twenty minutes. The other half of the stock and bread crumbs put in another stew pan and cook twenty minutes. Strain the liquor from the first pan into the second, pressing all the juice from the oysters, then cook ten minutes longer. Reserve half the cream; put the remainder in a double boiler; mix the butter and flour together until smooth and creamy. When the contents of the stew pan have cooked ten minutes, rub them through a fine sieve and return to the pan. Add the butter and flour; stir the mixture until it boils, then add the hot cream, and set in a cooler place. Beat the yolks and cold cream, stir into the mixture, and cook one minute, (stirring). Use whole spices.

AN EXCELLENT OYSTER STEW
Mrs. A. S. Averill.

One quart of oysters; 1 quart of milk; 1 teaspoon of flour; salt pork, butter, salt, pepper.

Cut the slice of pork into tiny bits and fry it; add the flour and simmer a few minutes. Then add the oysters and their juice, and allow them to plump in the hot mixture. Heat the milk, season it with butter, pepper and salt, add it to the oysters, and serve very hot.

FISH CHOWDER
Mrs. E. M. Ross.

Fish, weighing 10 or 12 pounds; 1½ pounds salt pork; 16 or 18 good-sized potatoes; 1 quart of boiling milk; 12 or 14 hard crackers; 3 pints of water; 2 tablespoons salt; 1 teaspoon pepper; a little flour; a couple of onions, if desired.

This is said to be Daniel Webster's recipe for chowder. Have the fish well cleaned, leaving on the skin; cut into slices an inch and a half thick, using only the breast, which is the best part for chowder. Cut the pork into thin slices, and put into a very large pot, and fry out all the fat; take out the pork, leaving the fat in the pot. Add the three pints of water, then put in a layer of the fish, covering as much of the surface of the fat as possible. Slice the potatoes thin and put in a layer of them; sift in the salt, pepper and flour, then a layer of pork cut in strips, another layer of fish and what potatoes may be left. Fill the pot with water until it covers the whole. Put over a good fire and let it boil twenty-five minutes. Take the boiling milk and put in the crackers, add to the chowder, and let boil five minutes more. It is then ready to serve.

LONG ISLAND CLAM CHOWDER
Mrs. E. Verona May.

Clams; 1 pound of salt pork; 7 onions, medium size; 9 potatoes; 2 quarts of boiling water; 1 quart of boiling milk; ½ cup of butter; 4 cups of oyster crackers; a pinch of thyme; salt, pepper.

Chop the pork and brown in the kettle until crisp. Then add the chopped onions and cook slightly, next the chopped potatoes and boiling water. Cut out the tough part of the

clams and chop it; add the clams and their liquor. Boil
thirty minutes, then add the milk, salt, pepper, butter, thyme,.
and crushed crackers. Excellent.

CLAM CHOWDER

Mrs. R. M. Widney.

Six tablespoons pickled pork; 2 medium-sized onions;
1 dessertspoon butter; 2 tablespoons flour; 1 quart clams;
1 quart milk; 1 pint cream; 1 quart potatoes; 1½ pints
toasted bread; salt and thyme.

Fry the pork, (cut into dice), onions and butter thoroughly; then add flour; brown well and place on the back
of the stove. Put clams over the fire in their own liquor;
when they have boiled three minutes, strain them and return
the liquor to the fire; add to the liquor the fried pork and
onions, milk, cream, and the potatoes—cut into dice, and
salt to taste. When about to send to table, add the clams
chopped fine, toasted bread cut in dice, and a little thyme.

FISH CHOWDER

Mrs. H. C. Austin.

One pound salt pork, cut into strips; 4 pounds cod or sea
bass; chopped onions; parsley; summer savory; pepper;
crackers.

Soak the pork in cold water five minutes; cover the bottom of the pot with this. Cut the cod or sea-bass into pieces
two inches square, and lay enough of this over the pork to
cover it; then the chopped onions, (this may be omitted, if
desired), parsley, summer savory, pepper and crackers. Repeat this layering until your fish and pork are used. Cover
with cold water, and boil gently for an hour. Then take out
the thick part with a skimmer, and, after thickening the
other with a little flour and butter, pour it over that you
have skimmed out.

DUMPLINGS

One pint of flour; 1 scant cup sweet milk; ½ teaspoon salt; 2 teaspoons Cleveland's Baking Powder.

Sift the baking powder, salt and flour together, and mix with the milk into a dough soft enough to handle easily. Roll out half an inch thick; cut out with a biscuit cutter, and drop into the boiling stew and boil ten minutes.

FISH

M. B. W.

Fish should never be allowed to stand; but should be cleaned immediately, in strongly-salted water. After they are cleaned, they should be washed with a cloth wet in salt water, then wrapped, sprinkled with salt and put in a cool place. Fish should never be soaked; nor put in an ice-chest, as any food which may be in the chest will absorb the odor. Ice may be placed around, but should not touch the fish; ice and water have a tendency to soften fish; a soft fish is unfit to eat.

BAKED WHITE FISH
Mrs. E. H. Sanderson.

Steam a white fish until tender; remove bones; sprinkle with salt and pepper; shred.

Dressing: Heat 1 pint of milk, ¼ pound flour, cook. When cold, add two eggs, ¼ pound butter. Season with a little grated onion and parsley. Bake in alternate layers of fish and sauce. Sprinkle top with crumbs and butter, and brown Garnish with slices of lemon and hard-boiled eggs, and serve with more sauce.

BAKED SHAD
Practical Housekeeping.

Open and clean the fish; leave on the head, if preferred; cut out the backbone, from the head to within two inches of the tail, and fill with the following mixture: Stale bread crumbs; 1 large onion; 2 ounces of butter; salt, pepper, a little parsley and 2 yolks.

Soak the bread in water, squeeze dry, mince the onion and fry in butter. Add the bread, butter, and seasoning of pepper, salt and parsley. Heat thoroughly. After taking from the fire, add the yolks, well beaten. Stuff. When the fish is filled, wind it with tape, place in baking pan, baste slightly with butter, and cover bottom of pan with water. Serve with egg sauce.

BAKED HALIBUT
Juliet Corson.

A halibut, weighing three or four pounds; 1 quart of tomatoes; 1 medium-sized onion; garlic, size of a dried pea; salt, pepper, butter, bread crumbs.

The fish is to be cleaned and washed; the fins and tail trimmed; then laid in a baking dish in which it can be sent to the table; or in a pan from which it can be removed without breaking. The tomatoes and onion are to be peeled, sliced and placed in the pan with the fish, also the garlic—minced very fine, and a palatable seasoning of salt and pepper. The fish is to be dusted with fine sifted crumbs and dotted with butter. Bake half an hour in a moderate oven. Either fresh or canned tomatoes may be used.

BAKED FISH
Mrs. M. B. Welch.

A fish weighing from four to six pounds is a good size to bake. It should be cooked whole to look well.

Make a dressing of bread crumbs, butter, salt and a little salt pork, chopped fine, (parsley and onions if you please); mix this with one egg. Fill the body, sew it up and lay it in a large dripper; put across it some pieces of salt pork, to flavor it; put a pint of water and a little salt in the pan. Bake it an hour and a half; baste frequently. After taking up the fish, thicken the gravy and pour over it.

[This is a good way to bake Barracuda or any California fish.—Eds.]

DRY STUFFING FOR BAKED FISH
Mrs. F. W. King.

One cup of cracker crumbs; ¼ cup of melted butter; 1

saltspoon of salt; 1 saltspoon of pepper; 1 teaspoon of chopped onion; 1 teaspoon of parsley; 1 teaspoon of pickles; 1 teaspoon of capers.

Stuff the fish, and, when baked, served with Hollandoise Sauce, prepared as follows :

One half cup of butter; ½ cup of boiling water; 2 lemons, (the juice); 2 eggs, (yolks); ½ teaspoon of salt; a speck of cayenne.

Beat the butter to a cream, add the yolks, lemon juice, cayenne and salt, set the bowl in a pan of boiling water, stirring constantly until the sauce thickens.

TO COOK COARSE-GRAINED FISH, (Sculpin excepted)
Mrs. Carl Schutze.

One sliced onion; 6 pepper-corns; 6 corns all-spice; 3 cloves; 1 bay leaf; 1 piece of lemon peel; ½ cup vinegar.

Pour into a fish kettle, or large shallow pan, sufficient water for cooking the fish. Salt it well. Add onion, pepper-corns, cloves, all-spice, bay leaf and lemon peel. To do away with the odor of kelp, if any there be, add the vinegar. Boil all this before putting the fish in. Set the kettle where it will keep just under boiling heat—for three-quarters of an hour. Drain and serve with sauce.

EGG SAUCE FOR FISH

Two tablespoons flour; 2 tablespoons butter; 1 cup milk; 1 cup fish water; 1 egg.

Rub flour and butter together; boil; but not long enough to become yellow. In another dish, boil fish water and milk, from which the cream has not been taken; add to the butter and flour, and stir altogether till smooth; season with salt if necessary. Let the sauce simmer till ready for use; add the egg last—boiled hard and chopped fine.

BOILED FISH
Mrs. E. R. Smith.

Wrap fish in a cloth and boil three-quarters of an hour in

a kettle of hot water with salt enough for seasoning. Remove cloth carefully and place the fish upon a platter.

SAUCE FOR FISH

Milk; corn starch; 3 hard-boiled eggs; butter.

Heat the milk in sauce pan, afterward thicken with corn starch; add the eggs, chopped fine. Season with butter. Pour over the fish.

Any kind of large fish may be used. Barracuda is a favorite.

HALIBUT AU GRATIN
Mrs Frank Phillips.

One pint cooked halibut; 1½ cups sweet cream or milk; 1 cup bread crumbs; 1 tablespoon flour; 2 tablespoons butter; ¼ teaspoon pepper; ½ teaspoon onion juice; 1½ teaspoon salt.

Break the fish into flakes with a fork. Sprinkle with half the pepper and one teaspoon of salt. Mix lightly. Heat the milk in a small sauce pan, mix the flour and one spoon of butter. Stir it in the boiling milk, cook one minute; add the onion juice, pepper and salt. Remove from the fire. Put in dish in layers, the last, a layer of cream sauce. Sprinkle with bread crumbs and the remainder of the butter. Cook fifteen minutes. More heat is required on the top than at the bottom.

HALIBUT MÂITRE d'HÔTEL

Three pounds of halibut; 1 tablespoon butter; 1 tablespoon chopped parsley; bread crumbs, egg, salt, pepper.

Cut the halibut in pieces three inches square; dip each in beaten egg, then in sifted bread crumbs. Fry in lard to a rich brown. Rub the butter to a cream, add lemon juice, parsley, salt and pepper. Mix, and spread on the hot squares of halibut. Set in the oven just long enough to melt the butter, then serve. A delicious breakfast dish.

FISH 'a la CREAM
Mrs J. J. Meyler.

Two pounds of fish; 1 quart milk; 1 spoonful butter; 2 spoonfuls flour; ½ onion; lemon, tobasco sauce, salt.

Boil halibut or coarse grained fish fifteen minutes. Remove the skin, pick in pieces. Sprinkle with salt. Put three-fourths of the milk in a custard boiler to heat. Mix the butter and flour with the remainder of the milk, and cook until quite thick; then add the onion, finely chopped, and two drops of tobasco sauce. Put alternate layers of fish, and dressing in a baking dish, with a slice of sweet rind lemon quartered over the dressing. Have the dressing cover the entire top. Bake slowly half an hour. Garnish with slices of lemon.

CREAM FISH
Miss Delia Clemons.

Six pounds of fish boiled, cooled and picked in pieces.

Sauce—1 quart of milk; 1 onion, cut fine, tied in a bag and boiled in the milk. Rub a teacup of butter in enough sifted flour to make the milk like rich cream. Stir into the boiling milk and cook thoroughly. Season with salt, pepper, and finely chopped parsley. Mix with the fish. Sprinkle bread crumbs over the top, and bake a few minutes.

FRIED FISH OF ANY KIND
Mrs. H. C. Austin.

Clean, wash and dry the fish; lay in a large flat dish; salt and dredge with flour. If the fish is large and thick slice it; have ready a frying pan of hot lard or butter; put it in and fry to a good brown.

A NICE BREAKFAST DISH
Mrs. A. C. Jones.

Broil sardines delicately, and serve on toast with lemon.

BROILED TROUT
Every-Day Cook Book.

Clean, and split them open; season with a little salt and cayenne; dip in whipped egg, dredge with flour and broil over a clear fire. Serve with sauce.

BOILED TROUT

Put the fish in boiling salted water, with a dash of vinegar in it; remove all scum as it rises, and boil the fish until their eyes protrude. Lift without breaking. Drain. Serve on a napkin. To be eaten with shrimp, or anchovy sauce.

FISH TOAST
Mrs M. G. Moore.

Salted fish—1 tablespoon butter; 1 tablespoon flour; 1 cup sweet milk; 1 hard boiled egg; some toasted bread; pepper.

Shred fish into small pieces; freshen in cold water. Heat butter in frying-pan; stir in the flour; cook; add one cup or more of sweet milk, eggs, chopped fine, and last the fish, after first draining from the water. Add a little pepper, and pour over a nice dish of toast. The sauce is excellent with baked potatoes.

BREADED SMELTS
Juliet Corson.

Smelts; milk; cracker dust; beaten egg.

The smelts should be wiped dry, then dipped in milk, rolled in cracker dust, dipped in beaten egg, rolled again in cracker dust, and fried brown in smoking hot fat. When taken from the fat lay them upon brown paper a moment to free them from grease.

FINNAN HADDIE.
Mrs. C. C. Carpenter.

Half pound finnan haddie, picked and braized in butter; 1 cup cream; 1 hard-boiled egg, cut in small pieces; the yolk of 1 raw egg; 1 teaspoon of grated Edam cheese; thicken with flour. Season to taste, cook seven or eight minutes, and serve in chafing dish.

SALT FISH PUDDING—(Breakfast Dish)
Mrs. B. C. Whiting.

Should you have some Alaska salmon left over, or a little mashed potato, or boiled rice, or both, instead of throwing

away, butter a pudding dish and put in alternate layers of the
potato, rice, and fish, then grated bread crumbs over the top,
and pour over a cup of sweet cream, or drawn butter, then
bake. You can add pepper and more salt if necessary. Hard-
boiled eggs chopped and a little fish sauce is an improvement.
Garnish with sliced lemon and parsley.

BOILED SALMON
Every-Day Cook Book.

The middle slice of salmon is best. Sew the fish neatly in
a bag made of mosquito net, put in boiling salted water. Boil
gently, allowing a quarter of an hour to the pound. When
done unwrap, being careful not to break the fish, and lay it
upon a hot dish. Have ready a large cup of drawn butter,
very rich, in which has been mixed a tablespoon of minced
parsley, and the juice of a lemon. Garnish with parsley, and
sliced eggs.

SALMON LOAF
Mrs. W. W. Ross.

One cup bread crumbs; 1 can salmon; 4 tablespoons melted
butter; 4 eggs; salt and pepper to taste.

Remove all bones and pieces of skin from fish. Stir together with other ingredients and turn into a greased pan, and
steam one hour. Serve with following sauce.

Sauce for Salmon Loaf—1 cup boiled cream; 1 tablespoon
corn starch, *heaped*; 1 tablespoon melted butter; yolk of 1 egg.

Thicken the cream *after* it is boiled with the corn starch,
wet with salmon juice; add butter and yolk of egg well beaten.

SALMON LOAF
Mrs. E. F. C. Klokke.

One can salmon; 4 eggs; 1 cup bread crumbs; butter size
of an egg, melted and cooled; pepper, salt. Steam half an
hour.

Sauce—1 egg, or yolks of two; ½ cup butter; ½ cup of
boiling water; 1 lemon, juice only.

ESCALOPED SALMON
Mrs. Adolf Ekstein.

Bread crumbs; salmon; milk; flour; butter; pepper; salt.

Place in baking dish alternate layers of bread crumbs, and salmon picked to pieces. Thicken some milk with a little flour; season with butter, salt and pepper. Pour over the fish while hot. Bake till brown.

ESCALOPED SALMON
Mrs. Augusta Robinson.

One egg; ½ cup of milk; a few drops Worcestershire sauce; bread crumbs.

Remove bones from a piece of boiled salmon. Fill a baking dish with alternate layers of bread crumbs and salmon; top layer of crumbs. Season each layer of crumbs with salt, pepper and small pieces of butter. Beat the egg separately and well, add milk and Worcestershire sauce. Pour over the escaloped salmon. Bake fifteen minutes with cover, then remove cover, and brown five minutes.

Codfish may be used in the same way very satisfactorily as a breakfast dish.

COLD SALMON
Mrs. E. F. C. Klokke.

Six laurel leaves; handful of parsley; ½ lemon, sliced; 1 onion, good-sized, sliced; 1 carrot, sliced; 1 spoonful white pepper—whole; ½ spoonful cloves; plenty of salt, vinegar, water, lettuce, sliced egg, mayonnaise.

Boil the parsley, laurel leaves, lemon, onion, carrot, pepper, cloves, and salt, in equal parts of vinegar and water. In this while boiling lay the cuts of salmon, which should be one and one-half inches thick. Cover and cook slowly from five to ten minutes. Place the salmon on platter to cool. Garnish with sliced eggs, sliced lemons, and lettuce. Serve with mayonnaise.

ROASTED CODFISH
Mrs. M. G. Moore.

Select a thick piece of dry codfish; do not wash or soak it; toast both sides to a deep brown; pound it to pieces with a dull knife   Pour boiling water over it, and let it simmer a few minutes, drain off the water; repeat this operation two or three times.   Drain, season with pepper and butter, and set it in a hot oven for a few minutes.   Delightful with baked potatoes.

CODFISH BALLS
Mrs. A. C. Radford.

Codfish; mashed potato; butter; sweet milk; a beaten egg.

After washing and soaking the fish, mince it fine; and boil twenty minutes.   Turn off the water, cover again with fresh boiling water, and boil another twenty minutes.   Drain it dry and spread upon a dish to cool.   Add an equal quantity of mashed potato; work into a stiff batter, by adding a lump of butter, sweet milk, and egg.   Flour your hands, and make the mixture into balls; drop into boiling lard, or good drippings, and fry them to a light brown.

CODFISH BALLS
Mrs. T. J. Carran.

Equal quantities of codfish and mashed potato; red beets —cooked; salt pork.

Carefully pick and wash the codfish, mix thoroughly with the potato and chopped beets, work into balls, brown in the fat of salt pork, and garnish with bits of fried pork.

TO COOK CODFISH
Mrs. C. G. Dubois.

Two-thirds quart of codfish; 1 pint cream; ½ pint milk; 1 tablespoon flour; 1 egg; 2 tablespoons milk; butter, size of butternut.

Shred the codfish; soak till fresh; place in saucepan with cream and the milk; boil once.   Beat egg and flour together, with the milk; add same to the fish, stirring constantly till done.   Season with butter.   Serve on toast.

ESCALOPED CODFISH

Two cups cold mashed potatoes; 1 pint sweet milk; 2 raw eggs; lump of butter, size of a walnut; salt; pepper; codfish.

Pick codfish in pieces, and soak in lukewarm water over night, or for several hours; change the water a few times. Mix the potatoes, milk, eggs, codfish and butter thoroughly. Season with salt and pepper, if necessary. Bake in buttered dish one half hour.

TURBOT 'a la CRÊME
Mrs. C. J. Ellis.

Boil a cod or bass; after it is cooked, and cold, remove the bones. Chop very fine, and season with salt and pepper.

Sauce—One pint of milk; 3 tablespoons of flour; a very little chopped onion; parsley; nutmeg; salt; pepper; 2 tablespoons of butter.

Mix the milk and flour; put in a stewpan over the fire. Add the seasonings, and when thick, the butter; then put in a dish a layer of fish, and a layer of sauce, until it is full. Cover with bread crumbs, and bake half an hour.

FISH TURBOT
Mrs. F. W. King.

One cup of sweet milk; 2 tablespoons of flour; 1 tablespoon of butter, large; 2 eggs; any kind of cold fish; pepper, salt.

Let the milk come to the boiling point, add the flour, butter, pepper and salt to taste. Cool it and add the eggs well beaten. The fish should be freed from bones, and picked in pieces. Put in an escalop dish, first a layer of dressing, then of fish; repeat until the dish is full. Sprinkle the top with cracker crumbs and bits of butter. Bake a light brown.

TURBOT
Mrs. L. W. Wheeler.

Cod, halibut, or any kind of white fish; one cup of milk; 1 tablespoon of butter; 1 teaspoon of flour; 1 egg; pepper; salt; a little chopped onion, and parsley.

Rub the butter and flour together, scald the milk and add to them, and cook until it thickens; add the beaten egg. Cook a few minutes longer, then stir in the onion and parsley. Steam the fish ten minutes, pick it fine, season with salt and pepper. Put a layer of fish in a dish, cover with the dressing. Repeat until the dish is filled. Cover the top with a layer of bread crumbs, and bake twenty minutes.

OYSTERS 'a la POULETTE
Mrs. Hancock Banning.

One dozen oysters; ½ ounce of butter; 1 gill of cream; ½ of a lemon; 1 teaspoon of dissolved flour; yolk of one egg; salt; chopped parsley.

Scald the oysters in their own liquor; drain; add to the liquor the salt, butter, lemon juice, cream and flour. Add the beaten yolk, and stir until it thickens. Place the oysters in a hot dish; pour the sauce over them, adding a very little chopped parsley.

ESCALOPED OYSTERS
Mrs. A. S. Averill.

One can of oysters—choice; 1 dozen soda crackers; salt; pepper; butter; 1 egg; 1 cup of milk.

Drain the oysters; crush the crackers, (but not too fine); cover the bottom of a baking dish with the crumbs; cover it with a layer of oysters, seasoned with salt and pepper; cover it with crackers, dotted thickly with butter. Repeat until the dish is nearly filled, having the last layer of crackers and butter. Beat the egg with the milk and pour over the dish. Bake half an hour, until delicately browned. Serve at once.

CREAM OYSTERS
Mrs. J. W. McKinley.

One can fine, large oysters; 1 pint cream; ½ cup cracker crumbs, rolled fine; pepper, salt and butter to taste.

Put the oysters and cream into separate kettles to heat.

The oysters, when the edges curl, are to be taken from the juice in the kettle and put on a platter to keep warm. Sift the cracker crumbs into the cream, add the oyster juice. Season with pepper, salt, and more or less butter, as the richness of the cream may require. Pour over the oysters and serve very hot. This is nice served on slices of toast.

CREAMED OYSTERS
Mrs. S. C. Hubbell.

One pint oysters; 1 tablespoon melted butter; 1 tablespoon flour, rounding; 1 cup hot milk; salt, pepper—cayenne, lemon juice, celery salt.

Mix butter and flour; pour on the hot milk slowly, beating well; seasoning with salt, pepper—cayenne, celery salt, and a little lemon juice. Parboil the oysters, drain, and add to the sauce.

DEVILED OYSTERS
Marion Harland.

One quart fine oysters; cayenne pepper; lemon juice; some melted butter; egg, beaten light; ½ cup rolled cracker.

Wipe the oysters dry, and lay in a flat dish. Cover with a mixture of melted butter, cayenne pepper (or pepper sauce), and lemon juice. Let them lie in this for ten minutes, turning them frequently; roll in the crumbs, then in the beaten egg, again in the crumbs, and fry in mixed lard and butter, made very hot before the oysters are dropped in.

FRIED OYSTERS
Mrs. M. J. Danison.

Three eggs; a few crackers; butter; salt.

Drain oysters, spread them upon a cloth and press another upon them to absorb all moisture. Have ready yolks of eggs well beaten; in another dish, finely crushed crackers. Dip oysters, alternately in the egg and crackers, rolling over so as to become well incrusted. In the frying pan heat sufficient butter to entirely cover the oysters. Fry both sides quickly to a light brown. Dry in colander before serving. Salt to taste.

BROILED OYSTERS
"76."

Finely rolled crackers; some melted butter; salt.

The oysters, after being strained, are rolled in cracker crumbs; then shaken gently on a rough towel. Dip in melted butter; roll in cracker crumbs and broil on gridiron. Serve hot.

CURRIED OYSTERS
Practical Housekeeping.

One quart of oysters; ½ cup of butter; 2 tablespoons flour; 1 tablespoon curry powder.

Drain the liquid from the oysters into a sauce pan, add butter, flour, and curry powder well mixed. Boil; add oysters and a little salt. Boil up once, and serve.

OYSTER ROLL

Cut a round piece of bread six inches across, from the top of a well-baked round loaf. Remove the inside, leaving a crust half an inch thick. Make a rich oyster stew, put in the crust first a layer of the oysters; then of bread crumbs. Repeat until it is filled. Put the cover on top. Glaze the loaf with the beaten yolk of an egg. Place in the oven for a few moments. Serve very hot.

OYSTER PIE

Two pounds of veal; 1 quart of oysters; suet, flour, butter, salt, pepper, biscuit dough.

Cut the veal, and a small piece of suet into small pieces. Boil until well done. Thicken the stock with flour, remove from the fire, add oysters, some bits of butter, pepper, and salt. Place in buttered baking dish and cover with a crust, prepared as for baking powder biscuit. Bake until the crust is done.

OYSTER PATTIES
Mrs. A. C. St. John.

Pie crust; oysters; butter; pepper, salt.

Line gem pans with rich pie crust, and bake in a quick

oven. Have ready a stew made of either canned, or fresh oysters, quite thick, and well seasoned. Remove the crusts from the pans, fill with the oysters, and serve hot. These with baked potatoes are good for luncheon.

One pint of oysters makes one dozen patties.

OYSTER SHORT CAKE
Mrs. Susie G. Hill.

One and a half cups flour; 1 tablespoon lard; ½ teaspoon Cleveland's baking powder; a pinch of salt; sweet milk; butter size of an egg.

Mix baking powder, salt and lard in the dry flour; add just enough milk to make a dough that will roll out. Spread on butter, roll it again, and repeat until all the butter is used. Bake in two layers in a quick oven.

Filling—1 quart of oysters; 1 tablespoon butter; ½ cup of sweet milk; 3 crackers, salt, pepper.

Season the oysters with butter, salt and pepper. Stew them a few minutes, add the milk, and when it comes to the boiling point, add the cracker, finely rolled. Place between and on top of the cake.

OYSTER COCKTAIL
Miss Ruth Childs.

Three tablespoons of tomato catsup; 6 tablespoons oyster liquor; 2 teaspoons Worcestershire sauce; 2 teaspoons pepper sauce; 3 lemons, juice only; a little salt; 175 California oysters. Mix and serve.

OYSTERS IN ICE
Mrs. Hugh W. Vail.

Take a block of ice one-and-a-half feet long by one foot wide. Melt the center with a plate full of hot water. Place several oysters in the hollow, and slices of lemon around the top. Set the ice on a napkin, and garnish with watercress, or parsley.

DEVILED LOBSTER
Mrs. Chas. Howland.

One can lobster; 2 tablespoons flour; 2 tablespoons butter; 1 teaspoon mixed mustard; 1 pint milk; 1 onion; crumbs, cayenne pepper and salt.

Beat flour, butter, and seasoning together. Stir in the boiling milk. Add the chopped lobster, cook two minutes, then pour into a baking dish. Cover with crumbs and brown in the oven.

STEWED LOBSTER
Mrs. J. H. Norton.

Two lobsters freshly boiled; ½ pint sweet cream; 3 eggs; 1 ounce melted butter; salt, pepper—cayenne.

Pick the meat from the lobsters, cut in dice, about half an inch in size; put into a sauce pan with the butter, and other seasoning. Cook five minutes. Add the cream, into which the eggs have been beaten. Let it come almost to the boiling point, when it will be ready to serve, on slices of toast if preferred. To be eaten hot.

LOBSTER a la NEWBERG
Mrs. C. E. Thom.

Four pounds lobster; 3 hard-boiled eggs, (yolks); ¼ pound butter; ⅓ cup cream; 1 large tablespoon flour; salt, pepper to taste.

Remove the yolks of the eggs, mash fine, with 2 tablespoons of the cream. Rub the butter smooth with the flour, and put in a farina boiler. When the butter is melted add the cream, and stir until scalding hot. Add the yolks of eggs and the lobster. Season with salt and red pepper; stir gently until thoroughly heated.

CREAMED LOBSTER
Mrs. S. C. Hubbell.

One pint lobster; 1 cup milk; 1 cup cream; 2 tablespoons flour; salt, cayenne pepper.

Cut the lobster in small pieces. Thicken the milk and

cream, with the flour; season to taste.   Let it boil up once, and add the lobster, which should be thoroughly heated; when ready to serve.

CRAB FOR LUNCHEON
Mrs. Charles Forman.

Six spoons of minced crab; 2 spoons cracker crumbs; 2 hard-boiled eggs, chopp.d fine; ½ lemon; nutmeg, cayenne pepper, salt.

Mix the crab, cracker and eggs.   Add the juice of the half lemon, a dust of nutmeg, cayenne and salt to taste.

One spoon butter; 1 spoon flour; 1 spoon onion, finely minced; 1 pint stock or water; 2 sprigs parsley.

Warm the butter in a sauce pan.   Sprinkle in the onion and parsley.   Cook thoroughly without browning, then add the flour, stirring constantly until cooked; then the boiling stock or water.   Beat thoroughly to prevent lumping.   Mix with the prepared crab, place in a buttered dish, and bake twenty minutes.   Serve on a platter surrounded by noodles prepared as follows:

Two eggs; 2 spoons of cold water; flour.

Make eggs, flour, and water into a stiff dough, kneading it twenty minutes at least; roll it out very thin; sprinkle lightly with flour, and fold over closely like a jelly roll.   Cut into fine strips, separate lightly, and let them dry on the pastry board for an hour or more.   Put these, an handful at a time into boiling salted water.   Skim out when done. Keep them warm until enough are cooked.   Heat a spoonful of butter in a pan, add a spoonful of cracker crumbs; brown lightly and mix it thoroughly through the noodles.   Surround the crab, placing all in the oven for a moment, that it may be evenly heated.

DEVILED CRAB
Mrs. R. R. Glassell.

12 crabs; 1 onion; 1 dozen mushrooms; 1 teacup cracker crumbs; 1 teacup cream; 1 egg; 1 lemon; butter; pepper; cayenne.

Boil the crabs half an hour, then pick out flesh and fat,

discarding the deadman's fingers. Heat in a saucepan a lump of butter—size of an egg. Chop one onion fine and fry until brown. Add the prepared crab meat, and the mushrooms. Moisten the cracker crumbs with the cream and the egg yolk; add lemon juice. Salt to taste, and a thick sprinkle of cayenne. Stuff the crab shells, cover with crumbs, putting a small lump of butter on top of each. Bake twenty minutes.

N. B.—Two California crabs equal a dozen Eastern crabs.

CRAB a la CREOLE
Mrs. Hugh W. Vail.

1 crab; 2 green peppers; butter, size of a walnut; 1 onion; 1 tomato, (large); 2 tablespoons of flour; cream; pepper; salt; toasted bread.

Chop the pepper and onion very fine. Add the butter and tomato, (skinned), and simmer them for ten minutes in a saucepan, rubbed with onion before using. Add pepper and salt. Mix the flour with enough cream to look like drawn butter; add the tomato sauce to this. Let it come to a boil, then add the picked crab, and serve immediately on slices of toast.

CRAB EN COQUILLE
X. Y. Z.

Pick the meat from the shells, mince and mix it with a cream sauce. Season with salt and pepper. Put the mixture in the crab shell, as in a scallop shell; cover with buttered cracker crumbs, and bake until brown.

TERRAPIN

Four terrapins; 8 ounces butter; 4 tumblers cooking sherry; 4 eggs —yolks only; flour; salt; cayenne; black pepper.

Wash the live terrapins in several waters, until perfectly clean; throw them into a pot of boiling water, allowing to each one teaspoon of salt. Cook until so tender that the legs can be easily pulled off. Take them out. Remove the top shells, the sand bag, and the gall, (very carefully). Cut the remainder into small pieces—rejecting nothing but the intestines and skinny portions. Put it in a stewpan, with the sherry, and the butter, cut in pieces and rolled in flour. Season with cayenne, black pepper and salt. Let it come to a boil, and just before serving, stir in the beaten yolks.

This is sufficient for eight or ten persons.

DEVILED SHRIMPS
Mrs. Willard H. Stimson.

One tablespoon of butter; 1 tablespoon of flour; $\frac{1}{2}$ pint cream; 2 yolks; 2 tablespoons catsup; $\frac{1}{2}$ teaspoon mustard; pepper; cracker crumbs.

Mix flour and butter in a saucepan—without burning; add the cream, stirring constantly until thoroughly cooked and smooth. Pepper to taste, and stir in the yolks, slightly beaten. When cold, add the mustard moistened with the catsup. Mix the shrimps with the dressing. Fill the shells. Dust with cracker or bread crumbs, and bake until brown.

TIMBALE OF SHRIMP
Mrs. Ezra T Stimson

To each pint of shrimps allow one tablespoon of butter; 2 tablespoons of flour; 2 tablespoons of chopped parsley; 1 teaspoon of salt; 1 saltspoon of pepper and a dash of cayenne; 2 cups of cream or milk; 3 hard-boiled eggs.

Melt the butter, add the flour and stir until smooth; add the cream and stir constantly until the mixture thickens; add the eggs, after having passed them through a sieve; then the shrimps chopped fine, or rather small pieces; then the seasoning. Fill timbale cases; cover top with bread crumbs and bits of butter and brown in hot oven.

FRIED FROGS LEGS
Mrs. Lincoln.

Remove the skin from the hind legs—which is the only

part used. Dip in crumbs, seasoned with salt and pepper; then in egg, and again in crumbs. Wipe the bone at the end; put in a basket, and fry one minute in smoking-hot fat. Drain and serve. Some parboil them in boiling salted water and a little lemon juice before frying.

ENTRÉES

SWEETBREAD PATTIES
Mrs. I. N. Van Nuys.

Four sweetbreads: ½ pint mushrooms; ½ lemon; 2 table-spoons of butter; 2 tablespoons of flour; ½ pint of cream; 1 teaspoon of salt; a pinch of pepper; a grating of nutmeg.

Squeeze the lemon juice over the sweetbreads and dice them. Melt the butter with the flour in a porcelain sauce-pan, stirring carefully, without browning. Add cream, salt, pepper and nutmeg; then the mushrooms and sweetbreads. Fill pattie cases—procured at the confectioners. Garnish the dish with parsley.

BRAIN PATTIES
Mrs. J. H. Norton.

Two sets of brains; 1 bottle of mushrooms; French peas; drawn-butter sauce; pepper; salt; nutmeg.

Boil, clean, and chop the brains very fine. Season with pepper and salt. Have ready the drawn-butter sauce—quite rich and thick. Stir the brains into the sauce, that they may get heated thoroughly. Chop the mushrooms fine and add to the sauce. Fill the pastry shells with the mixture, plac-ing on the top of each pattie French peas that have been heated, and seasoned with salt and pepper. Grate a little nutmeg on the patties before putting on the peas.

Delicious as an entrée.

CHICKEN PATTIES
Every-Day Cook Book.

Cooked chicken; ½ pint of milk; 1 teaspoon of corn starch; 1 teaspoon of butter; salt; pepper; puff paste.

Mince the chicken; season well; stir into it a sauce made of the milk, thickened with corn starch, seasoned with butter, salt and pepper. Line small pattie tins with rich puff paste. Bake in a brisk oven. Fill with chicken. Return to the oven for a few minutes to brown slightly.

IMITATION PATTIE DE FOIE GRAS
Marion Harland.

Livers of 4 or 5 fowls and as many gizzards; 3 tablespoons melted butter; 1 chopped onion; 1 tablespoon Worcestershire, or other pungent sauce; salt and white pepper to taste; a few truffles—if you can get them.

Boil the livers until quite done; drain and wipe dry, and, when cold, rub them to a paste in a Wedgewood mortar. Let the butter and onion simmer together very slowly at the side of the range for ten minutes. Strain them through thin muslin, pressing the bag hard to extract the full flavor of the onion, and work this well into the pounded liver. Turn into a larger vessel, and mix with it the rest of the seasoning, working all together for a long while. Butter a small china or earthenware jar or cup, and press the mixture hard down within it, interspersing it with square bits of the boiled giz-zards, to represent truffles. Of course, the latter are pref-erable; but, being scarce and expensive, they are not always to be had. If you have them, boil them and let them get cold before putting them into the pattie. Cover all with melted butter, and set all in a cool, dry place.

This pattie is a delicious relish, and is more easily attain-able than would at first appear. The livers of a turkey and a pair of chickens or ducks will make a small one, and these can be saved from one poultry day to another, by boiling them in salt water, and keeping in a cool place. Or, one can often secure any number of giblets, by previous application at the kitchen of a restaurant or a hotel.

MUSHROOM PATTIES
Mrs. T. A. Lewis.

One tablespoon butter; 1 tablespoon flour; 1 can mush-rooms; salt and pepper.

Cook together the butter and flour, stir in gradually the

liquor from the mushrooms that has been heated to boiling, then add the mushrooms and season with salt and pepper. Fill pattie shells with the creamed mushrooms and brown in oven. Serve hot.

CREAMED SWEETBREADS
Mrs. H. J. Fleishman.

Half pound calves' sweetbreads; 2 tablespoons flour; 2 tablespoons butter; 2 tablespoons tomato pulp, thick; 1 tablespoon chopped mushrooms; 1 teaspoon sugar; cream, pepper, salt to taste; boiling milk.

Boil the sweetbreads in salt water. Mix flour and butter. Add sufficient milk and cream to make a thick sauce. Add tomato, mushrooms, sugar, pepper, and salt.

Brains may be cooked in the same way.

THE QUEEN'S SWEETBREADS
Mrs. W. J. Elderkin.

After carefully preparing your sweetbreads, parboil them, then cut in slices about one inch in thickness. Dip quickly into melted butter, then cover with finely grated cheese. Dip these into the yolks of well-beaten eggs, then in finely prepared bread crumbs. Fry in very hot lard, a golden brown. Serve very hot with tomato sauce and finely chipped celery.

VEAL OR CHICKEN CROQUETTES
Mrs. C. C. McLean.

One pint minced veal or chicken; ½ pint milk; 1 tablespoon butter; 2 tablespoons flour; 1 tablespoon chopped parsley; pepper, salt.

Mix the butter and flour, stir it into the milk, cook until it thickens. Add the meat, pepper, salt and parsley. When cold shape in molds and fry in deep lard or butter.

CHICKEN CROQUETTES
Mrs. Charles Carpenter.

One large chicken; 1 set of calves' brains, or sweetbreads; 1 pint cream; ¼ pound butter; 4 yolks of eggs; juice of half a lemon; salt, pepper, cayenne, mace, flour, bread crumbs.

Free the chicken meat from the bones; mince it fine, add
the parboiled brains, or sweetbreads, rub all to a smooth
paste.   Add the cream, butter, and seasoning.   Put over the
fire in a porcelain-lined kettle.   When it boils, add an handful of flour.   When it becomes a stiff paste stir in the yolks
and juice of the half lemon.   Boil up once.   Let the paste
cool over night, closely covered.   Roll out in a cool place, in
small bolsters.   Dip in powdered bread crumbs, then in egg,
then in crumbs again.   Fry in new lard, very deep.

CHICKEN CROQUETTES
Mrs. S. C. Hubbell.

Half pound chicken, chopped and seasoned with salt, pepper, cayenne, celery salt; lemon juice; onion juice; chopped
parsley; cream sauce to make quite soft.

Keep on ice until hard, then roll, dip in crumbs, beaten
egg, and again in crumbs, fry in hot lard.   Serve with thin
cream sauce and green peas.

Cream sauce—Two tablespoons melted butter; 2 tablespoons corn starch, heaping; 1 pint hot milk; salt, pepper,
celery salt, cayenne.

Mix butter, and corn starch.   Add the milk slowly, beating well, and season.

TIMBALE OF CHICKEN
Mrs. T. A. Lewis.

Half pound cooked chicken; 1 gill cream; whites of five
eggs; 1 teaspoon salt; a little cayenne pepper.

Chop the chicken very fine, then pound it to a paste, adding
gradually the cream.   Then add the whites of three eggs, beat
each one well into the mixture before adding another.   Add
the salt and cayenne pepper.   Stir in carefully the
whites of two eggs beaten to a stiff froth.   Have your timbale
cups well buttered; fill half full with the mixture, stand them
in a pan of hot water and bake in a moderate oven twenty
minutes.   Serve hot with cream mushroom sauce.

TONGUE CROQUETTES
Mrs. J. H. Norton.

One tongue, good size; 2 eggs, beaten; small quantity potatoes, cooked; melted butter; Worcestershire sauce, celery salt, salt, pepper.

Boil the tongue very tender, chop very fine. Add the potatoes chopped, the eggs and a small quantity of melted butter; season. Make into any shape desired. Roll in beaten egg, then in cracker dust, fry in hot lard to a light brown. Garnish with green and serve.

SHAD ROE CROQUETTES
Miss Parloa.

One pint cream; 4 tablespoons corn starch; 4 shad roe; 4 tablespoons butter; 1 teaspoon salt; the juice of two lemons; a slight grating of nutmeg, and a speck of cayenne.

Boil the roe fifteen minutes in salted water, then drain, and mash. Put the cream on to boil. Mix the butter and corn-starch together, and stir into the boiling cream. Add the seasoning and roe. Boil up once, and set away to cool. Shape, and fry.

OYSTER CROQUETTES

One can oysters; 1 set brains; 1 egg; bread crumbs, parsley, butter, salt, cracker crumbs, cayenne pepper.

Dry the oysters, chop them fine; add the brains and enough bread crumbs to mold; add the beaten egg, a little butter, the parsley chopped, cayenne and salt. Make in shapes, roll in cracker crumbs and fry.

POTATO CROQUETTES
Mrs. Alice Curtain.

Four or five potatoes; butter and cream; 1 egg; cracker crumbs; oil or lard; salt.

Boil and mash thoroughly the potatoes, season to taste with butter, salt, and cream. Beat to a cream, then add the well-beaten white of the egg. Make into rolls, dip into the beaten yolk of the egg, then into cracker crumbs. Put into a wire basket and fry in deep hot lard until brown.

RICE CROQUETTES
Miss Parloa.

One large cup of cooked rice; ½ cup milk; 1 egg; 1 table-spoon sugar; 1 tablespoon butter; ½ teaspoon salt; a slight grating of nutmeg.

Put the milk on to boil, add rice and seasoning. When it boils up add the egg, well-beaten. Stir one minute, then take off and cool. When cold, shape, roll in egg and crumbs. Serve very hot. Any flavoring can be substituted for the nutmeg.

CHEESE CROQUETTES
Mrs. F. S. Hicks.

Ten ounces Roquefort cheese; 5 ounces butter; sweet cream; cayenne pepper.

Mix the cheese and butter, (which should not be highly salted), with enough cream to give the mixture the consistency of paste; use the cayenne with discretion. Shape like small croquettes, and serve with water crackers and coffee.

LAMB CHOPS WITH NOODLES
Mrs. J. W. McKinley.

To make the noodles; break a large egg into a bowl, and beat into it a little more than half a cup of flour and one-fourth teaspoon of salt. Now work this dough with the hands until it becomes smooth and like putty. Sprinkle a moulding board with flour and roll the dough as thin as possible. It should be like a wafer, then roll it up, and with a sharp knife cut it into very thin slices. Shake out these little slices on the board, and let them dry for half an hour or more. Put on the stove a large saucepan containing two quarts of boiling water. Add a tablespoon of salt, and after turning the noodles into the water, cook them rapidly for twenty-five minutes, then drain off all the water. Have the chops cut from the ribs. Trim them, and season with salt and pepper. Broil for eight minutes over clear coals. Heap the noodles in the center of a warm dish. Arrange the chops around them. Over the noodles sprinkle fried bread crumbs.

How to fry crumbs—To prepare them, dry pieces of bread, until they will crumble between the fingers. Place the bread on a board and crush lightly with a rolling pin. Most of the crumbs should be so coarse that they will not pass through a flour sieve. Place a frying pan containing two level table-spoons of butter on the fire, and when the butter becomes hot add the crumbs. Stir constantly until the crumbs are brown and crisp.

ROULETTE OF VEAL
Mrs. A. C. Jones.

Small, thin veal steaks; bacon: parsley: onion.

Spread the steaks with the finely minced parsley, and onion: roll, and fasten them with tooth picks. Let them stand two or three hours. Brown thin slices of bacon in a hot sauce pan. Add a little water. Put in the veal, cook it very slowly one hour, adding a little water if required. Take out the veal when done, and make the gravy, by creaming one tablespoon of flour with one teaspoon of butter, pouring into it, little by little, some of the hot gravy in which the veal was cooked, then pouring this slowly into cream, when it is ready to serve.

BEEF ROLL
Mrs. Mary E. Flanders.

Two pounds round steak, chopped fine: 2 well-beaten eggs; 3 rolled soda crackers; ½ cup butter; season with salt and pepper, and a little sage; put in a square bread tin and bake, basting often.

MEAT PIE
Mrs. S. J. Peck.

Cold meat: salt; biscuit dough; water: tablespoon butter.

Remove the bone and gristle from cold roast beef, steak, or any other meat. Chop it fine. Turn into a pan. cover with water, add butter and stew it a few minutes. Season to taste. Line a deep baking pan with a good biscuit dough. Pour in the meat, put on top crust, and bake.

VEAL LOAF
Mrs. Lou Ward.

Six pigs feet; 8 pounds veal; salt, pepper.

Boil separately, until the meat can be picked in pieces. Use sufficient water to give a quart of liquid from each. Then boil all together in one kettle until thick enough to press. Season with salt and pepper in the last boiling. Press over night.

BEEF LOAF
Mrs. E. M. Ross.

One and a half pounds lean steak, chopped fine; 2 eggs; 1 cup rolled crackers; 1 small teaspoon pepper; 1 teaspoon salt; butter.

Mix all together and mold into a loaf. Spread bits of butter on top and bake carefully. Cut into thin slices when cold. Nice for school lunches or picnics.

MEAT LOAF
Mrs. E. W. Clark.

3 pounds raw beef, chopped at the market; 3 eggs; 3 large crackers, rolled fine; 3 tablespoons of melted butter; 1½ teaspoons of salt; a shake of pepper; a little clove and nutmeg. Bake two hours and a quarter in a moderate oven.

HAMBURG LOAF
Mrs. M. H. Williams.

3 pounds chopped beef; 1 cup milk; 6 soda crackers; 2 eggs; salt and pepper to taste.

Put the beef, milk, soda crackers—rolled fine, the well-beaten eggs, salt and pepper into a large bowl, and mix thoroughly and bake in a well-buttered bread pan one hour, in a moderate oven.

RAGOUT OF LIVER
Mrs. C. J. Ellis.

Put a little lard into a saucepan, and when hot, throw in half an onion minced fine, one or two sprigs of parsley, chopped, and slices of calf's liver. Turn the liver several times, allowing it to cook well, and imbibe the flavor of the onion and parsley. When cooked, place it by the side of the fire. In another saucepan make a sauce as follows: Put in a piece of butter, the size of a large hickory nut, when it bubbles, sprinkle in a heaping teaspoon of flour, stir it until it assumes a fine brown color, then pour in a cupful of boiling water, stirring it well with the egg whisk; add salt, pepper, a tablespoon of vinegar and a heaping tablespoon of capers. Drain out the slices of liver, put in the sauce, and keep hot till ready to serve.

CALF'S LIVER EN BROCHETTE

Cut thin slices of liver, and of bacon, into pieces three inches square. Put alternate slices of liver and bacon on skewers, and broil over coals until done and brown. Season with salt, pepper, butter, and a little lemon juice.

Kidneys are delicious, cooked in the same way.

KIDNEY STEW
Miss Delia Clemons.

Two beef kidneys; 1 onion; 4 cloves; ½ pod of red pepper; salt.

Put all together, in sufficient water to cover; boil once; skim; then let simmer three hours, until tender. Next morning, cut them open; remove all fat, and cut in small pieces. Put a large spoonful of butter in a skillet; sift in a little flour; brown; then turn in the kidneys and gravy. Stir until it thickens a little. Serve hot.

CHICKEN PIE
Mrs. M. Pickering.

One chicken; 1 tablespoon of salt; 1 tablespoon of butter; 1 tablespoon of flour; water.

Cut the chicken in pieces; boil until tender, in just enough water to cover it, adding the salt when half done. Take out the chicken, thicken the liquid with the flour and butter rubbed together. Season with salt and pepper; boil five minutes.

Crust—One quart of flour; 1 cup of butter; 2 teaspoons of Cleveland's baking powder; make into dough, adding a little salt. Roll one-half of this one quarter of an inch in thickness. Line a deep dish, allowing an inch to turn over the top crust; put in the chicken and gravy. Cover. Wet the edge and fold over the under crust; press them firmly together. Cut a hole in the center. Spread soft butter over the top. Make an ornament to fit the center and bake until done.

OLD VIRGINIA CHICKEN PIE
Mrs. E. M. Ross.

Spring chicken; sliced bacon; 1 teacup bread crumbs; 1 pint of rich cream; 1 tablespoon butter; yolks of three hard-boiled eggs; salt and pepper.

Make a rich pastry, line a deep tin pan with it, put in chicken with other ingredients, cover with a top crust and bake slowly one hour.

CHICKEN PIE
Katherine Duncan Lewis.

Pastry—one pint of flour; 1 coffeecup of butter and lard, mixed; ½ teaspoon of salt.

Chop well in wooden chopping bowl, then mix into a stiff dough, with ice water, (never touch with the hands, and have the butter frozen), roll out, fold up and put on ice for half an hour.

One chicken; 2 tablespoons of butter; 2 tablespoons of flour; one cup of oysters; salt; pepper; celery seed; 1 pint chicken broth.

The chicken should be boiled, cut in pieces, and laid in the baking dish, with the gravy—made of the butter and flour cooked together, to which is added the pint of hot liquor in which the chicken has been boiled. Add salt, pepper, celery seed, and oysters. Cover with the pastry. Bake thirty or forty minutes. No bottom or side crust.

CHICKEN 'a la MERINGO
Mrs. C. H. Walton.

Two chickens; salt pork; 2 tablespoons of butter; 2 table-spoons of onions; 4 tablespoons of flour; 1 quart white stock or water; 1 cup of strained tomato; 1 cup of mushrooms; olives.

Singe and cut up the chickens. Roll the pieces in flour and fry them brown in pork fat. Brown the onions in the butter, add flour and stock, simmer five minutes; season; add the tomato, pour over the chicken. Cook twenty minutes. Add mushrooms and olives.

JELLIED CHICKEN
Mrs. W. G. Whorton.

One chicken; 2 tablespoons gelatine; hard-boiled eggs; salt; pepper.

Boil the chicken in as little water as possible until the meat falls from the bones, chop fine; season with salt and pepper. Put in a mold a layer of chicken, then a layer of sliced eggs; alternate these until the mold is nearly full; Boil down to one half the liquor which is left in the pot. While warm, add the gelatine; when dissolved, pour over the chicken. Set in a cool place to jelly.

PRESSED CHICKEN
Mrs. J. W. Gillette.

Two chickens; 1 cup of butter; 1 tablespoon of salt; 1 teaspoon of pepper; 1 beaten egg; a little parsley; hard-boiled eggs.

Boil the chickens until the meat separates from the bones. Chop the meat. Boil the liquor until it is reduced to a cupful. Add to this the butter, salt, pepper, parsley and beaten egg. Stir this mixture into the chicken. Lay slices of boiled egg in a dish, press in the chicken. Serve, garnished with celery tops.

CREOLE FRICASSEE

Mrs. E. M. Ross.

Cut chicken, or any other fowl, into pieces, and allow it to lie in cold *salted* water for 30 minutes, take out and dry with a towel. Rub each piece with a little black and red pepper and dredge them lightly with flour. Have two table-spoonfuls of ham fat boiling hot in the saucepan, brown the chicken in this. When well-browned on both sides, put in a few rings of onions, and when these are pale brown, add a pint and a half of hot water—celery, salt and pepper to taste; cover closely and cook gently until the chicken is tender. The creoles color this gravy very often with Chili pepper, which gives it a fine red color.

SALMI OF DUCK

Juliet Corson.

Dress and cut the duck in small joints before cooking. Roast it brown in its own fat. Dust with dry flour, which is also browned. Cover with boiling water, and stew slowly until tender. A palatable seasoning of salt and pepper, and a cupful of olives are to be added at any time.

SALMI OF DUCK

Mrs. Carl Schutze.

At elegant dinners, when duck is served, only the breast is used. The portions that remain can be prepared for luncheons as follows:

Cut the joints neatly, remove every bit of meat from the bones, crack and put them in a stew pan, with the bits of skin, add 1 tomato, sliced; 1 onion, sliced; 1 carrot, sliced; a few bits of celery, salt, pepper and a very little Spanish pepper. Cover with water and stew slowly two hours, (a longer time will do no harm). In another saucepan brown sufficient flour and butter for sauce for the meat. Strain the liquid from the stew, pour it boiling on the flour and butter. Rub the vegetables through a sieve and add them, and then put in the duck meat, let it get very hot, then serve. On no account let it boil. Spanish pepper should be used cautiously, as a little goes a good way.

BRAINS

Miss M. E. McLellan.

Brains; vinegar; laurel leaves; onions; beefsteak; cloves; flour; butter; pepper; salt.

Scald and skin the brains, cover with vinegar; add a few laurel leaves, two or three cloves and a little onion. Let them stand several hours. When ready to cook, pour off the vinegar and stew them in water about twenty minutes. Make a gravy of beef stock, a little flour and butter. Season with pepper, salt and a little vinegar. Put the brains in the gravy and cook them a few minutes. Serve.

BRAIN FRITTERS

Mrs. A. C. Doan.

One pair beef brains; put in cold salt water for ten or fifteen minutes to remove the blood. Wash them, boil in salted water for fifteen minutes. When cold, cut in slices about half an inch thick. Dip in batter made as follows:

One egg, well beaten; 1 cup sweet milk; 1 cup flour; and a little salt; fry in *very hot* lard until brown. Serve hot.

CREAM FRITTERS

Mrs. R. L. McKnight.

Six macaroons; 6 eggs; ½ pint cream; 2 ounces sugar; ½ lemon.

Pound the macaroons in a mortar, mix them with the sugar, and grated rind of the half lemon. Beat the yolks soft; and the whites of two eggs to a stiff froth and add. Add the cream; mix well. Fry the fritters a light brown on both sides. Sift sugar over them and serve immediately.

GREEN CORN FRITTERS

Mrs. W. W. Lord.

One quart corn; 1 teacup flour; 2 eggs; butter, milk.

Use sufficient milk to make a batter, and fry in hot butter, one tablespoon to one fritter.

LOBSTER CUTLETS
Mrs. C. H. Walton.

One pint lobster meat, cut fine; 1 saltspoon salt; 1 salt-spoon mustard; 1 cup thick cream sauce; a little cayenne.

Mix, and spread half an inch thick on a platter. Cut in the shape of cutlets. Roll in crumbs, then in egg, and again in crumbs. Fry in smoking hot fat. Drain, and serve with a claw to represent the bone.

NUT SANDWICHES
Mrs. C. C. Converse.

Bread, butter, English walnuts; Swiss cheese; salt.

Cut thin slices of delicately buttered bread into fancy shapes. Spread them with walnuts chopped very fine and mixed with grated Swiss cheese, slightly salted. Put two together.

MACARONI PUDDING
Mrs. H. Z. Osborne.

One-third package (best white) macaroni; ⅓ cup butter; 1 cup grated cheese; ½ cup sweet milk; 1 egg; salt and pepper to taste.

Break macaroni into small pieces, and put into a sauce pan of boiling water. Boil for half an hour. Then drain off all of the water and season with the butter, pepper and salt, and half of the grated cheese. Put this into a buttered pudding-dish, and sprinkle the remainder of the cheese over the top, and pour the milk and egg (thoroughly beaten together) over all, and bake twenty minutes.

Baked Macaroni with Cheese and Tomatoes
Mrs. W. B. Holcomb.

Two-thirds cup of cracker crumbs; 1 cup macaroni; cheese, tomatoes, milk, butter; salt, pepper.

Break into half-inch pieces enough macaroni to fill a cup. Put it into a kettle of boiling salted water, and cook rapidly for one-half hour. Put in a baking dish a layer of macaroni, then a layer of grated cheese, then a layer of tomatoes, until a sufficient quantity is used.   Pour over this mixture enough milk to cover, season with salt, pepper and butter.   Cover the whole with cracker crumbs, moistened in melted butter. Bake until the crumbs are a light brown.

POULTRY AND GAME

M. B. W.

In *roasting* or *boiling* whole any fowl, truss it.

To broil, split the body down the back, and lay it open.

Cut the joints, do not break the bones, when preparing a fowl for fricassee.

The longer fowl or game can be kept perfectly sweet, before cooking, the more tender it will be.

ROAST TURKEY
Mrs. W. G. W.

The turkey should be carefully plucked, singed with white paper, neatly drawn, washed inside, and thoroughly dried with a cloth. Cut off the neck close to the back, leaving enough of the skin to turn over on the back. Cut off the legs in the joints, draw out the strings from the thighs, and flatten the breast bone—to make it look plump. Fill the breast and body with the dressing, sew up carefully, truss firmly. Dredge with flour and put in the oven. Baste freely, first with butter and water, then with the gravy in the pan. Roast to a golden brown, allowing twenty minutes to the pound. To prevent scorching, lay a piece of buttered brown paper over the breast. Serve with cranberry sauce and gravy.

PLAIN DRESSING FOR ROAST TURKEY
Mrs. W. G. W.

One large or two small loaves of stale bread; ¾ pound of butter; 1 teaspoon of salt; 2 teaspoons of sage; 1 teaspoon of pepper; Use only the soft part of the bread, finely crumbed, and work in the butter without melting.

CHESTNUT DRESSING FOR ROAST TURKEY
Mrs. W. G. W.

Shell thirty large chestnuts, boil them two or three minutes, throw them into cold water, and remove the brown skin. Cover again with boiling water and cook them slowly one hour. Dry, mash and mix them with a plain bread and butter dressing, omitting the sage. Serve turkey with chestnut sauce.

Oyster Stuffing for Roast Turkey
Mrs. W. G. W.

Make a bread and butter dressing, leaving, out the sage. Drain the liquor from a quart of oysters. Put in first a spoonful of the dressing, then two or three oysters; until the turkey is filled. Be careful not to break the oysters.

TURKEY DRESSING
Mrs. Frank Phillips.

One pint of grated bread crumbs, 1 tablespoon of butter; 1 pound of currants; 1 egg; a little milk.

Put the crumbs and butter in a hot oven ten minutes, then take out and add the currants, (which have been boiled and dried), the egg and milk.

STUFFING FOR TURKEY
Mrs. C. H. Walton.

Soft bread or cracker crumbs; season with thyme, salt and pepper; moisten with ½ cup of hot butter, and hot water enough to make it quite moist. Mix in about ½ pound of chopped English walnuts.

ROAST TURKEY
Mrs. J. H. Jones.

When the turkey is made ready to roast, fill the breast and body with a dressing made of grated bread crumbs; ½ cup melted butter; pepper; salt and sage. One raw egg added makes the dressing cut smoothly.

Rub the outside of the turkey well with fresh lard or a little butter and salt. Roast from two to four hours, according to size. Serve with cranberry sauce.

BONED ROASTED TURKEY
Mrs. W. J. Brown.

Slit the skin down the back, and raising one side at a time with the fingers, separate the flesh from the bones with a knife; when the legs and wings are reached, unjoint them from the body, and cut through to the bone, then turn back the flesh and remove the bones. The turkey may be reshaped, by stuffing with any dressing preferred, sew together. press the wings close to the back, tie firmly. Baste often with water, seasoned with salt and butter. Roast until thoroughly done. Carve across in slices. Serve with cranberry sauce, or jelly.

BOILED TURKEY
Practical Housekeeping.

Wash the turkey thoroughly, and rub it with salt; fill with a dressing of bread and butter, seasoned with sage, salt and pepper, mixed with a pint of raw oysters, (chopped). Tie the legs and wings close to the body. Place in boiling salted water, with the breast downward. skim often. Boil about two hours, but not until the skin breaks. Serve with oyster sauce.

DEVILED TURKEY
Mrs. C. J. Ellis.

Cut the legs and thighs from a roasted turkey. Score them deeply, and rub in plenty of mustard. Pour over them the gravy and juice of meat. Pepper and salt liberally; put in Worcestershire sauce, cayenne pepper and a dash of garlic. Let it stand all night to become thoroughly impregnated. Before breakfast put in stew pan on fire and stew thoroughly, pouring the juice with plenty of butter in the stew pan.

MARYLAND FRIED CHICKEN
Juliet Corson.

To prepare the chicken; remove the feathers, singe it, wipe it with a wet towel. Draw it without breaking the intestines, and there will be no need of washing it. Cut it in joints, as for fricassee; dip each joint quickly in cold water, then at once roll it in flour, seasoned with salt and pepper, covering it thoroughly. Melt lard in a large, shallow frying pan, covering the bottom a quarter of an inch deep. When the fat begins to smoke, put in the chicken, leaving spaces between the pieces. Fry slowly until it is a light brown, and tender. Allow three-quarters of an hour for preparing the entire dish.

FRIED YOUNG CHICKEN
Mrs. W. H. Pendleton.

Flour, butter, lard, salt, chicken.

Cut the chicken in pieces; salt, roll in flour and fry slowly in equal quantities of hot butter and lard, until of a fine brown.

BROILED CHICKEN
Practical Housekeeping.

Cut the chicken open on the back, lay on the meat board, and pound until it will be flat on the gridiron. Broil over coals until of a nice brown. It will cook much better if covered with a pie tin, pressed down with a weight, so that all parts of the chicken may lie close to the gridiron. While the chicken is broiling, boil the liver, gizzard and heart in a pint of water; when tender, chop fine, add flour, butter, pepper, salt. Stir a cup of sweet cream in the water in which they were boiled. When the chicken is cooked, dip it in the gravy while hot, return it to the gridiron for a minute, then put it in the gravy, boil half a minute, and serve hot. Cook quail in the same way.

ROAST GOOSE
Miss Parloa.

Stuff the goose with a dressing made as follows:

Potatoes boiled, peeled, and mashed fine and light; 1 tablespoon salt; 1 teaspoon pepper; 1 teaspoon sage; 2 tablespoons of onion juice; 2 of butter. Truss, and dredge well with salt, pepper and flour. Roast before the fire, (if weighing eight pounds), one and one-half hours; in the oven, one and one quarter hours.   Make gravy as for turkey.   No butter is required for goose, it is so fat.   Serve with apple sauce.

ROAST DUCK
Miss Parloa.

Ducks to be good must be cooked rare; for this reason it is best not to stuff.   If you do stuff them use the goose dressing, and have it very hot.   The better way is to cut an onion in two, and put in the body of the bird, then truss, and dredge with salt, pepper and flour, and roast, if before the fire, forty minutes, if in the oven, thirty minutes. The fire must be very hot, and the oven a very quick one.   Serve with currant jelly, and a sauce, made the same as for turkey.

ROASTED TEAL DUCK
Mrs. Anna Ogier.

Pick, clean, and hang the ducks two days.   Make a stuffing of bread crumbs, salt, pepper, onions, and a small piece of butter.   Lay them in a pan, dredge with flour, pepper and salt.   Baste frequently.

HOW TO DRESS A DUCK DRY
Mrs. Carl Schutze.

The feathers of a duck can be easily removed while the natural heat remains in it.

Select a heavy piece of board, longer and broader than the bird.   Drive two nails firmly in the top, and to these tie the duck securely, as soon as slaughtered. Set the board in slanting position on the table.   Scald wings and tail that the larger feathers may be removed easily.   Pick breast and back first.   Work as rapidly as possible, using both hands.   Hold the bird first by the wings, then by the feet over a quick blaze so as to remove hairs.

Place the edge of a knife-blade under pin-feathers and remove by grasping them between thumb and blade.

BREAKFAST QUAIL
J. A. Graves.

Prepare the birds by opening in the back, place them in a
dripping pan, season with salt, pepper, and a generous supply
of butter; add enough water to cover the bottom of the pan,
then place them in a hot oven.   Turn the birds frequently,
basting them with the seasoned water in the pan, which
gradually cooks down, making a fine gravy.   By constant
basting, the birds when well done and nicely browned, will be
rich and juicy and of a finer flavor than when broiled.

Serve on buttered toast.

BROILED QUAIL
Mrs. Adelia Hall.

Dress the birds carefully, and lay them a little time in
salted water. Split down the back, dry with a cloth, rub with
butter, and place them on a gridiron over a clear fire.   Turn
them frequently.   Dip them in melted butter, seasoned with
salt.   Lay slices of thin toast nicely buttered upon a hot dish,
place a bird, breast upward, upon each slice.   Garnish with
currant jelly.

ROAST QUAIL
Everyday Cook Book.

Pluck and drain the birds, rub them with butter, tie strips
of bacon over the breasts, and roast in the oven from twenty
to twenty-five minutes.

HUNTER'S STEW
J. A. Graves.

One dozen quail, (doves may be used); 1 gallon of water;
1 large onion; 2 pods of red pepper; tomatoes; potatoes; green
corn; bacon; celery; black pepper; salt.

Put the quail in a porcelain lined stew pan with close
fitting cover.   Add the water, pepper pods, a slice of bacon,
salt and black pepper to taste.   Cover and boil one hour,
then add the onion quartered, the celery chopped, corn cut
from the ear, tomatoes, and potatoes, and more water if

required. Stew one hour and a half. Regulate the quantity of vegetables according to taste. Corn and tomatoes add much to the flavor. A few rabbits, quartered and cooked with the birds is an improvement. Canned corn may be used if fresh is not in season.

LARDED AND ROASTED GROUSE
Mrs. Frank E. Phillips.

Clean, and rinse quickly in cold water. Season with salt and pepper. Dredge with butter and flour. Put one onion inside, roast half an hour in hot oven.

Serve with bread sauce and fried bread crumbs. Any fowl can be cooked in the same way.

PIGEON PIE
Everyday Cook Book.

Clean and truss three or four pigeons. Rub outside and inside with a mixture of pepper and salt. Fill with bread and butter stuffing or mashed potatoes. Sew them up. Butter, and line with pie crust, the sides of a pudding dish, and lay in the birds. For three large tame pigeons, cut quarter of a pound of sweet butter, strew this over them, with a large teaspoon of salt, a small teaspoon of pepper, and, if liked, some minced parsley. Dredge with a tablespoon of wheat flour, add water to nearly fill the pan, lay skewers across the top, cover with puff paste crust. Cut a slit in the middle. Ornament the edge. Bake in a quick oven one hour, then brush the crust with the yolk of egg beaten with a little milk, and finish baking. All small birds may be cooked in this manner.

WILD PIGEONS WITH OLIVES
Mrs. E. F. C. Klokke.

Clean, wash, and salt the pigeons. Brown them in hot butter, then stew them in broth or water for from forty-five to sixty minutes. Add broth or water from time to time to prevent burning. Boil pickled olives in water for from five to ten minutes, add them to the gravy; stew them a few moments and serve with the birds.

ROAST WILD DUCK
Mrs. W. G. W.

Before roasting, parboil them, with a small peeled carrot placed in each; this will absorb the fishy flavor which most wild ducks have. When parboiled, throw away the carrots, and lay the ducks in fresh water half an hour. Dry, and stuff with bread crumbs seasoned with pepper, salt and sage (or onion.) Roast until brown and tender, basting alternately with butter and water, and the drippings. When the ducks are taken up, add a teaspoon of currant jelly and a pinch of cayenne pepper to the gravy; thicken with browned flour, and serve in a tureen.

FRIED RABBIT
Mrs. J. W. Hendricks.

A young cottontail rabbit; bacon; flour; hot lard.

Soak the rabbit four or five hours in strong, salt water. Cut in pieces suitable for frying. Roll in flour, and drop into hot lard, to which two or three good-sized pieces of bacon have been added. Season well. Cook thoroughly and it will be as nice as chicken.

BARBECUED RABBIT

Two tablespoons vinegar; 1 tablespoon made mustard; pepper, salt, butter, parsley.

Clean and wash the rabbit; open it all the way on the under side. Lay it flat in salted water for half an hour. Wipe dry, and broil it, gashing the thick part of the back that the heat may penetrate it. When brown and tender, put it on a hot dish, add pepper, salt and butter; turning it over and over, that it may absorb the butter. Cover and set in the oven for five minutes. Heat the vinegar, and mustard; pour it over the rabbit; garnish with crisp parsley, and serve.

JACK RABBIT FRIED
Mrs. Carl Schutze.

Sufficient fat for cooking; a little chopped parsley; pepper, salt.

Dress rabbit and soak over night in very salt water. Joint. Cut the back across the spine into pieces two inches thick. Wipe pieces as dry as possible and immerse in deep fat, very hot. Four minutes time will cook the thinner pieces, and eight minutes will be required for the joint of the hind leg if very large. Watch carefully that the pieces do not burn. When done, dredge with salt, pepper and parsley. Lay on butcher's paper that the fat may be absorbed, and place in oven till ready for use. This way of cooking preserves the game taste liked by so many.

JACK RABBIT FRICASSEE
Mrs. Carl Schutze.

One onion; a few pepper corns; a little cream; a piece of butter; salt.

Dress rabbit, and soak over night in very salt water. When ready for use, joint; put it in a large saucepan with the onion, sliced, and sufficient water to cover. Boil five minutes before turning off the water. Season with salt and whole pepper corns. Remove rabbit and onion to a hot platter. Skim off pepper corns and thicken the gravy. Add cream and butter and boil once more before turning over the rabbit.

SQUIRRELS

Recipes for rabbit and squirrel are interchangeable. The large fat California squirrels have tender, savory meat.

MEATS

M. B. W.

Meat should not be allowed to remain in the paper in which it is sent from the market; the paper imparts a disagreeable taste, aside from absorbing the juices. Meat should be cut across the grain of the muscle. If necessary to clean, scrape fresh meat, or wash all over with a clean, wet cloth. Do not place meat *in* water. Wipe perfectly dry before cooking. Never put meat directly on ice; hang, or place on a dish in the refrigerator, not in the ice chamber.

Salt meats should be put to cook in cold water, fresh meats in boiling water. In boiling meats, if more water is required, add hot water, and be careful to keep the water on the meat constantly boiling.

BEEF 'a la MODE—Southern Style
Mrs. J. F. Conroy.

Seven to 10 lbs. beef round, shoulder is best; 1 tablespoon allspice; 1 tablespoon cinnamon; 1 tablespoon cloves; carrots, turnips, onions, garlic, bacon, fresh pork, 1 pint water.

Bind the beef with a strip of muslin to keep in shape. Cut five turnips and five carrots in strips about three inches in length, and a third of an inch in width; boil them, but not so tender that they will break. Cut pork into strips of the same size, make incisions in the beef an inch apart, in each of these put a piece of pork, of carrot, and of turnip, which have been rolled in the mixed spices; use small bits of garlic occasionally. When all are filled place in a spider with a pint of water; dredge with flour; bake slowly two hours; then add to the pan whole onions, carrots, and turnips; lay small pieces of bacon on the beef; bake another hour; the last half hour, baste with gravy prepared as follows:

One turnip: 1 carrot; ¾ pint water; ¼ pint currant jelly. Cook until thick: then strain.

Remove the cloth from the beef, and serve it on a dish with the whole vegetables placed around it, and small pieces of fat on top.

ROAST BEEF
A. C. B.

A sirloin or rib roast is best. Have the bones removed. Roll the meat and fasten in shape with skewers or tie with strong string. Place on a rack in a dripping pan and put in a very hot oven to sear it over in order to retain the juices. Keep the oven closed for about ten minutes, then open, dredge with flour, salt and pepper, and baste with the gravy. Turn the meat when necessary and baste often. Bake a six-pound roast one hour if liked rare, and an hour and a quarter if liked well done. Serve with gravy made from the drippings of the meat; or any favorite sauce.

LARDED FILLET OF BEEF
Mrs. M. B. Welch.

The fillet must be well trimmed and freed from fat and skin. Then lard it neatly; put the trimmings of pork or bacon, with which you have larded it, in the bottom of the dripping pan; pour into the pan a cup of good beef stock, or hot water, though the stock is much the better: sprinkle salt and pepper over the fillet, put it in the pan, and bake from half to three-quarters of an hour, according to the size of the fillet, basting frequently, and adding, if necessary, a little stock occasionally. Serve with mushroom sauce.

POTTED ROAST
Miss Carrie T. Waddilove.

Five pounds round steak; 2 large slices salt pork; 1 large onion (sliced): 4 cloves of garlic (cut fine); 4 bay leaves (crushed fine): 1 large carrot (cut in thin pieces): 4 stalks celery (cut thin); 4 drops tobasco; 1 teaspoon ground cloves; ½ teaspoon mace; 1 pint boiling water; 1 can French mushrooms; grated rind ½ orange; pepper, salt.

Place slices of salt pork in the bottom of a kettle; cover with onion, garlic, bay leaves, carrot, celery, tobasco, ground cloves, mace and orange peel.

Trim the steak well; bind together; make several incisions and put in them salt pork, pepper and salt. Place in boiling water for a few moments in order to retain juice; then take it out and put it on top of the ingredients in the pot and cover with the pint of boiling water. Lay a thick cloth over the pot, covering closely; boil constantly for three or four hours. About an hour before serving, uncover and set on back of stove; turn over the beef; do not thicken the gravy. Chop coarsely a can of French mushrooms and add to gravy about ten minutes before serving.

YORKSHIRE PUDDING—An Accompaniment for Roast Beef
Mrs. E. J. Curson.

One pint sweet milk; 4 eggs; 2 cups flour; 2 teaspoons Cleveland's baking powder; 1 teaspoon salt; drippings.

Beat whites and yolks separately. Mix the ingredients into a smooth batter. Pour drippings from the roast into a baking dish, add the batter, and bake twenty minutes. Serve immediately. It is not good except it be hot. This is better than the old way of baking in the pan with the roast.

BROILED STEAK
Mrs. R. M. Widney.

Steak to be good should be at least three-fourth inch thick. Trim, put in double broiler, and cook over a bed of clear coals for ten minutes if you wish a rare steak, from twelve to fifteen for a well-done steak. Turn constantly. Serve on a hot platter with first-class butter, pepper and salt. Do not stick a knife or a fork into the meat as this injures it. Many serve with mushroom, tomato and other sauces.

TO FRY STEAK
Mrs. T. F. McCamant.

A good tenderloin steak; salt, pepper, flour, suet.
Remove the gristle, and outside parts from the steak.
Pound well. Season and roll in flour, fry in smoking hot
suet a quarter of an inch deep. Turn it as soon as it browns.
When cooked remove to a hot platter and spread over it a
little butter.

Steak fried in this way, if not overcooked, is as wholesome as when broiled.

BEEF STEAK WITH ONIONS
Mrs. Anna Ogier.

Tenderloin steak or porterhouse; 2 large onions; 1 tablespoon of butter; cream, flour, pepper, salt.

Crisp the steak quickly on both sides, in a very hot, well-
greased frying pan. Remove it to a dish and keep it hot.
Chop and scald the onions, season with pepper and salt, fry
to a light brown; dredge with flour, and add cream or milk
sufficient to make a nice gravy. Let it come to a boil then
pour it over the steak.

STEAK SINOLAISE
Mrs. Hotchkiss.

Three and one half lbs. beefsteak; 1 tablespoon vinegar;
3 silver-skinned onions; salt, pepper, flour, lard, parsley,
thyme, sage, bay leaves, garlic.

The steak should be two and a half or three inches thick
and not too large to lie flat in a spider. Sprinkle with salt,
pepper, and vinegar. Make three or four incisions in it and
put small pieces of garlic in them. Let it stand thirty
minutes, then rub it on both sides with sweet lard, dredge
plentifully with flour. Fry brown on both sides, then sprinkle
it with the sweet herbs, and onions sliced thin, cover with
cold water, and stew slowly until tender in a closely-covered
spider. One and a half hours is required for a steak of this
size. Serve with plain boiled rice.

BRAISED BEEF
Mrs. Henderson.

Five ℔s. fresh beef, (not too lean) ; 1 onion, sliced ; 1 carrot, sliced ; 1 quart boiling water ; 2 or 3 sprigs of parsley; 4 cloves, a little celery; pepper, salt.

Cover tightly, cook three hours, adding a little boiling water if needed.

Serve with horseradish sauce.

BEEF OMELET
Mrs. W. W. Lord.

Three ℔s. beef (chopped fine); 3 eggs (beaten); 6 crackers (rolled fine); 1 tablespoon salt; 1 tablespoon melted butter; 1 teaspoon pepper; sage to taste.

Mix well and form into a loaf. Put a little water and bits of butter into the pan. Invert a pan over the top and bake an hour and a quarter, basting occasionally.

DRIED BEEF FRIZZLED IN CREAM
Mrs. F. H. Pieper.

Chipped beef; butter the size of an egg; a little flour; cream.

Melt the butter in a frying pan, stir the beef in it for two or three minutes, dust in a little flour; add the cream. Boil, and serve hot.

CORN BEEF BOILED
Mrs. W. J. Brown.

Put the meat in cold water. Boil five to six hours, then remove the bones. Wrap it in a napkin and put it in a cool place under a weight to press it. It will be more juicy if left in the liquor until cold.

LUNCHEON CORN BEEF
Mrs. M. G. Moore.

Thin slices corn beef; 1 tablespoon butter; 1 tablespoon flour; 1 tablespoon good vinegar; 1 cup of water.

Put into a frying-pan the butter and flour; cook; stiring

all the while. Add water and vinegar. Lay the corn beef into this and cook four or five minutes.

HUNTER'S ROAST
Mrs. R. M. Widney.

Leg mutton; 1 lb. bacon or salt pork. Cut the bacon in strips about three inches long; make slits, or pockets near the surface of the mutton, and insert the bacon in such a way that the fat from it will drain through the mutton while roasting.

Baste often; allow about 15 minutes to the pound.

TO FRY MUTTON
Mrs. T. F. McCamant.

Mutton; salt; pepper; sugar; nutmeg or cinnamon; flour; suet.

Take steak from the round of mutton; pound thoroughly; sprinkle with salt, pepper, a little sugar, a *very little* nutmeg or cinnamon, or both. Roll in flour, fry in hot suet.

Mutton prepared and cooked in this way will pass for venison at any table.

LEG OF MUTTON BOILED
Mrs. W. J. Brown.

Leg of mutton; boiling water; 1 tablespoon vinegar; salt; pepper.

Add the vinegar to boiling water; put in the mutton. When it comes to the boiling point set it on back of the stove and let it simmer two and one-half hours. Season with salt and pepper. Cook until tender, which will take from four to five hours.

Serve with caper, or egg sauce.

SADDLE OF LAMB
Mrs. Lincoln.

Trim off all the pink skin and superfluous fat. Remove the ends of the ribs, the cord, and veins along the back. Wipe, and rub the inside with salt, pepper and flour; place it in the pan, with the inside up, in order to thoroughly cook the fat. Baste and dredge often. When the fat is brown and crisp, turn, and cook the upper part till brown. Keep a buttered paper over it to prevent burning.

SHOULDER OF VEAL
Miss Frances Widney.

Two and one half lbs. veal; 1½ cup butter; 1 cup sweet cream; toasted bread; pepper; salt; cornstarch.

Heat the butter in a kettle; cut the veal in pieces; fry it brown in the butter, then add sufficient water to cook it. When done, thicken the gravy with the cornstarch, and add the cream. Serve on the toasted bread. This is sufficient for seven persons.

BREADED VEAL CUTLETS
Mrs. J. M. B.

Trim and flatten the cutlets; season with pepper and salt, dip in beaten eggs, then in rolled cracker. Fry rather slowly in butter or beef drippings. Serve on a hot platter, plain, or with tomato sauce.

HAUNCH OF VENISON—Old Kentucky Huntsman's Recipe

Haunch of venison; ½ lb. butter; salt and pepper.

Put the venison in a large kettle, cover with water, and boil until tender; drain off the water, put the butter with salt and pepper in the kettle, set over a moderate fire, and let brown, first on one side, and then on the other. Venison cooked in this way retains its natural flavor, and will be found delicious.

HAM BONES
Mrs. Jessie Benton Fremont.

"The Funeral of a Ham." This is the startling name the Germans give their final use of the unsightly "ham-bones" —too good still to be thrown away, but too ugly to bring to table.

The bone, itself, goes into the soup kettle and from the

broth it flavors, they take enough to stew *gently*, (*boiling fast, kills flavors and hardens meat*), the shavings of ham that had remained on the bone.

Put these in the broth with a Chili pepper, a very little garlic, soup-herbs and a laurel leaf—pungent, but sparingly used flavors, and let them assimilate by *slow*, steady heat. Then make mashed potatoes into a lining for a pudding-dish (you can also use boiled macaroni in the same way;) and lay in the stewed ham in light layers alternating with potatoes (or macaroni) and bake so it will look light and brown, like a potato soufflé. There may be some baking powder to make the brown top crust and sides, or cream, (I really do not know how it is done, but it should be brown and raised like a nice dish of baked mashed potatoes) and sent to the table in the dish in which it was baked. It is simple enough—most excellent and *flavorous*, or only fit for a railway eating-station—according to the intelligent patience of the cook.

BAKED HAM
Mrs. S. Speedy

Scrape, and wash a nice, plump ham. Mix a paste of flour and water. Roll it out about an inch in thickness, cover the entire ham with this, wetting the edges to make them adhere. Bake three hours.

BAKED HAM
Everyday Cook Book

Wash and scrape the ham, then cover with cold water and simmer gently, until the skin can be pulled off (probably two or three hours). When skinned, and in the dripping pan, pour over it one teacup of vinegar, and one of hot water in which one teaspoon of mustard has been dissolved. Bake slowly two hours, basting often. Then cover the ham all over to the depth of an inch with brown sugar, pressing it down firmly. Set it in a very slow oven. The sugar will soon form a thick crust. It should remain in the oven a full hour. Then remove from the pan, drain, and place upon a dish. When the ham is cool, but not cold, press it by turning another flat dish on top with a weight on it. Pressing makes the ham slice firmly.

BOILED HAM
Mrs. R. M. Widney

Take a ham weighing from twelve to fourteen pounds, wash thoroughly, cover with cold water, and cook slowly, from five to six hours. When nearly cold, remove the ham from the water in which it boiled and draw off the skin. Have ready six or eight well rolled soda crackers, with which is mixed about three tablespoons of sugar; spread over ham, place in a moderately hot oven, for thirty or forty minutes.

BROILED HAM
Practical Housekeeping.

Broil slices of ham on a hot gridiron until the fat runs out, and the meat is slightly brown; then drop the slices into a pan of cold water, drain and return to the gridiron; repeat several times until the ham is done. Place on a hot platter; add a little butter, and serve at once. Pickled pork and breakfast bacon may be broiled in the same way.

HAM FOR TOAST
Mrs. S. C. Hubbell.

One-fourth pound lean ham; 1 tablespoon cream or milk; 1 tablespoon melted butter; yolks of three eggs.

Mince the ham, and mix it with the other ingredients; then stir all together over the fire until the mixture thickens. Spread on hot toast.

HAM FOR SANDWICHES
Mrs. W. W. Ross.

Five pounds ham, boiled and cold; 2 pounds fresh beef tongue; 1 tablespoon white sugar; 1 teaspoon mustard, dry; 1 teaspoon pepper; 2 eggs.

Chop the ham and tongue very fine; add the sugar, mustard and pepper. Moisten the meat with the eggs, well beaten. Spread the mixture between thin slices of buttered bread. This quantity will make a hundred sandwiches.

ROAST PIG

Mrs. J. M. B.

Select a pig from four to six weeks old. Clean it thoroughly using a teaspoon of soda in the water you wash the inside with. Wipe dry and stuff with a dressing made of bread crumbs highly seasoned with butter, sage, salt and pepper. Sew it up. Skewer the fore legs forward, and the hind legs backward. Rub it over with butter, and sprinkle with salt, pepper and flour. Put it in a dripping pan with a little water and bake about three hours, basting often. It is not necessary to have the oven very hot at first; be careful not to let it burn. When done, place it on a platter; garnish with parsley and put an apple or small ear of corn in its mouth.

ROAST SPARE RIBS

Trim off the rough ends; crack the ribs across the middle, rub with salt, sprinkle with pepper, fold over, stuff with plain turkey dressing. Sew up tightly, put in dripping pan with a pint of water. Baste frequently, turning once, so that both sides may be of a rich brown.

TO FRY TRIPE

Take prepared tripe, wash and wipe dry. Cut it four inches square; dip first in egg, then in flour; fry slowly to a delicate brown, in butter. Add to the gravy a wine-glass each of vinegar and water; boil up and pour over the dish with the tripe.

BROILED TRIPE

Prepare tripe as for frying; lay on a broiling iron over a clear fire; let broil gently on both sides; Serve on a hot platter with plenty of butter. Garnish with lemon or parsley.

TO COOK A CALF'S HEAD
Mrs. T. B.

Tie the brains in muslin with sweet herbs. Boil brains, head, haslet, and feet, two hours, adding the liver the last hour. When nearly done take out the brains, and a portion of the lights. Chop them with a hard boiled egg, season with salt, pepper, and a little butter, add a little of the broth; dredge lightly with flour and cook sufficiently to make a nice sauce. Take up the rest of the meat, remove the bones, lay it on a dish, and pour the sauce over it.

SALT TONGUE
Miss Parloa.

Soak over night, and cook from five to six hours. Throw into cold water and peel off the skin.

FRESH TONGUE
Miss Parloa.

Put into boiling water to cover, with two tablespoons of salt. Cook from five to six hours. Skin the same as salt tongue.

BREAKFAST FRITTERS
Mrs. W. W. Ross.

One cup minced meat; 1 cup sweet milk; 1 tablespoon bread crumbs; 1 tablespoon flour; egg, pepper, salt.

Mix and season. Make into small cakes and fry them a light brown in deep fat.

MEAT CAKES
Mrs. S. J. Peck.

Three cups chopped meat; 1 cup mashed potato; 2 eggs, salt, pepper and sage.

To any cold meat chopped fine, add the potatoes, eggs and seasonings. Work all together; form into cakes, roll in flour and fry.

TO CORN BEEF

Mrs. S. C. Foy.

Take twelve or fifteen pounds of beef, cut from the round; cut it into four pieces; put into a jar or cask, and cover with brine made as follows: To one gallon boiling water, dissolve rock salt until, when cold, a fresh egg will float. Turn a plate over the meat, and press it down with a stone. One teaspoon of saltpetre will give the meat a red color. In about four days, pour off the brine, boil, skim, and cool, and pour over the meat again. Six days will corn thoroughly.

SAUCES

M. B. W.

Sauces are often a failure, because the flour is not sufficiently cooked. When the flour and water are mixed and
added to the boiling liquid, the sauce should boil at least ten
minutes.

A quicker and better way is to cook the dry flour in the
hot butter, thus insuring a smooth sauce, free from grease,
and of excellent flavor.

HOLLANDAISE SAUCE
Mrs. E. H. Sanderson.

Butter, size of ½ egg; 1 teaspoon flour; yolks of 4 eggs;
1 small lime or ½ lemon; salt, red and black pepper to taste.

Put butter in sauce pan, heat till it bubbles, then add
flour, stirring constantly; do not brown. Remove from fire;
stir in with egg whisk the yolks, well beaten. Return to
stove just a moment to set the eggs. Remove from the stove
and add juice of lime or lemon; Season. This must not boil
after the eggs are in or it will curdle. Must be made and
served at once. Fine for any fish.

A SIMPLE BROWN SAUCE
Mrs. Henderson.

One tablespoon minced onion; 1 teaspoon flour, heaped; ½
pint stock; a little butter.

Fry the onion in the butter until it takes color, then
sprinkle in the flour. When that browns add the stock.
Cook it a few minutes and strain.

DRAWN BUTTER
Mrs. W J. Brown.

Half cup butter; 2 tablespoons flour; 1 pint boiling water
or milk; 1 sprig parsley; salt; pepper.

Rub butter and flour together, put into a sauce pan with the boiling water; stir constantly until perfectly smooth, then add the parsley, season, and serve.

EGG SAUCE

Mince three or four hard-boiled eggs, and stir them into drawn butter. If too thick, add a little cream or milk.

CAPER SAUCE

Add two tablespoons of pickled capers to a drawn butter sauce. Good for boiled leg of lamb.

SAUCE TARTARE FOR MEAT AND FISH
Mrs. J. J. Ayers.

Half cup Howland's olive oil; 2 yolks of raw eggs; 3 tablespoons vinegar; 1 tablespoon mustard; 1 teaspoon sugar; 1 teaspoon salt; 1 teaspoon onion juice; ½ teaspoon pepper; 1 tablespoon cucumber pickles, chopped.

Beat the eggs, oil and seasoning together like mayonnaise, then add the pickles.

CHESTNUT SAUCE FOR ROAST TURKEY
Miss Parloa.

One pint shelled chestnuts; 1 quart stock; 1 teaspoon lemon juice; 1 tablespoon flour; 2 tablespoons butter, salt, pepper. Boil the chestnuts about three minutes; then plunge into cold water, and rub off the dark skins. Cook them gently in the stock until they will mash readily. Mash fine as possible. Cook the butter and flour in a sauce pan until a dark brown. Stir into the sauce and cook two minutes.

The chestnuts used are twice as large as the native nut. All first-class grocers keep them.

GIBLET SAUCE

Stew the neck, liver, heart, and gizzard in a little water, thicken with butter and browned flour. Season with pepper and salt; strain. Mince the heart and liver very fine and return to the sauce. Serve very hot.

OYSTER SAUCE
Miss Parloa.

One pint oysters, 3 tablespoons butter; 1 heaping table-spoon flour; 1 tablespoon lemon juice; salt, pepper, a speck of cayenne.

Wash the oysters in enough water with the addition of the oyster liquor to make a pint, boil, and skim. Stir the butter and flour in a sauce pan, until of a dark brown. Add the skimmed liquor, boil up· add the other ingredients, boil up once more, and serve.

SAUCE PIQUANTE FOR BOILED TONGUE
Mrs. T. F. McCamant.

One-half cup of vinegar; 2 large onions; 2 tablespoons sugar; 1 tablespoon butter; pepper, salt, water.

Slice the onions fine; stew them in the vinegar, and water enough to cover. Boil until tender, and mash them smooth. Add sugar and butter, cook until quite thick, stirring con-stantly; season with pepper and salt. This forms the base of several sauces. One is made by adding an equal quantity of the gravy from roast beef, mutton, or turkey.

BÉCHAMEL SAUCE
Mrs. Henderson.

One tablespoon flour; 3 or 4 tablespoons good thick cream; 1 pint of veal stock; ¼ of rather small onion; ¼ of a turnip; ¼ of a good-sized carrot; 2 sprigs parsley; ¼ of a bay-leaf; ½ a sprig of thyme; 3 pepper-corns; ½ lump of sugar; a small blade of mace; 1 oz. butter, size of walnut.

Put butter into a stew-pan, and when hot add to it all the ingredients but the stock, mace, flour and cream fry this slowly until it assumes a yellow color; do not let it brown, as the sauce should be white when done; stir in the flour, which let cook a minute, and add the blade of mace and the stock, (boiling) from another stew-pan. After it has all simmered about five minutes, strain it through a sieve without allowing the vegetables to pass through; return the strained sauce to the fire, reduce it, by boiling, about one-third; add the cream and the sauce is ready.

HORSERADISH SAUCE

One-half cup grated cracker; ½ cup grated horseradish; 1 cup cream; 1 tablespoon fat from cooked meat; salt, pepper. Simmer together fifteen minutes.
Serve with braised beef.

MUSHROOM SAUCE
Mrs. M. B. Welch.

Put a tablespoon of butter and a tablespoon of flour in a saucepan over the fire. Stir until the flour is well browned. Add very slowly the juice from half a can of mushrooms, and sufficient hot beef stock to make the sauce the proper thickness; season with pepper, salt and a teaspoon of lemon juice; Add a half can of mushrooms, simmer a few minutes, and serve.

MINT SAUCE
Mrs. Henderson.

Put four tablespoons of chopped mint; 2 tablespoons of sugar, and a quarter of a pint of vinegar into a sauce-boat. Let it remain an hour or two before dinner, that the vinegar may become impregnated with the mint.

CHESTNUT SAUCE
Mrs. Lincoln.

Remove the shells from one pint of large chestnuts; scald or boil them three minutes to loosen the skin. Remove the skin; break them in halves, and look them over carefully. Cook in salted boiling water or stock till very soft. Mash fine in the water in which they were boiled. Cook 1 tablespoon flour in two tablespoons brown butter, stir into the chestnuts and cook five minutes. Add salt and pepper to taste.

BREAD SAUCE FOR GAME OR MEATS
Mrs. Frank Phillips.

Two cups milk; 1 cup bread crumbs; 2 tablespoons butter; 1 teaspoon salt; ⅓ teaspoon pepper; ½ onion.

Dry the bread in the oven. Roll it into coarse crumbs; sift and put the part which goes through the sieve (about one third) to boil with the milk and onion. Boil ten or fifteen minutes. Add one tablespoon of the butter, and the seasoning. Skim out the onion. Fry the remainder of the crumbs in the rest of the butter, which must be very hot. Stir over a hot fire two minutes, being careful not to burn, cover the breasts of the birds with these. Pour the sauce around the birds, or serve separately.

THICK CREAM SAUCE FOR CROQUETTES, ETC.
Mrs. C. H. Walton.

One pint hot cream; ½ teaspoon salt; 2 even tablespoons butter; ½ saltspoon white pepper; 4 heaping tablespoons flour; ½ teaspoon celery salt; a few grains of cayenne.

Scald the cream. Melt the butter in a granite saucepan. When bubling, add the dry flour. Stir till well mixed. Add one third of the cream, and stir as it boils and thickens. Add more cream and boil again. When perfectly smooth, add the remainder of the cream. The sauce should be very thick, almost like a drop batter. Add the seasoning, and mix it while hot with the meat or fish.

VEGETABLES

All vegetables are best when fresh and crisp: celery, lettuce, cucumbers, and radishes should be kept in cold water. New potatoes should be prepared just before cooking and put on in boiling water. Old potatoes should be peeled and put into cold water an hour before cooking; then drain off the water and put into cold water and set over the fire; when they are barely done, drain off the water and set on back of the stove. A small quantity of cayenne pepper put into the water when cooking cabbage and onions will somewhat neutralize the disagreeable odor.

ASPARAGUS ON TOAST
Mrs. G. W. White.

Asparagus; soda; salt; pepper; butter; cream or milk; toasted bread.

Cut off the hard ends. Boil the rest whole with a very little soda in the water, which will preserve the color, make tender, and improve the flavor. Boil until tender. Season with butter, pepper and salt. Spread on hot buttered toast, and pour over it hot cream or milk.

AMBUSHED ASPARAGUS
Mrs. Willard H. Stimson.

Three bunches asparagus; stale light rolls; only the tops are used; 3 eggs; 1 pint milk; pepper; salt; a tablespoon butter.

Boil asparagus twenty minutes, and drain. Take out the inside of the rolls, and put the tops in the oven to dry. Stir the beaten eggs into the boiling milk with the butter, pepper and salt to taste. Add the asparagus, cut in small pieces, fill the tops with the mixture and serve hot.

ARTICHOKES
Mrs. Lincoln.

The Globe Artichokes are thick, fleshy-petalled flowers which grow on a plant that resembles the thistle. The thickened receptacle and scales of the involucre form the edible portion. Soak the artichokes, cut off the outside leaves, trim away the lower leaves, and the ends of the others. Cook in boiling salted water, with the tops downward, half an hour. Drain, remove the choke—or internal filamentous portion—and serve with drawn butter.

BEETS
Mrs. Henderson.

Be careful not to prick, or cut the skin before cooking, as they will then lose their color. Put them into boiling water, and boil until tender. If they are served hot, season them with butter, pepper, and salt; if cold, slice and pour vinegar over them, or cut in dice, and mix with other cold vegetables for a salad.

STRING BEANS
Mrs. W. B. Abernethy

One and a half quarts beans; 1 small onion; 1 tablespoon (rounded) lard; 1 heaping teaspoon sugar; salt, pepper, and a little flour.

String the beans carefully and break in small pieces. Put the lard in a large skillet and when very hot put in the onion, chopped fine, and cook brown ; have ready the beans thoroughly washed and drained, put in the skillet and cover very closely. Allow them to cook for ten or fifteen minutes, stirring once or twice to prevent burning; then cover with boiling water and cook until tender. If the water needs replenishing be sure it is boiling. When cooked season with salt, pepper, and teaspoon sugar, and sift in a little flour.

STRINGED BEANS
Mrs. Helen Widney Watson.

One quart beans; ½ cup cream, more is better; 1 table-spoon butter; salt, pepper.

String, wash, and slit the bean pods lengthwise, cover them with cold water, and cook until perfectly tender. Drain off any water that may remain. Cook dry, being careful not to burn. Add the butter. Stir for a moment or two, then add the salt, pepper and cream.

BOSTON BAKED BEANS
Mrs. W. J. Horner

One quart beans; 1 pound salt pork; 1 teaspoon saleratus; 1 teaspoon mustard; 1 teaspoon salt; 1 tablespoon molasses.

Soak the beans over night. In the morning bring them to a boil; adding the saleratus; then drain, and put them into an earthen pot with salt pork, molasses, mustard, and salt. Cover with water and bake four hours adding more water, as may be necessary.

BAKED BEANS
Mrs. Augusta Robinson.

Two cups beans; 1 scant teaspoon soda ; 3 tablespoons molasses; 3 inch square salt pork; pinch mustard.

Prepare the beans in the evening and let soak over night. In the morning drain off the water, put the beans in the bean jar, add the molasses, soda, mustard, and the salt pork ; cut in pieces, put on enough water to cover. Put the lid on the jar and allow them to simmer all day in a slow oven, watching that the beans do not get dry. This process may be hurried by parboiling the beans for about two hours before putting in the bean jar.

MASHED CARROTS
Mrs. W. G. W.

Carrots; butter; pepper; salt.

After scraping and washing the carrots lay them in cold water half an hour ; then cook tender in boiling water.

Drain, mash with a wooden beetle, work in a good sized piece of butter, season with pepper and salt. Heap in a vegetable dish, and serve very hot.

BOILED GREEN CORN
Mrs. W. G. Whorton.

Choose young sugar corn full grown but tender. Strip off the outer husks, turn back the innermost, carefully pick out the silk, recover the ear with the thin husk, tie it with thread, put into boiling salted water, and boil rapidly from twenty to thirty minutes, according to size and age of corn. Cut off the stalks close to the cob and send it to the table in a napkin.

Or, the corn may be cut from the cob after it is boiled, and seasoned with salt, pepper, and butter.

CORN OYSTERS
Mrs. Charlotte L. Wills.

One pint pulp ; ½ teaspoon salt ; 2 tablespoons lard or butter; a dash of cayenne or black pepper.

Score and press out pulp of sweet corn as for pudding ; mix well together with salt and pepper. Put the lard or butter in a frying pan. When hot, drop some of the mixture into it in little pats; brown, and turn. Serve hot with meats.

Makes a good dish for breakfast or luncheon.

CORN PUDDING
Mrs. J. J. Mellus.

One and one-half dozen ears green corn; 3 eggs; 1 teacup cream; one teaspoon sugar; ½ teaspoon salt; pepper; butter size of an egg.

Cut down the center of each row of kernels. Scrape out pulp, being careful not to get any of the husk. Add the salt, pepper, sugar, cream and beaten eggs. Bake until of a light brown.

GREEN CORN PUDDING
Mrs. E. M. Ross.

One dozen large ears of corn; 5 eggs; 1⅓ cup butter; 1 quart milk; 1 tablespoon sugar.

Grate the corn from the ears; mix it well with the beaten yolks of the eggs, then add the butter, sugar, a little salt, the milk, and last, the well beaten whites of the eggs. Bake slowly for an hour in a covered dish, removing the cover for ten or fifteen minutes before it is to be served, that it may brown.

CORN PUDDING—As made in Western Pennsylvania.
Mrs. Charlotte L. ~~Mills.~~ *Wills.*

One dozen ears sweet corn; 1 pint milk; 1 teaspoon salt; ¼ teaspoon black pepper; ½ cup butter.

Score the corn down the middle of each row; press out all the pulp, leaving the hull on the cob. Mix the pulp, milk, salt and pepper. Butter a pudding dish; pour in the mixture; cut up the remainder of the butter and put it in the pudding. Bake slowly one hour. Serve as a vegetable with meats. Less milk than a pint may be successfully used if the corn is young.

We now have a small wooden frame with steel knife and teeth fastened in it which scrapes the corn more easily and quickly.

STEWED CAULIFLOWER
Mrs. M. G. Moore.

One tablespoon butter; 1 tablespoon flour; 1 pint of boiling water; 2 tablespoons vinegar; 2 eggs (yolks only); a little salt and pepper; cauliflower.

Boil the cauliflower in salted water; remove from the fire before it becomes too tender; drain in sieve. Melt, without browning, the butter; stir in the flour; cook, stirring all the while. Then add slowly the boiling water, vinegar, salt and pepper. As soon as the mixture boils, put the cauliflower in it; stir in very carefully the yolks of eggs.

Serve at once.

CAULIFLOWER AND CHEESE
Mrs. M. G. Moore.

Cauliflower; 1 tablespoon cheese, grated; 1 oz. butter.

Boil cauliflower, not too tender. Remove from the fire

and place in baking dish in the oven. Put over the top the cheese and butter, melting it well into the vegetable and slightly browning.

Sauce:—Two oz. butter; 1 teaspoon flour; 2 teaspoons cream or milk; 2 oz. cheese (grated); 2 eggs (beaten).

Melt the butter, without browning; into this put the flour; slightly cook it, then add cheese, cream or milk, and eggs, well beaten. Stir over the fire until all is perfectly smooth. Do not permit it to boil. Pour over cauliflower.

CABBAGE
Mrs. E. F. Spence.

One cabbage; boiling salted water; $1\frac{1}{8}$ teaspoon soda. The cabbage should be fine and of medium size. Wash, quarter, and put it in a kettle of boiling salted water to which the soda has been added. Boil twenty minutes. Serve hot.

LADIES' CABBAGE
C. S.

Cabbage; 4 tablespoons cream; 1 tablespoon butter; 1 egg; pepper; salt.

Select medium sized heads that feel firm and heavy. Shave the cabbage very fine, and let it lie in cold salted water one hour. Drain and place in plenty of boiling water. Cook rapidly for ten minutes, then drain; add butter, pepper, salt and cream. Simmer until it is nearly dry. Just before serving, beat the egg to a cream; stir quickly into the cabbage; boil up once and serve.

HOT CABBAGE SLAW
Mrs. H. L. Parlee.

One cabbage; 1 teacup milk; ½ teacup vinegar; butter the size of a walnut; pepper; salt.

Slice the cabbage fine; put it in a sauce pan with the milk, butter, salt and pepper. When it boils, add the vinegar; cover closely and cook slowly until done. Less vinegar may be used or none at all. If cream is used instead of milk, less butter is required.

STUFFED CABBAGE
Mrs. M. J. Danison.

One head cabbage; some cooked veal or chicken; 1 egg, (yolk); salt; pepper.

Choose a large fresh cabbage and cut out the heart; fill with the veal, or chicken chopped very fine, highly seasoned, and rolled into balls with yolk of egg. Then tie the cabbage firmly together, (some tie a cloth around it,) and boil in a covered kettle two hours.

TO COOK EGG PLANT
H. F. G.

Peel, and slice as thin as possible; lay them in salt water for a few minutes; dry them on a cloth; dust with flour ; and drop them (three or four at a time) in hot lard. Fry quickly to a light brown like Saratoga chips. They are nice for breakfast eaten with tomatoes sliced in vinegar.

STUFFED EGG PLANT
Miss Carrie T. Waddilove.

Four egg plants ; 3 hard boiled eggs ; 1 fresh egg ; 1 slice onion; 1 tablespoon minced salt pork; 3 handfuls browned bread crumbs; 2 or 3 cloves; garlic; pinch sage; red pepper; salt; some white bread crumbs.

Scrape the egg plant from out the shell and chop with salt pork, browned bread crumbs, onion, garlic, sage, red pepper, salt. Fry in a little butter for five minutes; break in one fresh egg ; then add the chopped boiled eggs. Fill cases; cover with white bread crumbs. Bake ten or fifteen minutes. Soak egg plant in strong salt water several hours before using. This quantity is sufficient for eight persons.

HOME MADE HOMINY
Mrs. M. R. Congdon.

One can of lye potash; 1 quart water. Dissolve in an earthen vessel; when settled and clear, bottle for use.

One quart dry corn; 3 quarts water; 3 tablespoons potash lye.

Shell the corn, rejecting all shrivelled kernels; soak it over night. Boil half an hour in the water and lye; if at the end of that time the skins do not slip off easily, boil longer. Wash the corn in soft water until it is free from hulls; sometimes eight or ten waters are required. Then cook in a double boiler until soft. Salt to taste.

TO PREPARE HOMINY
Mrs. Cheever, Waukegan, Ill.

Two quarts wood ashes; 3 gallons water; 4 quarts corn; salt.

Boil the ashes in one gallon of the water for one hour; remove from the fire and add the remaining two gallons; be sure it is cold water; let it settle; skim it and then drain off the lye; put it in a kettle and add the corn. Boil until the skins crack; then drain off the water and wash in several waters, rubbing with the hands until the hulls are removed. Then cook in water with sufficient salt till tender.

HOMINY GRITS CROQUETTES
Mrs. Henry Smith.

One cup hominy grits; 3 cups milk; 1 teaspoon vanilla; beef drippings; 3 eggs; 1 teaspoon salt; 4 tablespoons sugar; bread crumbs.

Cook the grits with the milk in a double boiler until the milk has been entirely absorbed; then stir in two of the eggs well beaten, the salt, sugar and vanilla. Turn out to cool. When cold, form into cylinders; beat well the remaining egg and dip the cylinders first in the egg then in the bread crumbs and fry in smoking hot fat. Serve with powdered sugar. If not for desert, omit the sugar and vanilla.

MUSHROOMS
Mrs. W. J. McCloskey.

Pare the mushrooms and drop them into vinegar and water to prevent discoloration. The vinegar gives them a tart flavor and can be increased or diminished to taste. Put in a sauce pan sufficient butter to cover the mushrooms; when the butter is brown, drop them in and cook over a rapid fire until they begin to brown; then stir in flour and water mixed to a thin smooth paste. Season with salt and pepper. Cook from six to ten minutes. Long cooking toughens them.

BROILED MUSHROOMS
H. F. G.

Choose the largest sort; lay them on a small gridiron over bright coals, stalks upward. Broil quickly. Season with butter, pepper and salt.

FRIED MUSHROOMS
H. F. G.

Peel; put them in hot butter and heat thoroughly—much cooking toughens them. Season with butter, pepper and salt. Serve on buttered toast; a few drops of lemon juice on each mushroom is an improvement.

BOILED MACARONI
X. Y. Z.

Never make the mistake of washing macaroni before cooking it. If dusty, wipe it with a dry cloth, then plunge it in boiling salted water. Boil steadily until it softens sufficiently to break under gentle pressure. Drain in a colander and hold it under the cold water faucet until the glutinous coating is removed and the little tubes lie separately in the dish, then drain, and finish as desired.

ONIONS 'a la CRÊME
Mrs. A. C. Doan.

Onions; butter; bread crumbs; salt; pepper; sweet cream.

Boil the onions in salted water until tender. Butter a deep baking dish; fill alternately with a layer of bread crumbs sprinkled with pepper, salt, and bits of butter, then a layer of sliced onions, until full, having bread crumbs on top. Cover with sweet cream. Bake half an hour, or until brown. Serve hot in the same dish.

ESCALOPED ONIONS
Mrs. Mondini Wood.

Onions; cracker crumbs; cream; butter; pepper; salt.

Cook thirty sliced onions in salted water until very tender (they will be more delicate if the water is changed.) Put a layer of onions in a baking dish, then a layer of crumbs seasoned with butter, pepper and salt. Repeat until the desired amount is prepared, finishing with the crackers. Add a little of the onion water and sufficient cream to make very moist. Bake until a light brown.

BOILED ONIONS

Remove the tops, roots and thin outer skin. Put them in cold water and parboil. Drain, and cook them very tender in plenty of milk and water, salted. Drain again and put them in a hot dish. Season with salt, pepper, and bits of butter.

STUFFED OLIVES
Mrs. T. A. Lewis.

Open olives, take out pits, and stuff with chopped truffles.

CREAMED PARSNIPS
H F. G.

Parsnips; 2 tablespoons butter; pepper; salt; a little minced parsley; 3 tablespoons of cream; $\frac{1}{4}$ tablespoon of flour.

Boil the parsnips until tender. Scrape, and slice lengthwise. Put over the fire, the butter and other seasonings. Shake until the mixture boils, then add the cream, mixed with the flour, boil once, and pour over the parsnips.

PARSNIPS
Mrs. Alice Curtain.

Parsnips; 1 egg; salt; pepper; butter.

Peel the parsnips, cut thin and cook with a little water, until dry. Mash fine, and season with butter, pepper and salt; beat up the egg and mix with the parsnips while hot, then fry in butter, or beef drippings or a mixture of both, as you would potato croquettes. Excellent.

STUFFED PEPPERS
Mrs. Hugh W. Vail.

Large green peppers; bread crumbs; chopped meat; butter; grated cheese; tartare sauce.

Remove the seeds from the peppers. Mix the bread crumbs, meat, cheese, and butter. Stuff the pepper skins with the mixture and bake until brown. Serve with tartare sauce.

GREEN PEAS
H. F. G.

Lay them in cold water fifteen or twenty minutes *before* shelling. After shelling put immediately into boiling water, with one or two teaspoons of white sugar. Boil rapidly until the skin begins to shrivel, then turn them into a hot dish with a little salt, and a small lump of butter.

Peas should not be *cooked with* seasoning.

BOILED POTATOES

Wash the potatoes just before cooking, put them in cold salted water and boil until half done, turn the water off, and pour on fresh boiling salted water. Cook until soft. Take from the fire, put a tablespoon of cold water in the pot and pour it off. This method of cooking improves even poor potatoes, making them soft, and mealy.

POTATOES BAKED IN MILK
Mrs. E. W. Lucas.

Fill a baking dish with sliced potatoes, season with salt, pepper, and butter, cover with new milk. Bake in a slow oven, one and one-half hours.

POTATOES au GRATEN
Mrs. C. H. Walton.

Cut potatoes in cubes, mix with white stock and white sauce, cover with crumbs and bake.

POTATO PUFFS
Mrs. Owens.

One quart mashed potatoes; 2 eggs.

Beat the eggs light; beat the potato, nicely seasoned, until creamy; then dip up a spoonful of potato, immerse it in the egg and lay in a baking dish. Cover the bottom of the dish with these puffs, and brown evenly in a well-heated oven.

CREAMED POTATOES
Mrs. Owens.

Three tablespoons butter; 2 teaspoons flour; 1 teaspoon minced parsley; 1 cup cream, or milk.

Cut cold boiled potatoes in dice. Mix the butter, flour and cream in a saucepan. When the mixture comes to a boil, add the potatoes with pepper, salt and parsley. Boil up once and serve.

HASHED AND BROWNED POTATOES
Miss Ida A. Maynard.

One quart cold boiled potatoes; 1 teaspoon flour; salt, pepper, milk; 2 tablespoons butter.

Chop the potatoes, coarse; sprinkle with flour, season with pepper and salt and add a little milk to moisten. Melt the butter in a frying pan; add the potatoes, and cook slowly until brown on the under side. Fold, and turn out like an omelet.

STUFFED POTATOES
Miss Ida A. Maynard.

Six medium-sized potatoes; 1 tablespoon butter; a little hot milk; salt and pepper to taste.

Bake the potatoes; when done, cut off a small piece at each end, with a spoon, remove the inside, which mash, and beat well and moisten with the hot milk; add the butter, and season with salt and pepper to taste. Fill the skins with this mixture and brush with melted butter. Brown in the oven.

CREAMED POTATOES
Mrs. A. L. Allen.

Six potatoes; 1 cup milk; 1 tablespoon butter; 1 teaspoon salt; 4 eggs, whites only; a speck of cayenne; grated cheese.

Boil the potatoes in their skins, peel and mash them while

hot; add the butter, milk and cayenne.   Beat until light, whip the whites to a stiff froth, stir gently into the potatoes. Put them in baking dish, dust with grated cheese, bake in a quick oven until of a golden brown.

RAW POTATO CAKES
Mrs. Owens.

One quart grated potato ; 4 eggs ; 1 tablespoon flour ; 1 teaspoon Cleveland's baking powder.

Peel, and grate the potatoes on a coarse grater as quickly as possible.   Mix with the eggs well beaten, then the flour, baking powder, and a pinch of salt.   Fry by spoonsful in a frying pan, in hot lard.   Turn like griddle cakes.   Serve hot.

BAKED POTATOES

Select potatoes of equal size, wash and wipe dry with a cloth.   Bake in a quick oven and serve as soon as done.

POTATO CROUQUETTES
Marion Harland.

Beat mashed potatoes soft, with milk and a little butter ; whip in the yolk of an egg for every cupful.   Season with salt and pepper.   Let all get cold and stiff.   Make into croquettes, roll in flour, and fry in deep fat.

ESCALOPED POTATO
Mrs. Nellie King

Three cups mashed potato, hot ; ½ cup milk ; 2 table-spoons butter; raw egg; pepper; salt; breadcrumbs.

Beat together the potato, milk, egg, butter, pepper, and salt.   Fill a baking dish with this mixture.   Sprinkle the top with bread crumbs, and bake fifteen minutes covered.   Then remove the cover and brown five minutes.

PARISIENNE POTATOES
Mrs. Hugh W. Vail.

Cut raw potatoes into small balls, fry them in very hot lard and sprinkle with salt.

DUCHESS POTATOES
X. Y. Z.

Eight large potatoes: 1 tablespoon butter; 2 eggs; salt; cracker crumbs; flour.

Boil and mash the potatoes; mix them with the butter, salt and raw yolks; stir all together over the fire. When cold, roll out, using sufficient flour to prevent its sticking to the board; make into shapes according to fancy. Beat the white of one egg with one tablespoon of cold water; dip the potato in this, roll in cracker crumbs and fry in hot lard.

FRENCH POTATOES
Mrs. Orr Haralson.

Potatoes: 2 eggs; ½ teaspoon salt; ⅓ teaspoon pepper: 2 tablespoons flour.

Select small new potatoes of uniform size; scrape them clean and white; roll them in batter made after recipe given above. Put a layer in a wire basket and place in a kettle of smoking hot fat until cooked.

MASHED POTATOES
H. F. G.

Potatoes are not good for mashing until they are fully grown. Peel and lay them in cold water for an hour before boiling. Put them in salted boiling water and boil rapidly until done (not overdone); then turn them quickly into a colander; drain dry; return them to the dry kettle; mash them smooth; season with salt, a little white pepper, generous piece of butter, and one, two or three tablespoons of sweet cream. Set the kettle over the fire, and with a strong spoon, stir the potatoes until creamy and very light. Serve hot as possible.

MASHED POTATOES BAKED

Heap creamed mashed potatoes upon a flat dish, shaped into a mound or pine apple: brush lightly with beaten white of egg; brown delicately, garnish the edge of the plate with parsley.

LYONNAISE POTATOES
H. F. G.

One quart cooked potatoes; 3 tablespoons butter; 1 tablespoon chopped onion ; 1 tablespoon chopped parsley ; salt ;
pepper.

Fry the onion in the butter until it is slightly browned,
then add the sliced potatoes, well salted and peppered. When
thoroughly heated, add the parsley, and cook two minutes.

The onions may be omitted.

SARATOGA POTATOES
Mrs. W. W. Widney.

Pare, and slice potatoes thin as possible, lay them in ice
water for an hour. Then dry them on a cloth. Drop the
slices, few at a time, in deep hot lard, or better still cottolene.
Fry to a delicate brown. Take up with a skimmer, lay them
on clean soft paper. Sprinkle with salt. and set them in the
open oven, to preserve their crispness. Serve either hot or
cold.

BOILED RICE
X. Y. Z.

Wash the rice, drain, and put in boiling salted water.
Boil twelve minutes, drain, cover with a thickly folded towel,
set in the oven, leaving the door open, and steam it until the
grains are dry and bursting.

SUMMER SQUASH
Mrs. M. R. Sinsabaugh.

Young squash ; egg ; cracker crumbs ; corn meal; salt;
pepper; butter, and lard.

Select solid squash, that have not begun to form seed, cut
them in slices a quarter of an inch in thickness, lay them in
salt and water for a few minutes. Dip each slice into beaten
egg, roll in fine cracker crumbs and Indian meal, well salted
and peppered. Fry in hot olive oil, or butter and lard mixed.
Fry briskly at first, afterwards more slowly until tender.

BAKED HUBBARD SQUASH
O. G. M.

Cut in pieces, scrape out the seeds and soft part. Bake from one to one and a half hours, according to the thickness of the squash. To be eaten with butter and salt, like baked potatoes.

SPINACH
Mrs. W. G. Kerckhoff.

Four bunches spinach; 1 cup water; ½ tablespoon salt; 2 tablespoons butter; 2 tablespoons dried bread crumbs, or 1 tablespoon flour; ½ cup cream.

Pick apart leaf by leaf the spinach, and wash thoroughly; put into a large stew pan with the water, cover closely and cook for fifteen minutes; then add the salt and cook five minutes longer. Remove from fire, turn into a colander, and press out as much water as possible; then put into chopping tray and mince very fine. Put butter into frying pan; when melted, add bread crumbs or flour; stir the mixture until it becomes smooth and frothy; then add the chopped spinach and cook for five minutes, stirring constantly; then add the cream and cook for one minute.

SPINACH WITH CREAM
Mrs. R. L. McKnight.

Spinach; cream; sugar; nutmeg; stale bread; salt.

Pick the leaves from the stalks; wash thoroughly; boil in covered sauce pan with just sufficient water to prevent burning; add salt, and turn frequently while cooking. When tender; drain and chop fine, and return to the sauce pan with sufficient boiling cream to moisten; add a sprinkling of sugar and a grating of nutmeg. Stir it until thoroughly hot; then pile it high in the center of a hot dish. Garnish around the base with rings of stale bread fried in boiling fat. Serve very hot.

BAKED SALSIFY
Miss M. E. McLellan.

Salsify; bread crumbs; milk; butter; pepper; salt.

Boil the salsify until the skin comes off easily. Remove

the skin; slice. Put into a dish a layer of salsify, and a layer of bread crumbs with a little butter, pepper and salt on each layer; repeat until the dish is full, having the crumbs on top. Then pour over it as much milk as the dish will hold and bake until brown or from thirty to thirty-five minutes.

BOILED SWEET POTATOES
X. Y. Z.

Wash, and put them in salted boiling water, cover close, and boil rapidly half an hour, longer if the potatoes are large.

BAKED SWEET POTATOES
X. Y. Z.

Boil the potatoes, until they are two thirds done, then peel, and cut them lengthwise in two or three slices. Lay them in a buttered baking pan, sprinkle with sugar and bits of butter, and bake until they are nicely browned.

BROILED TOMATOES
Mrs. M. B. Welch.

Select tomatoes not over ripe, halve them crosswise, dip the cut side into beaten egg, then into wheat flour, and place them upon a greased gridiron. When well browned, turn them and cook the skin side until thoroughly done. Put butter, pepper, and salt on the egg side and serve upon a platter.

ESCALOPED TOMATOES
Mrs. Adolf Ekstein.

Bread crumbs; tomatoes; butter; little sugar; pepper, salt. Put a layer of the bread crumbs in a buttered pudding dish, then a layer of sliced tomatoes (canned ones will do) season with butter, pepper, salt, a little sugar; then a layer of the crumbs, and so on finishing with a layer of crumbs. Bake three quarters of an hour.

FRIED TOMATOES FOR BREAKFAST
Mrs. T. S. Stauway.

Cut large smooth tomatoes in slices half an inch thick;

dip them in powdered bread crumbs and fry them a light brown in half butter and half lard.

STUFFED TOMATOES
H. F. W.

Twelve large smooth tomatoes; 1 cup bread crumbs; 1 tablespoon butter; 1 tablespoon sugar; 1 teaspoon salt; 1 teaspoon onion juice; a little pepper.

Arrange the tomatoes in a baking pan; cut a thin slice from the smooth end of each, scoop out as much of the pulp and juice as possible, without spoiling the shape. Mix this with the other ingredients. Fill the tomatoes, put on the tops, and bake slowly, three quarters of an hour. Slip a pancake turner under them and lift gently on to a hot platter. Garnish with parsley.

BAKED TOMATOES
Mrs. W. W. Widney.

Tomatoes; butter; salt; pepper.

Cut a piece the size of a quarter dollar from the stem end of large smooth tomatoes, put in each a salt spoon of salt, half as much pepper, butter the size of a nutmeg; set them in a pan and bake nearly an hour.

Particularly good with lamb, or mutton chops.

BAKED DICED TURNIPS
Mrs. Adolf Ekstein.

Turnips, cooked in salted water; cream gravy; cracker crumbs.

Cut the turnips into dice, and cook in the salted water; when done, put into a colander and douse with cold water; then place in a baking dish and pour the cream gravy over them, cover with cracker crumbs and bake until brown.

EGGS AND CHEESE

BOILED EGGS
H. F. W.

Put the eggs in cold water over a moderate fire; if desired soft, they will be sufficiently cooked by the time the water reaches the boiling point; if hard, leave them in the water fifteen minutes, keeping it just below the boiling point. Cooked in this way the yolks will be dry, mealy and healthful.

BAKED EGGS
Mrs. A. C. Doan.

Six fresh eggs; 6 tablespoons rich sweet cream; pepper, salt.

Grease an agate pie pan thickly with butter. Break into it the eggs, and pour the cream between them. Season to taste, and bake them for four minutes in a hot oven.

BEAUREGARD EGGS
Mrs. Fannie H. Shoemaker.

Five eggs; 1 tablespoon corn starch; 5 squares of toast; ½ pint milk; butter size of a walnut; salt and pepper to taste.

Boil the eggs twenty minutes, remove the shells. Chop the whites fine, rub the yolks through a sieve. Do not mix them. Rub the butter and cornstarch together, and stir into the boiling milk. Add the whites, salt and pepper; lay the toast on a hot dish, cover it with the white sauce, then with a layer of yolks, repeat once. Sprinkle the top with a little salt and pepper. Stand it in the oven for one or two minutes, then serve.

EGGS BRONILLE
H. F. W.

Six eggs; ½ cup cream; 2 mushrooms; 3 tablespoons butter; 1 teaspoon salt; a little pepper; a slight grating of nutmeg.

Dice the mushrooms, and fry them one minute, in one tablespoon of the butter. Beat eggs, cream, pepper and salt together; add the butter and mushrooms. Put this mixture in a saucepan over a moderate fire, stirring it until it begins to thicken, then take from the fire and beat rapidly until it becomes thick and creamy. Then heap on slices of toast, garnish with toast points and serve immediately.

CURRIED EGGS
Mrs. Chas. Capen.

Four eggs; 1 teaspoon chopped onion; 1 tablespoon butter; 1 heaping tablespoon flour; ½ tablespoon curry powder; 1 cup cream; salt; pepper; bread crumbs. Boil the eggs half an hour; shell, and slice into a shallow dish. Fry the onion in the butter, being careful not to burn it; add flour, and curry powder. Pour the cream on slowly. Add salt and pepper to taste. Simmer until the onion is soft, then pour over the eggs, cover with buttered bread crumbs and brown, in the oven. Serve hot.

ESCALOPED EGGS
Miss H. B. Freeman.

Melt a small piece of butter and two very thin slices of cheese in a frying pan; break in the number of eggs you wish to use; drop small pieces of butter over them, season with salt and pepper, and then sprinkle thickly over the top nice bread crumbs; place in the oven and let remain until the yolks are of a jelly-like consistency, then serve.

ASPARAGUS OMELET FOR BREAKFAST
H. F. W.

Four tablespoons cream; 4 tablespoons asparagus; 4 eggs.
Beat the eggs with the cream, and proceed as for plain omelet, when ready to fold, spread over it the asparagus: the soft heads, which have been cooked, cut up, and heated in a little butter.

BAKED OMELET
Mrs. W. J. Brown.

Six eggs; 1 cup sweet milk; 2 tablespoons flour; butter size of an egg; a pinch of salt.

Stir the flour into a little of the milk; add the rest of the milk and the yolks well beaten, mix thoroughly. Just before cooking stir in the stiffly beaten whites. Heat the butter in a spider or earthen baking dish, being careful not to burn it; pour in the mixture and bake about ten minutes in a moderate oven. Loosen it with a knife and slip it on a hot platter and serve.

TOMATO OMELET
Mrs. J. H. Jones.

Six eggs; 1 cup milk; 1 tablespoon flour; pinch salt.

Beat the whites and yolks separately. Mix the flour and milk; add the yolks and then the well-beaten whites, and a tomato which has been previously boiled, mashed, strained and seasoned. Place in a well-buttered dish and bake in a quick oven five minutes.

CHEESE OMELET
Mrs. Anna O'Melveny.

Beat 6 eggs very light, whites and yolks separately. Add to the yolks 1 small cupful of warm milk, salt and pepper, and lastly and lightly, the whites and some rich grated cheese.

Have a good sized lump of butter heating in the frying pan, and when very hot pour in the mixture, taking care that it does not scorch. As soon as it sets, put in the oven covered, and bake about eight minutes. When done turn over on a hot platter and serve at once.

A DELICIOUS OMELET
H. F. W.

One small cup bread crumbs; 1 cup sweet milk; 3 eggs; 1 tablespoon butter; a little salt.

Soak the crumbs in the milk over night. In the morning

beat the whites and yolks separately, adding the yolks and
and salt first, then the whites. Stir lightly, and pour into a
shallow frying pan, in which is the hot butter. Fry a light
brown and serve at once. It should be folded almost as soon
as it begins to set, in order to have it light and tender inside.
Substitute cold mashed potato for the crumbs and you have
potato omelet. It may be baked if preferred.

FRIAR'S OMELET
X. Y. Z.

Ten large apples; 1 egg; butter; sugar; bread crumbs.

Peel, slice, and stew the apples, seasoning them to taste,
with butter and sugar, when cool beat in the egg. Butter
thickly the inside of a plain mold that will hold three pints.
Over the butter put an half inch layer of bread crumbs, then
pour in the apple sauce; cover with a thick layer of crumbs;
bake in a moderate oven until brown. Turn out of the
mold, dust with powdered sugar. Serve hot with cream or
sauce.

EGG OMELET
Mrs. John L. Truslow, Santa Barbara.

To each person allow 1 egg; 1 even teaspoon butter; 2
tablespoons sweet milk, salt and pepper to taste.

Break the whites of eggs in pudding dish and beat well.
Beat the yelks till light; add melted butter, salt, pepper, and
milk; turn into the whites stirring all the time. Bake in
nice oven ten or fifteen minutes and serve immediately.

WELSH RAREBIT
H. W. W.

One half ℔ American cheese ; 1 tablespoon butter ; 1 gill
milk; 1 egg, yolk; salt; pepper; mustard.

Grate the cheese, put in a sauce pan with the butter, a
little mustard, pepper, and salt. When the cheese begins to
melt, stir in slowly the milk ; when smooth add the yolk.
Spread the mixture on slices of buttered toast and serve in a
chafing dish.

RAREBIT `a la SOYER

Mrs. C. J. Ellis.

One half ℔ rich cheese ; 2 oz. butter ; 1 teaspoon mustard (made); salt, little; cayenne, plenty; 2 eggs (beaten).

Stir with *wooden spoon.*

Cut cheese into small cubes, as nearly as possible of a size. Put eggs in after it is nearly cooked. Serve on hot toast, on *very hot* plates.

CHEESE BALLS

O. G. M.

Bread crumbs; salt; pepper; grated cheese; 1 egg.

Equal quantities of bread and cheese; season. Mix into a paste with the egg, roll into balls, and fry in boiling oil, butter, or cottolene.

CHEESE CAKES

Mrs. M. B. Welch.

One and one half ounces butter; 1½ ounces sugar; 1 egg; five drops of almond essence; grated rind of a lemon; a sprinkle of nutmeg; 1 ounce of cracker crumbs; 4 tablespoons milk.

Bake in patty pans lined with puff paste.

CHEESE FONDU

Mrs E. R. Smith.

One fourth ℔ of cheese ; 1 gill of milk; 3 eggs ; butter, pepper, salt.

Grate the cheese, and heat it in the milk until it is perfectly melted. Remove from the fire, add the eggs (beaten) and seasoning. Put butter in dish and set to melt. When melted pour in the cheese mixture. Heat in a moderate oven until it stiffens.

A good luncheon dish.

CHEESE FONDU

E. P. T.

To 2 tablespoons of slightly browned flour, add ½ saltspoon mustard, ½ saltspoon white pepper, a few grains cayenne. 1 tablespoon butter, 1 saltspoon soda, ½ cupful skimmed milk and ¼ ℔ grated cheese. Heat over boiling water until the cheese is melted, add quickly 3 well beaten eggs, stir until smooth, put in patty pans or paper cups, bake quickly and serve very hot.

CHEESE RAMAKINS
Mrs. Fannie H. Shoemaker.

Four tablespoons grated cheese ; 2 tablespoons butter ; 1 gill milk ; 2 ounces bread ; 3 eggs, yolks of two, whites of three; ⅓ teaspoon mustard; cayenne and salt.

Boil the bread and milk, stirring until smooth. Add the butter and cheese, stirring over the fire one minute. Remove from the fire, add the yolk and seasoning ; then carefully stir in the stiffly frothed whites, pour into a buttered dish and bake fifteen minutes in a quick oven.

CHEESE STRAWS
Mrs. C. B. Woodhead.

One cup flour; 1 cup grated cheese: 2 oz. butter; pinch of salt; a dash of cayenne ; water to make of the consistency of pie crust dough.

Roll in sheets quarter of an inch in thickness, cut in strips, and bake in a moderate oven.

CHEESE CROQUETTES
Mrs. F. S. Hicks.

Ten ounces Roquefort cheese ; 5 ounces butter: cream ; cayenne.

Mix the cheese with the butter, which should be fresh and not too highly salted, add enough cream to give it the consistency of paste. Make it hot with cayenne, but not too hot. Mould in the shape of small croquettes, and serve with water crackers, and coffee.

CHEESE AND EGG TOAST
Mrs. M. G. Moore.

One tablespoon cheese ; ½ pint cream or milk : 2 eggs; butter; salt, pepper; slices of toasted bread.

Cut the cheese into small pieces ; put it into the cream or milk; boil until melted. Season with salt, pepper and butter, add eggs (well beaten), and remove from the fire, stirring for a few moments. Spread over the slices of toast.

CHEESE SOUFFLE

H. F. W.

Six ounces Parmesan cheese ; 1 saltspoon dry mustard ; 1 saltspoon white pepper; 2 ounces butter; a pinch of cayenne ; 1 gill milk; 2 tablespoons flour; 6 eggs.

Grate the cheese, put it in a sauce pan with the mustard, pepper, and cayenne. Stir into this mixture the flour and butter; then add the milk slowly. Put the sauce pan on the fire and stir the contents until a thick rich cream is formed, being careful that it does not boil. Remove from the fire, add the well beaten yolks, then the whites, stiffly frothed. Pour the mixture into a pudding dish and bake in a moderate oven twenty minutes. Serve immediately.

CHEESE WITH RICE

One cup rice ; 2½ cups boiling water ; 1 tablespoon salt ; ¼ ℔ cheese; cayenne; milk; cracker crumbs; butter.

Rub the rice through several waters; put it in the boiling salted water. Steam until tender, stirring with a fork instead of a spoon so as not to break the kernels. When the rice is done, put a layer into a buttered pudding dish, dot it with shavings of cheese and a speck of cayenne. Repeat until the rice and cheese are used, having the top layer of cheese. Add milk to half the depth of the contents of the dish, cover with buttered cracker crumbs and bake until the cheese melts.

This can be served as an entrée with lamb or as a breakfast dish.

BREAD

A. C. B.

There are three important requisites in the composition of good bread : — good flour, good yeast, and thorough kneading. Flour should be white and dry, and sifted before using. The bowl or pan in which a bread sponge is mixed should be thoroughly wrapped in a thick cloth, flannel being preferable.

BREAD
Mrs. W. H. Perry.

One cake Royal yeast ; 6 cups water; ½ cup milk ; 1 teaspoon salt; a small piece of butter; flour.

Make a thin batter of flour and three cups of water; to this add the yeast which has been softened in warm water. When light, add the salt, butter, milk, three cups of water, and flour enough to make very stiff. Let it rise over night. In the morning add more flour. Knead thoroughly and make into loaves. This recipe will make most delicious rolls.

YEAST BREAD
Mrs. M. S. Mathison.

One cake Magic yeast ; 1 pint lukewarm water ; 1 quart new milk ; 1 quart cold water ; 1 tablespoon salt ; 2 tablespoons sugar; flour; butter or lard.

At noon soak the yeast in the warm water fifteen minutes, then stir in flour sufficient to make a stiff batter. Set it in a warm place (not too warm) until very light. In the evening scald the milk and add it, with the water, salt, sugar and flour, enough to knead. Knead it half an hour, then rub the top of the dough with butter or lard, to prevent its drying. In the morning knead another half hour, divide into six loaves, and when sufficiently light bake one hour in a hot oven. When taken from the oven, wet the tops of the loaves with sweet milk, to soften the crust.   Do not wrap the bread in cloths until it is cold.

POTATO YEAST
Honora Fogarty.

Four large tablespoons flour ; 1 tablespoon salt ; 1 table-spoon sugar; ½ salt spoon ginger ; 4 potatoes, medium size ; 2 quarts water.

Cook the potatoes in the water ; when done, mash them and add with the water to the other ingredients. Stir thoroughly. When cool add 1 cake of Magic yeast soaked in ½ cup cold water.

YEAST BREAD
Honora Fogarty.

One quart lukewarm water ; 1 pint yeast ; 1 tablespoon salt.

Make a sponge, cover carefully, let it stand until very light, then mix it stiff.   Let it rise one hour ; mold into loaves.   Let it rise again; bake one hour at least.

This quantity will make four loaves and a pan of biscuits.

GOOD BREAD
H. F. W.

One cake Magic yeast ; 1 tumbler warm water ; 4 table-spoons flour; 1½ cups boiling water; flour; warm water.

Soak the yeast in tumbler of warm water thirty minutes. Mix the measured flour in the boiling water. Stir till like cream.   When lukewarm add the yeast; keep this in a warm place twelve hours. Then add two pints warm water, *beat* (not stir) fifteen minutes. Then set it in a warm place to rise over night. In the morning heat the batter, until lukewarm. Add flour; knead until it does not stick to the board, When light, mold into loaves.   Bake in a moderate oven forty-five to sixty minutes.

BREAD STICKS
Mrs. John Wigmore from Miss Parloa.

Four cups flour; ¼ cup butter; 1 cup boiled milk; ¼ cake

compressed yeast ; 3 tablespoons cold water ; 1 tablespoon sugar; 1 teaspoon salt, scant measure; white of 1 egg.

Melt the butter in the milk. Dissolve the yeast in the water. Beat the white of egg to a stiff froth. Add all the ingredients to the flour. Knead well, and let the dough rise over night. In the morning make into balls the size of large walnuts. Roll these into sticks a foot long. Place them two inches apart in long pans. Let them rise half an hour in a cool place. Bake twenty-five minutes in a moderate oven. They should be quite dry and crisp.

RYE BREAD
Mrs. T. D. Stimson.

One quart boiling milk; a little salt; 2 tablespoons butter ; 2 tablespoons sugar ; ¼ cake compressed yeast ; ½ cup corn meal; rye flour; wheat flour.

Add butter, sugar and salt to the milk. When it is luke-warm; add the yeast, dissolved in a little sweet milk, the corn meal, and rye flour, until it is stiff as can be stirred with a spoon. Let this stand until morning ; then knead. When light, make into loaves, using a little wheat flour on the board, and put in pans to rise. This makes two loaves of very nice bread.

OATMEAL BREAD
Mrs. T. W. Brotherton

One cup oat meal ; 1 cup warm water ; ½ cup sugar ; 1 tablespoon melted butter ; ¼ cake compressed yeast ; wheat flour.

The oat meal should be cooked and salted as for the table. In the evening add the other ingredients, stirring in all the wheat flour possible. Let it rise over night. In the morning stir in more wheat flour; put in pans. Let it rise again, then bake in a moderate oven one hour.

ROLLS
Mrs. C. W. Pendleton.

One pint milk ; 2 tablespoons sugar ; 1 tablespoon lard, large; ½ cake compressed yeast; 1 quart flour; 1 pinch salt ; warm water; soda the size of a pea.

Scald the milk, add lard and sugar. Dissolve the yeast in a little warm water. When the milk is cool add the yeast and flour. Let this batter stand over night. In the morning add flour to make a dough. Knead this, adding the salt and soda. Let it stand two or three hours, then knead again and mould. I make mine round, and turn one side over the other. Let them rise one and a half hours. Bake in a moderate oven.

FRENCH ROLLS
Marian Harland.

One pint milk; 2 eggs; 4 tablespoons yeast; 3 tablespoons butter; 1 teaspoon salt; 3 pints flour; or enough to make a soft dough; 1 tablespoon white sugar.

Warm the milk slightly, and add to it the beaten eggs and salt. Rub the butter into the flour quickly and lightly, until it is like yellow powder. Work into this gradually, with a wooden spoon, the milk and eggs, then the yeast. Knead well, and let it rise for three hours, or until the dough is light and begins to crack on top. Make into small rolls; let them stand on the hearth twenty minutes before baking in a quick oven. Just before taking them them up, brush over with white of egg. Shut the oven door one minute to glaze them.

SWEETENED FRENCH ROLLS
Mrs. E. B. Millar.

Two cups milk; 1 cup home-made yeast; 3 tablespoons sugar; 1 tablespoon butter; 1 egg.

To the milk, yeast, and beaten egg, add sufficient flour (into which the butter should be worked) to make a stiff batter. Mix well. Let it rise over night. In the morning knead it (not too much). Roll out into rounds, fold over, lay in a pan, cover closely, and set them in a warm place, until very light. Bake quickly in a moderate oven.

VIENNA ROLLS
Juliet Corson.

Four lbs. flour; 3 pints milk and water; ½ ounce of salt;

1¾ ounces fresh compressed yeast. These proportions are for an ordinary family.

Place the flour in the bread bowl, and in it put the milk, water and salt; mix with the liquid enough of the flour to make a very thin batter; next rub the yeast to powder between the hands, and mix it into the batter; cover the bread closely and let it stand for three-quarters of an hour. At the end of that time mix in the rest of the flour smoothly, and let the dough thus made stand again, closely covered, for two hours and a half, until it is light and elastic; then cut into pound pieces, and each pound into twelve equal parts; flatten these small pieces of dough into squares three quarters of an inch thick, fold their corners to the center, pinch them down to hold them, and turn the little rolls thus made over on a board covered with cloth; let them stand about ten minutes, turn them up again on a baking sheet, and put them into a hot oven and bake quickly for about fifteen minutes; when half done brush them with milk, return them to the oven and finish baking them.

PARKER HOUSE ROLLS
Mrs. T. D. Stimson.

One pint boiling milk; 1 heaping tablespoon butter; 1 heaping tablespoon sugar: 1 even teaspoon salt; ¼ cake compressed yeast; best wheat flour.

Add butter, sugar, and salt to the boiling milk, let it cool until lukewarm, then add the yeast, and stir in the flour gradually until thick enough to knead. Knead ten minutes, cover with a cloth, place a heavy pan, or molding board over it; let it stand until morning. Knead again, and let stand until ten o'clock, then roll out, cut with a biscuit cutter, butter half of the upper side and lap over the other; put in a pan, leaving plenty of room between; when light bake twenty minutes. This makes three dozen rolls.

BEATEN BISCUIT
Mrs. J. W. McKinley.

One pound flour; 2½ ounces lard; a pinch of salt; water to make a stiff dough.

Lay the dough on a molding board, and beat with a rolling pin, adding flour as it softens. Beat until the dough will crack as it is pulled apart. It will require about five hundred strokes. Make into biscuit the size of a large walnut, and bake in a moderate oven.

BAKING POWDER BISCUIT
Martha Bashor.

Two pints flour; 1 tablespoon lard or butter; 2 teaspoons Cleveland's baking powder—heaped; sweet milk.

Knead little as possible. Bake in a quick oven.

CREAM BISCUIT
Mrs. J. M. Stewart.

One quart flour; 1 coffee cup sour cream; 2 heaping teaspoons Cleveland's baking powder; ½ teaspoon soda; a little salt; sweet milk.

Mix the baking powder in the dry flour, and stir it into the cream with the soda and salt. Use enough sweet milk in mixing to make the dough roll easily. Bake in a hot oven.

The above makes a superior crust for strawberry shortcake. Roll the dough in two equal parts. Put them together, spreading butter between, that they may separate easily when baked.

TWIN BISCUIT
Miss Ida A. Maynard.

One pint flour; ½ teaspoon salt; 2 teaspoons Cleveland's baking powder; 1 tablespoon butter; milk.

Sift together flour, salt and baking powder. Rub in the butter. Add enough milk to make a soft dough. Roll thin. Cut into rounds with a small cutter. Spread these with softened butter, then cut more rounds, and put one on top of each of the buttered ones. Bake about ten minutes in a very hot oven.

GRAHAM SHORTCAKE
Mrs. T. W. Brotherton.

One half cup butter; 1 cup sugar; ½ cup water or milk; 3 well-beaten eggs; 1 cup graham flour, (sifted); ½ cup white flour; 2 teaspoons Cleveland's baking powder, sifted with flour.

Delicious with strawberries or raspberries. Cream an improvement. To be baked in layers—berries added just before serving.

BROWN BREAD
Mrs. Vida A. Bixby.

Two cups corn meal; 1 cup graham flour; 1 cup white flour; 2 cups sour milk; 1 cup molasses; 2 eggs; 1 teaspoon soda; salt; 1 cup raisins.

Mix together the corn meal, graham and white flour. Add milk; molasses, eggs, soda, and a little salt. Raisins should be put in last, if used at all. Their use is optional. Steam four hours. Brown in oven one half hour.

BOSTON BROWN BREAD
Mrs. J. J. Mellus.

Two cups corn meal; 1 cup rye flour, or sifted graham; 2 cups sweet milk; 1 cup sour milk; ½ cup molasses; ½ teaspoon salt; 2 tablespoons melted butter; 1 teaspoon soda, dissolved in a ⅓ cup of hot water.

Pour the mixture into a buttered tin and steam three hours, then bake twenty minutes, leaving on the cover. Be careful to keep the water boiling.

STEAMED GRAHAM BREAD
Mrs. H. Z. Osborne.

One and one half teacups sour milk; 1 egg; 1 teaspoon saleratus; ½ cup sugar; ½ cup molasses; ½ teaspoon salt; shortening, the size of an egg.

Stir in enough graham flour to make a thin batter, then add the egg well beaten, and stir in wheat flour until the batter is thick. Put it in a well-greased tin. Steam two hours, then brown it in the oven.

SOUTHERN RICE BREAD
Mrs. S. T. Rorer.

Three eggs; 1½ pints milk; 1 teaspoon salt; 1 pint white

corn meal; 1 tablespoon melted butter; 1 cup cold boiled rice; 2 teaspoons Cleveland's baking powder.

Mix and beat well. Add the baking powder last. Bake in round, shallow pans (well greased) thirty minutes. Serve hot.

THE REAL OLD CORN PONE
Mrs. M. A. Gibson.

Corn meal; molasses; salt; boiling water.

Make a thin mush; when cool, stir in meal until about as thick as graham bread dough--(a stiff batter). Add a little salt, and a *little* molasses to sweeten. Pour into a well-greased Dutch oven, and put in a warm place to rise. When light, it will be raised in the middle and break in little cracks all over the top, have the coals of fire ready to put on top and under the oven. · Stand it with one side to the fire for a short time, then turn it a little, and continue turning it until every part has been exposed to the fire. When carefully made this is delicious.

CORN BREAD
Mrs S. J. Peck.

Two cups sour milk; 1 cup flour; ½ cup warm water; 2 eggs; ½ teaspoon soda; 1 teaspoon salt; corn meal.

Mix flour, milk, salt and eggs. Stir in sufficient meal to make a stiff batter. Add the soda, dissolved in warm water, last. Pour the mixture into a hot pan well greased. Bake to a nice brown. To be eaten hot.

STEAMED CORN BREAD
Mrs. D. S. Dickson.

Two cups corn meal; 2 cups buttermilk; 1 cup syrup; 1 cup flour; 1 teaspoon soda, (dissolved).

Steam three hours.

CORN PONE
Mrs. R. C. Hunt.

Two cups corn meal—heaped; 1 cup flour; 2½ cups sweet milk; 2 tablespoons white sugar; 1 tablespoon lard; 2 teaspoons Cleveland's baking powder; 1 teaspoon salt; 3 eggs.

Beat all together very thoroughly, adding the stiffly frothed whites of the eggs last. Pour into a well-greased dripping pan and bake in a hot oven. Good.

SOUTHERN HOE CAKE
Mrs. James Foord.

Two cups corn meal—fresh; 1 teaspoon salt; boiling water. Scald the meal by pouring boiling water on it. It should not be stiff. Pour into a shallow pan, making the cake half an inch thick. Bake in a hot oven until of a light brown.

JOHNNY CAKE
Mrs. Z. L. Parmelee.

Two cups yellow corn meal; 1 cup flour; ½ cup molasses; ¼ cup shortening; 2 cups sour milk; 1 teaspoon soda; a pinch of salt.

Beat the mixture thoroughly, and pour into tins, that it may be an inch or more in thickness, before baking. While baking, after it begins to brown, brush the top with melted butter. This is a great improvement.

Sweet milk and two heaping teaspoons of Cleveland's baking powder may be used instead of sour milk and soda.

JOHNNY CAKE
Mrs. I. H. Preston.

Half cup brown sugar; ½ cup butter and lard—mixed; ½ cup wheat flour; ½ pint sweet milk; 2 teaspoons Cleveland's baking powder—heaped; ½ teaspoon salt; 2 eggs.

Corn meal to make a batter. Mix the ingredients as for cake. Bake three quarters of an hour.

TEA MUFFINS
Mrs. A. C. Radford.

One quart flour; 1 pint milk; 3 eggs well beaten; 2 tablespoons melted butter; 2 teaspoons Cleveland's baking powder.

Mix the baking powder with the flour; add the eggs, butter and milk. Bake in buttered rings in a quick oven.

OATMEAL MUFFINS
Mrs. C. C. Converse.

One cup cooked oatmeal; 1 pint flour; ½ pint milk; ½ cup lukewarm water; ¼ of a yeast cake; 1 tablespoon sugar; 1 teaspoon salt.

Scald the milk, add sugar and salt. Cool. Add the yeast dissolved in the water, then the flour mixed with the oatmeal. Beat thoroughly and let it rise, then beat again. Fill the pans two-thirds full. Set in a warm place twenty minutes. Bake thirty minutes in a moderate oven.

MUFFINS, No. 1
Mrs. S. E. Smith.

One pint warm milk; flour; lump of butter, the size of an egg; ½ cup yeast; salt.

Sufficient flour should be used to make a stiff batter. Let it rise over night. In the morning before baking, it should stand in tins half hour. Quick oven.

MUFFINS, No. 2
Mrs. S. E. Smith.

One cup milk; 3 cups flour; 4 teaspoons melted butter; 2 eggs; 1 teaspoon soda; 2 teaspoons cream tartar.

Dissolve soda in the milk.

FLOUR MUFFINS
Mrs. H. E. Smith.

One and half cups sweet milk; 3 cups flour; 1 tablespoon sugar; 1 tablespoon melted butter; 2 teaspoons Cleveland's baking powder; 1 egg; a little salt.

Bake in muffin rings.

ENGLISH MUFFINS
Mrs. I. N. Van Nuys.

Four cups flour; 2 cups milk; 1 tablespoon sugar; 3 teaspoons Cleveland's baking powder; 1 teaspoon salt; 2 eggs.

Bake in rings on a hot griddle.

ENGLISH MUFFINS
Mary Roach.

One pint lukewarm potato water ; 2 tablespoons mashed potato; 1 large cup yeast; flour; corn meal.

Mix like soft bread dough. When very light, roll and cut with a large cutter, sprinkle corn meal over the molding board, leave the muffins upon it until light ; then bake on a pancake griddle until quite crisp.

CORN MUFFINS
Mrs. Jerome Curtin.

Two cups flour ; 3 cups milk ; 1 cup corn meal ; ½ cup butter; 2 tablespoons sugar; 2 teaspoons Cleveland's baking powder; salt.

Lard may be used instead of butter. Bake in gem pans.

CORN MUFFINS
Mrs. J. H. Jones.

One half cup butter ; 1 cup sugar, scant ; 2 cups flour ; 4 eggs; 1 pint milk; 1 cup Indian meal; 2 teaspoons Cleveland's baking powder.

Cream the butter and sugar, add the eggs, then flour, milk, etc. Bake ten or fifteen minutes in a quick oven.

GRAHAM GRITS OR CORN MUFFINS
Mrs. Augusta Robinson.

One cup white flour ; 1 cup graham grits or corn meal ; 1 small tablespoon sugar or molasses; 1 egg; 1 small tablespoon melted butter; ½ teaspoon salt; 1 teaspoon soda; 2 teaspoons cream tartar; sweet milk enough to make a stiff batter.

Bake in a fairly hot oven. This recipe makes eight or ten muffins.

WAFFLES
Mrs. W. H. Perry.

One cake Royal yeast ; 2 teacups milk ; ½ teaspoon salt ; ½ teaspoon baking soda; 1 egg; flour; warm water.

Dissolve the yeast in a little warm water, add the milk,

salt, and flour enough to make a thin batter. In the morning stir in the soda and egg (well beaten). Bake in waffle irons.

WAFFLES
Mrs. A. S. Averill.

One pint buttermilk ; 1 tablespoon sugar ; 2 tablespoons melted butter; 1 teaspoon soda, scant; 2 eggs; flour: salt.

Stir flour into the buttermilk until the spoon can rest on top of the batter. Add sugar, butter, salt, and soda, and just before baking, the eggs well beaten.

These, as all other kinds of warm breakfast cakes, are better if mixed over night, adding the soda and eggs in the morning.

WAFFLES
Mrs. W. B. Holcomb.

One quart flour ; 3 teaspoons Cleveland's baking powder ; ¹⁄₂ cup butter; 3 eggs; a little milk.

Sift flour and baking powder together. Rub in the butter, add sufficient milk to make a stiff batter. Eggs beaten separately are added last. Waffle irons should be hot and filled two thirds full.

WAFERS
Mrs. H. K. S. O'Melveny.

One pint flour, prepared is best; 1 cup milk; 1 tablespoon butter; 1 teaspoon salt.

Rub butter and salt into the flour, wet with the milk, roll as thin as possible, cut into rounds with a cake-cutter, and roll again, thinner than *possible*—they should be translucent. Transfer them to a floured pan and bake in a quick oven until delicately browned. Very dainty.

GRAHAM GEMS
Mrs. E. R. Smith.

Two large spoons sugar ; 2 eggs ; 1½ cups sour milk : 1 teaspoon soda ; a good sized piece of butter.

Rub the sugar and butter together, then add eggs, milk, and soda. Buttermilk may take the place of sour milk. This recipe will make one dozen gems.

GRAHAM GEMS
Mrs. W. B. Holcomb.

One and a half pints graham flour ; 1 egg ; sweet milk ; 3 teaspoons Cleveland's baking powder; 1 tablespoon butter ; 1 tablespoon sugar.

Mix the baking powder in the flour, rub in the butter, add salt, sugar, and the beaten egg. Stir these ingredients to a batter with milk. Drop in hot gem pans and bake in a quick oven.

CORN GEMS
Mrs. W. M. Dickson.

Two cups corn meal ; 2 cups flour : 2½ cups sweet milk ; 2 eggs; ½ cup butter. 1 tablespoon sugar; 2 teaspoons cream tartar; 1 teaspoon soda.

AUNTY'S BANNOCKS

One pint meal ; 1 pint milk ; 1 pint water ; 2 tablespoons sugar; 5 eggs. a little salt.

Scald the meal in the water, add the eggs while hot, bake one hour. Good.

JOLLY BOYS
Mrs. S. T. Rorer.

One pint yellow corn meal; ½ cup butter; 3 eggs; 1 pint warm milk; 1 yeast cake; 2 tablespoons warm water; ¼ cup sugar; flour.

Scald the meal (it should be moist, not wet). Cream the butter, add the eggs well beaten, then the milk (scalded, and cooled). Beat, add meal, yeast (dissolved in two tablespoons of water), sugar, and flour to make a soft dough. Cover, and set in a warm place over night, or until very light. Make into balls the size of English walnuts, place on a floured cloth, and when light (about an hour), fry in smoking hot fat. Dust with powdered sugar, and serve.

FRITTERS
Mrs. Homer Cooke.

One pint sweet milk; 2 eggs; ½ teaspoon Cleveland's

baking powder; 1 small teaspoon salt; flour; hot fat; maple molasses.

Use sufficient flour to make a thin batter; fry in hot fat, and serve with maple molasses.

DELICIOUS PUFFS FOR TEA
Mrs. C. C. McLean.

One pint sweet milk; 6 eggs; a large pinch of salt; flour. Beat the yolks until they are very light; stir in the milk, salt, frothed whites, and flour to make a batter about the consistency of boiled custard. Bake in gem pans in a quick oven.

POP OVERS
Mrs. H. E. Smith

Two eggs; 2 cups milk; 2 cups flour; a pinch of salt.

Beat very light, drop in hot gem pans, bake half an hour in a quick oven.

GRIDDLE CAKES
Miss M. E. McLellan.

One quart sour milk; 1 teaspoon salt; 1 teaspoon soda; 1 tablespoon sugar; 2 eggs; flour.

Mix over night, using enough flour to make a very stiff batter; in the morning, add the sugar, the soda dissolved in warm water, and the eggs well beaten.

ADIRONDACK GRIDDLE CAKES
H. F. W.

One pint sour milk; 1 pt. flour; 2 eggs; 1 teaspoon soda; 1½ teaspoon salt.

Mix flour and milk together; stand over night. In the morning add eggs well beaten, soda, and salt. Bake on hot griddle. A delicious griddle cake.

RICE GRIDDLE CAKES
Miss M. E. McLellan.

One small cup boiled rice; 1 cup sifted flour; ¾ cup milk; 1 tablespoon sugar; 1 beaten egg; a little melted butter; salt; 1 teaspoon Cleveland's baking powder.

Sift the sugar and baking powder with the flour. Beat the eggs separately, and add the whites last. If a half pint cup is used, two eggs will be needed.

CRUMB CAKES
Mrs. T. W. Brotherton.

One and one third cups crumbs of stale bread; 3 cups sweet milk; 3 eggs; 1 dessert spoon Cleveland's baking powder; flour.

Soak the crumbs in the milk over night. In the morning add baking powder, eggs well beaten, and flour sufficient to make them of the right consistency for baking on a griddle.

WHEAT CAKES
Mrs. Homer Cooke.

One cup of buttermilk; 1 teaspoon soda; flour; salt.

To every cup of rich buttermilk, add one small level teaspoon of soda; salt to taste, with sufficient flour to make a thin batter; beat until light.

FLANNEL CAKES
Mrs. M. Hagan.

One quart flour; 1 egg; ½ teaspoon soda; sour milk.

Make a batter of the milk and flour; beat the egg with the soda until very light, and add it to the batter.

CORN MEAL PANCAKES
L. C. Goodwin.

One pint sour milk; 1 cup flour; 1 cup corn meal; 1 teaspoon soda; 2 eggs; a little salt.

Beat whites and yolks separately, adding the whites last.

CAKE

Miss Farmer, Boston Cooking School.

In making cake only the best materials should be used ;
and these, with accurate measurements and care in baking,
can hardly fail to produce good results.

Pastry flour should always be used, and fine granulated
sugar, unless otherwise specified.   If bread flour is used
instead of the pastry, less is required ; allowing a difference
of one tablespoonful for each cupful called for by the recipe.
The materials should first be brought together and prepared
and the pans buttered.   Use clarified butter for this, procuring
it by melting the butter and carefully turning it off so that
the salt which sinks to the bottom, may be left behind.   It is
easier to use a small brush in buttering.   The pans may be
papered, if liked, but a thin dusting of flour is just as good,
dredging the pan with flour and then shaking out all that
one can, leaving only as much as will be taken up by the
butter, which will be only a fine dust.   Square or round pans
are best for cake, as they are more easily handled and the
cake bakes more evenly.   The cake should not be poured into
the pan, but put in by spoonfuls, one in each corner first and
then in the center, smoothing it over and having the sides
and corners, if anything higher than the center, as they will
cook quicker and shrink more.   For baking cake a rather
moderate oven is required for most kinds.

No thermometer has as yet been invented which can satisfactorily test the heat of the oven, and it must be tested by
the hand or by flour, which if nicely browned in five minutes,
will show the temperature to be just right.   If too hot, the
heat may be reduced in any way most convenient, not,
however, by placing water in the oven unless absolutely
necessary as the moisture generated will interfere with the

proper baking of the cake. Baking cake may be divided into four stages. In the first quarter the cake should begin to rise. In the second, it should rise more and brown slightly. In the third it should rise to its full height, double its height when first put in the oven, and brown more. In the fourth quarter it should finish baking and shrink from the pan, which shows it is done. This last test does not apply to bride or pound cake, which should be tested with the finger. If it leaves a depression the cake is not thoroughly baked, but if it is firm to the touch it is done. A cake should be watched carefully in the baking, timing by the clock, and turning the cake as often as necessary; only making sure that each motion is a gentle one.

FRUIT CAKE

Mrs. Charles Silent.

Twelve eggs; 1 ℔ butter; 1 ℔ brown sugar; 1¼ ℔s browned flour; 1 cup molasses; 3½ ℔s raisins; 2 ℔s currants; 2½ ℔s citron ; ½ cup currant jelly dissolved in ½ cup hot water; 1 teaspoon soda; 1 teaspoon cloves; 1 teaspoon cinnamon; 1 teaspoon nutmeg; 1 teaspoon mace; ½ teaspoon ginger.

Cream the butter and sugar. Beat the eggs, whites and yelks separately. Add the beaten yelks to butter and sugar. Add the soda to the dissolved jelly and hot water. Mix the fruit with the browned flour and mix all together adding the spices last. Bake in a very slow oven for four hours.

FRUIT CAKE

Mrs. Anna O'Melveny.

Two coffee cups butter ; 4 coffee cups sugar ; 8 eggs, well beaten ; 1 coffee cup sour milk ; 5 coffee cups sifted flour ; 1 ℔ raisins, well stoned; 1 heaping teaspoon soda ; 1 large nutmeg, grated ; 1 teaspoon each cloves, cinnamon, and allspice ; 1 teaspoon each lemon, and vanilla; 1 ℔ English currants, well washed; ½ ℔ citron, sliced thin.

Dissolve the soda in two tablespoons of hot water. Cream butter and sugar together till perfectly smooth. After all the ingredients except the fruit are put together, beat thoroughly.

When the fruit is prepared roll it in flour.   Then stir into the
cake batter until well mixed.   If you like the flavor of
crushed orange peel, add a tablespoonful.   This quantity will
make four, two-quart pans of cake.   Bake in a slow oven.

BLACK FRUIT CAKE
Mrs. J. E. Murray.

One cup butter ; 3½ cups brown sugar ; ½ cup molasses ;
1 cup milk ; 4 cups flour ; 4 eggs ; 1½ teaspoons Cleveland's
baking powder ; 1 ℔ raisins ; 1 ℔ currants ; ½ ℔ figs ; ¾ ℔
citron; 2 teaspoons each cloves, cinnamon and allspice.
Bake slowly.

PLAIN FRUIT CAKE
Miss S. E. Smith, St. Johns, New Brunswick, Canada.

One large cup butter ; 2 cups dark brown sugar ; 1 cup
molasses; 1 cup water; 3 eggs; 3 heaping cups raisins; 1 cup
currants; 4½ cups flour; 1 teaspoon soda, dissolved in water;
a little sliced citron and spice to taste; figs if desired.

PORK CAKE
Dr. Chase, Ann Arbor.

One ℔ fat salt pork entirely free of lean or rind ; 1 ℔
raisins seeded and chopped fine; ¼ ℔ citron shaved very thin;
2 cups sugar; 1 cup molasses; 1 teaspoon soda, powdered and
put in molasses; 1 oz. each, nutmeg and cloves; 2 oz. cinnamon; flour, sifted, enough to give the ordinary consistency of
cake mixture.

Chop the pork very fine ; pour over ½ pint boiling water.
Add other ingredients and bake slowly.   Try with broom
straw.   When nothing adheres it is done.   If properly cared
for will be nice and moist two months after baking.

THREE PLY CAKE
Mrs. E. D. Major.

Two cups sugar; 3 cups flour ; ½ cup butter ; 1 cup milk
or water; 3 eggs, beaten yelks and whites separately ; 1 teaspoon Cleveland's baking powder ; 1 cup raisins; 1 cup currants;
a little citron; 1 teaspoon molasses; spice to taste.

Beat butter and sugar together, add milk or water, then yelks of eggs, flour and yeast powder ; lastly whites of eggs and flavoring.

Take one third of mixture into another dish and add to it the fruit and spices. Bake in three layers, with fruit layers in center, and join while warm either with jelly or white icing.

WALNUT CAKE
Mrs. M. E. Kerr, Orange.

Two cups granulated sugar ; ½ cup butter ; ⅔ cup milk ; 3 eggs ; 3 cups sifted flour ; 1 heaping teaspoon Cleveland's baking powder ; 1 cup nut meats, chopped a little ; 1 cup seeded raisins, chopped a little.

Sift the baking powder with the flour. Put together in the usual way. Fill the cake pan with a layer of the cake, then a layer of raisins upon that, then strew over with a handful of nut meats, and so on until the pan is two thirds full. Bake in a moderate oven.

WALNUT FILLING FOR ANY LAYER CAKE
Miss Kate Stevens.

Whites of two eggs beaten stiff; 1 cup of walnuts cut fine with a knife ; 1 cup seeded raisins ; 8 tablespoons pulverized sugar; flavor with Watson's extract.

Make a thick syrup of the sugar, when it ropes, pour it over the whites, beating all the time. Beat till nearly cool, then add raisins and nuts and spread between layers.

NUT CREAM CAKE
Mrs. M. R. Sinsabaugh.

Three eggs; 1 cup sugar ; 1 heaping teaspoon Cleveland's baking powder; 5 tablespoons hot water; 1¼ cups flour, well sifted.

Beat the yelks of the eggs and sugar well together, add hot water and stir in the flour slowly. Then add the whites of the eggs beaten to a stiff froth, and bake in two layers in an oven rather hotter than for loaf cake.

Cream for above cake : Chop enough English walnuts

(quite fine) to make one cupful and stir into one half pint of whipped cream, sweetened and flavored with lemon, to taste. Spread this between the layers and ice the top.

NUT CAKE
Mrs. Burdette Chandler.

One-half cup butter; 2 cups sugar; 3 cups flour; 1 cup sweet milk; 3 eggs, beaten separately; 2 teaspoons Cleveland's baking powder. Flavor with lemon.

Filling: One cup nuts, chopped finely; 3 eggs, whites only, beaten stiff. Stir together; adding enough sugar to make filling sufficiently stiff.

Bake cake in layers, and spread filling between.

NUT CAKE
Mrs. A. T. Tuttle.

One pound flour; 1 pound butter; 1 pound pulverized sugar; 10 eggs; 1 pound any kind of nuts chopped fine; 1 pound raisins; 1 pound currants; ½ pound citron; 2 nutmegs. Flavor to taste Beat all together very hard. Bake three hours Cover top with icing.

FIG CAKE
Mrs. A. C. Goodrich.

One cup butter; 2 cups sugar; 3 cups sifted flour; flavor with vanilla; 1 cup milk; 4 eggs—yelks and whites beaten separately; 3 teaspoons Cleveland's baking powder.

Take ½ the batter, pour into two jelly tins and on each put a layer of split figs, *seeds* up. To the other half of the batter add 2 tablespoons molasses, 1 cup seedless raisins, ½ cup currants, 1 teaspoonful cinnamon, ½ teaspoon of cloves, a little more flour, and bake in two jelly tins. Put the layers together with frosting—having a fig cake on top.

FIG CAKE
Mrs. Willard H. Stimson.

Four eggs—whites only; ½ large cup milk; ⅔ cup butter;

1½ cups sugar; 3 cups flour; 1 teaspoon Cleveland's baking powder.

Filling for same.—Two eggs—whites only; 1½ pounds figs—chopped; 1 cup raisins—seeded; 1 cup walnut meats; powdered sugar to make a good icing; flavor with vanilla.

BANANA CAKE
Mrs. Homer Cooke, Waukegan. Ill.

One and one half cups granulated sugar; ½ cup butter; ⅔ cup sweet milk; 2 cups sifted flour; 1½ teaspoons Cleveland's baking powder; flavor to taste.

Bake in two layers in large sized tins. Put sliced bananas on one layer of cake, cover with thick layer of whipped cream—sweetened to taste, then layer of cake and another layer of banana and whipped cream.

This cake should be eaten fresh.

MARSHMALLOW CAKE
Mrs. Homer Cooke, Waukegan, Ill.

Take any favorite recipe for cake and make two good layers, putting one in the oven before the other; flavor with lemon.

Use banana marshmallows—if you can get them. Have them a little warm and place them as close as you can crowd them on the first layer of cake. Try to have the other layer just ready, so it will go together hot. Make a lemon icing of the white of one egg, same quantity of lemon juice and sufficient confectioners' sugar to make it the proper consistency.

This cake is better to stand a day or two before eating.

BLACKBERRY CAKE
Mrs. W. J. Brown, Miss Eva Williams.

One cup granulated sugar; ¾ cup butter; 3 eggs; 1 cup blackberry jam; 3 tablespoons sour cream; 1½ cups flour; 1 teaspoon soda; 1 teaspoon cinnamon; 1 nutmeg (grated).

Beat the butter, sugar and yolks of the eggs to a cream; then stir in the jam, sour cream, soda, flavoring, flour and the well-beaten whites of the eggs. Bake in two layers and put together with boiled frosting.

This is a delicious cake. Raspberry or strawberry jam can be used in place of blackberry.

FROSTING FOR BLACKBERRY CAKE
Mrs. W. J. B.

Two cups granulated sugar; ½ cup hot water; whites of 2 eggs.

Boil the sugar and water until it threads from the spoon; then pour gradually into the stiffly-beaten whites of the eggs. Beat rapidly to prevent its being grainy. When the right consistency, spread quickly, as it soon becomes too stiff to spread smoothly.

CRANBERRY CAKE
Mrs. Gerrard Irvine.

Three cups sugar; 1½ cups butter; 1½ cups sweet milk; 1½ pounds raisins; 6 eggs—beaten separately; 2 teaspoons Watson's lemon extract; 7 cups flour; 2 quarts cranberries; 3 teaspoons Cleveland's baking powder.

Bake very slowly 1½ hours. Mix as any cake. Cook cranberries. Remove seeds and skins, and sweeten as for cranberry sauce. Add to cake mixture. Bake in loaf.

POUND CAKE
Mrs. D. M. Welch.

One pound butter; 1 pound flour; grated peel of 1 lemon; 1 pound sugar; whites of nine eggs; yelks of seven.

Cream the butter. Add the sugar and well-beaten yelks, (beat these until very light); then mix in alternately the flour and stiffly-beaten whites, and add the grated lemon peel. Bake in a moderate oven.

POUND CAKE
Mrs. W. T. Carter.

One pound pulverized sugar; ¾ pound butter; 10 eggs— well beaten; 18 ounces flour.

Rub the butter and sugar well together with the hand, add the eggs gradually, and beat well. Flavor with lemon and then add the flour, stirring gently. Bake in buttered and paper-lined molds in moderate oven.

POUND CAKE
Miss M. E. McLellan.

Four eggs—their weight in butter, in powdered sugar and in flour; a small half teaspoon Cleveland's baking powder.

Cream the butter and sugar together. Add the eggs beaten—not separately; flavor with mace and extract of lemon. Bake in cups or gem tins, and cover with icing when cold.

WHITE CAKE
Miss Farmer, Boston Cooking School.

One half cup butter; 1½ cup sugar; ½ cup milk; 5 eggs—whites only; 2 cups flour—sifted before measuring; 1½ teaspoons Cleveland's baking powder; ¼ rounding teaspoon cream tartar; 1 teaspoon vanilla.

Cream the butter in a warm bowl, and add gradually the sugar and milk, also the whites of the eggs beaten until stiff. Sift the flour together with the baking powder and cream tartar, and add with the vanilla. Beat thoroughly to give fineness of texture, and bake half hour in shallow pans. When done, spread marshmallow paste between and also on the top.

This will be found an especially nice white cake, and with the marshmallow filling, which is something new, makes a very attractive cake.

MARSHMALLOW PASTE - for the above

Three fourths cup sugar; ¼ cup milk; ½ teaspoon vanilla; ¼ pound marshmallows; 2 tablespoons hot water.

Stir the milk and sugar together and boil *without* stirring for six minutes—counting the time from the moment it begins to boil all over the surface. Melt the marshmallows, and add

2 tablespoons of hot water, cooking over hot water until smooth, stirring meanwhile. Combine the two mixtures, and beat until stiff enough to spread. Add the vanilla last. If the sugar is stirred while boiling, it is apt to granulate.

WHITE PERFECTION CAKE
Mrs. R. C. Hunt.

Two cups sugar; ¾ cup butter; 1 cup sweet milk; ½ cup corn starch; 3 cups flour; 8 eggs—whites *only*, (beaten very stiff); 2 teaspoons Cleveland's baking powder; any flavor desired.

Beat butter and sugar to a cream, then add the milk, then the flour and corn starch, with the baking powder mixed with them. Beat until smooth and white as cream, then add flavoring, and, last of all, *stir* in the whites. Do not beat them in, and do not beat the cake after the whites are in. Bake in a moderate oven.

This cake may be made richer by adding ¼ pound citron sliced *very* thin, floured and added just before baking.

DELICATE CAKE
Mrs. Burdette Chandler.

One cup butter; 2 cups sugar; 1 cup sweet milk; 3 cups flour; 5 eggs—whites only; 4 even teaspoons Cleveland's baking powder. Flavor with lemon.

DELICATE CAKE
Mrs. F. M. Van Doren.

One and half cups sugar; ⅔ cup butter; ⅔ cup sweet milk; 1 teaspoon cream tartar; ½ teaspoon soda; 2½ cups flour; 1 pound raisins, stoned and chopped, and laid in middle of cake; whites of 6 eggs.

Rub butter and sugar to a cream.

BRIDE'S CAKE
Mrs. A. S. Baldwin.

Three cups powdered sugar; 1 cup butter; 2 cups flour; ⅔ cup corn starch, and cup filled up with flour; ½ cup

sweet milk; 3 teaspoons Cleveland's baking powder; 14 eggs
—whites only.

Flavor with rose or bitter almond.   Bake little over three
hours.

SNOW CAKE
Mrs. Gerrard Irvine.

One half teacup butter; 1 teacup sugar; 1½ teacups flour
—sifted with 1 teaspoon Cleveland's baking powder—twice;
½ cup sweet milk; 4 eggs—whites only.

Flavor with lemon.   Cream the butter and sugar *well*
together.   Add the milk, then the flour and lemon extract.
Beat thoroughly, then add the well-beaten whites of the eggs.
Stir them gently in, and bake in moderate oven, being careful
not to open oven door for 20 minutes.

SNOW CAKE
Mrs. Vaughn.

One cup sugar; ½ cup butter; ½ cup sweet milk; 1½
cups flour; 4 eggs—whites only—well beaten; 1 teaspoon
Cleveland's baking powder.

Flavor with vanilla.

SUNSHINE CAKE
Mrs. F. S. Hicks.

Whites of 11 eggs; 1½ cups granulated sugar, measured
after sifting; yolks of 6 eggs; 1 cup flour, measured after sifting; 1 teaspoon cream tartar; 1 teaspoon orange extract.

This is made almost exactly like angel cake.   Beat the
whites of eggs to a stiff froth and gradually beat in the sugar.
Beat the yelks in a similar manner, add to them the whites,
sugar, and flavoring.   Finally stir in the flour.   Mix quickly
and well.   Bake for 50 minutes in a slow oven. Use a pan the
same as for angel cake, with little knobs on the corners so
that when the cake is turned upside down it will not be flat on
the table, but will allow a current of air to pass around it.

ANGEL CAKE
Miss Mary Dickson. Petaluma.

Whites of 11 eggs, beaten to a stiff froth; 2 cups sugar, sifted once; 1½ cups flour, sifted *seven* times; then add 1 teaspoon cream tartar and *sift again*; 1 teaspoon vanilla or bitter almond.

When the eggs are ready, put the sugar in gradually, beating it well; then add the flour slowly, add flavor.   Beat all very hard, and pour into an ungreased pan.   Bake forty or fifty minutes in a moderate oven. When done turn the pan with cake, upside down across another pan or dish, so it will not sweat. Do not take it out of the pan till it is cold. The baking pan should be new, or one that has never had milk or grease of any kind in it.

ANGEL CAKE
Mrs. Weiside, (Pastry Cook at Glenwood.)

One cup flour; 1 teaspoon cream tartar; 1½ cups sugar; 11 eggs, whites only; 1 teaspoon flavoring.

Sift the flour with the cream tartar twice. Whip the eggs to a stiff froth, add the sugar and beat a great deal. Stir in flour with a spoon. Flavor. Bake in a moderate oven.

Mrs. Weiside has made this cake successfully for fifteen years, and says if the directions are followed no extra care in baking is needed.

FEATHER CAKE
Mrs. Wm. J. Robinson, Moncton, Canada.

Four eggs, whites only; 1½ cups sugar; ½ cup butter; 2 cups flour; 1 cup milk; 1 teaspoon cream tartar; ½ teaspoon soda. Flavor to taste.

Beat the butter and sugar together with a little of the milk, add half the flour in which the cream tartar and soda have been thoroughly mixed, then the remainder of the milk and flour with flavoring, and lastly the eggs beaten to a stiff froth. Bake in a moderate oven.

CORN STARCH CAKE
Mrs. T. C. Griswold.

Two cups sugar; 1 cup butter; 1 cup corn starch; 2 cups flour; 1 cup milk; 6 eggs, whites only; 1½ teaspoons Cleveland's baking powder. Flavor to taste and bake one hour if in one cake. A shorter time if in two.

JENNY LIND CAKE
Mrs. F. M. Van Doren.

Two cups sugar; 1 cup butter; 1 cup sweet milk; 1 cup flour; 3 teaspoons Cleveland's baking powder; 12 eggs, *whites only.*

SPONGE CAKE
Mrs. D. L. Whipple.

One and one-half cups of sugar; 3 eggs, beaten thoroughly; 1½ cups flour, sifted three times with ½ teaspoon salt, and 2 teaspoons Cleveland's baking powder; add flour so prepared to the eggs and sugar, beat well; add ⅔ cup boiling water last and bake in medium oven.

CREAM SPONGE CAKE
Miss Ella Kerr, Orange.

One cup sugar; 3 eggs; ⅔ cup sweet cream; 1½ cup flour; 1 teaspoon Cleveland's baking powder.

Beat the eggs and sugar together, add the cream then the flour and baking powder. Flavor with lemon.

SPONGE CAKE
Mrs. L. A. Bradish.

Two cups sugar; 1 cup flour; 1 cup boiling water; 2 even teaspoons Cleveland's baking powder; 4 eggs.

Beat the eggs and sugar thoroughly. Sift the baking powder into the flour and stir into the sugar and eggs, add a pinch of salt and flavoring, pour in the boiling water and bake immediately.

SPONGE CAKE
Mrs. D. M. Welch.

One pound pulverized sugar; ½ pound sifted flour; 1 salt-

spoon salt; 10 eggs, beaten separately; grated rind and juice of
1 lemon.

Beat both yelks and whites very thoroughly; blend them
lightly and quickly together; add the sugar gradually, then
the lemon juice, rind and salt, lastly the flour. Do not beat
the mixture after the flour is added.

PREMIUM SPONGE CAKE
Miss Lois Dickson, Petaluma.

Three eggs, well beaten; 1 cup sugar; ⅓ cup milk; 1⅓
cups flour; ½ teaspoon soda; 1 teaspoon cream tartar; a pinch
of salt; flavor to taste.

SPONGE DROP CAKE
Mrs. W. T. Carter.

Twelve eggs, yelks only; 1 teaspoon extract lemon; 1
pound sugar; 1 pound and 4 ounces flour; ½ ounce carbonate
of ammonia.

Put the sugar in a wooden bowl, adding the yelks of the
eggs one or two at a time, and beating with your hand.
When all are in, rub thoroughly together, then add the carbonate of ammonia, finely pulverized; if necessary dissolve in
a little milk; add flavoring, and then the flour, stirring gently.
Drop on well-buttered and floured tins, in bits the size of a
walnut and bake in a quick oven. When cool cover the drops
with "Royal icing," either tinted, prepared with chocolate or
plain as you may fancy. The chocolate icing is prepared by
adding melted chocolate to the plain icing.

LEMON CAKE
Mrs. W. J. Brown.

One cup butter; 3 cups sugar; 5 eggs, whites beaten separately; 1 cup sweet milk; 4 cups sifted flour; 1 teaspoon cream
tartar; 1 teaspoon soda; or 1½ teaspoons Cleveland's baking
powder and ½ teaspoon soda; the grated peel and juice of one
lemon.

Beat the butter, sugar and yolks of eggs to a cream, stir in
the other ingredients, adding the well-beaten whites of eggs

last. This is a delicious cake and will make two good-sized loaves.

LEMON CAKE
Mrs. W. M. Dickson.

Three-fourths cup butter; 1½ cups sugar; ¾ cup sweet milk; 2½ cups flour; 3 eggs; 1 teaspoon soda; 2 teaspoons cream tartar.

For jelly; take 1 coffee cup sugar· 2 tablespoons butter; 2 eggs; juice of 2 lemons.

Beat all together and boil until the consistency of jelly. For orange cake use oranges instead of lemons.

LEMON CAKE
Mrs. J. W. Gillette.

One cup sugar; ½ cup butter; ½ cup milk; 2 cups flour, sifted; 1 teaspoon Cleveland's baking powder; 2 eggs. Flavor with extract of lemon. Bake in layers.

For the jelly—2 coffee cups of sugar; 2 eggs; 2 tablespoons butter; 2 lemons, juice only.

Mix lemon juice with the sugar, butter and eggs; boil to the consistency of jelly. Orange may be used in the same way.

ORANGE CAKE
Miss Ida Maynard, Colorado Springs.

Half cup butter; 2 cups sugar; 1½ oranges; ½ cup cold water; 5 eggs, yelks of only four; 1½ teaspoons Cleveland's baking powder; 2½ cups flour, sifted with the baking powder.

Cream the butter, add the sugar slowly and beat well, then the yelks of eggs well beaten. Add to this the juice of the oranges and the grated rind of one; then the water, then flour and beat well. Now add the whites of 5 eggs beaten stiff, and bake in a buttered pan 30 minutes.

Orange frosting—Take the grated rind and juice of one orange. Let it stand 20 minutes, then add the unbeaten white of one egg and enough confectioner's sugar to make it stiff enough to spread.

ORANGE FILLING—for Layer Cake
Mrs. H. K. S. O'Melveny.

Two oranges; 1 lemon; grate the rinds and add the juice; 1 cup cold water; 1 cup sugar; 1 tablespoon corn starch mixed in some of the water. Boil until smooth; and cool before putting on the cake.

NEAPOLITAN CAKE
Mrs. W. W. Ross.

One and one-half cups sugar; ½ cup butter; ½ cup milk; ½ cup flour; 3 eggs. Into this mixture stir chocolate custard made as follows:

Eight tablespoons Ghirardelli's grated chocolate; 5 tablespoons granulated sugar; ½ cup of milk. Cook until it thickens a little and beat until cool. Stir this into cake part thoroughly. Add to this mixture 1½ cups flour and 2 teaspoons Cleveland's baking powder. Beat thoroughly. Bake in three layers. Put white icing between the layers and on top.

CHOCOLATE CAKE
Miss Ruth Childs.

One and one-half cups butter; 1 cup white powdered sugar; 1 pound brown sugar; 6 eggs—yelks and whites separately; 1 cup sweet milk; 3 cups flour; ¼ pound sliced blanched almonds; 2 teaspoons Cleveland's baking powder; ⅓ cake Ghirardelli's chocolate; 1 lemon; 1 teaspoon cloves; 1 teaspoon allspice; 1 teaspoon cinnamon; 1 pound chopped raisins.

Bake slowly one hour and a half.

CHOCOLATE CAKE
Mrs. W. J. Brown.

One cup sugar; ½ cup butter; ⅔ cup sweet milk; 2 cups sifted flour; 4 eggs—whites only; 1½ teaspoons Cleveland's baking powder; 1 square Ghirardelli's chocolate—grated; flavor with vanilla.

Beat sugar and butter to a cream, then add milk, flour and baking powder and stir well. Add whites of eggs well-beaten. Bake in three layers, two of white and add the grated chocolate to the third. Bake in a moderate oven. Place the dark layer between the two white ones. For the chocolate frosting, make a syrup of two cups granulated sugar; 8 tablespoons water; boil till it threads from the spoon. Have the whites of two eggs beaten to a stiff froth, and beat rapidly while pouring in syrup—that the frosting may be smooth, then add 1 square of grated chocolate, and beat till thick enough to spread.

This quantity is sufficient to put between the layers, and also to cover the cake.

If cocoanut cake is desired, bake cake in three layers with no chocolate, and put no chocolate in frosting. Put frosting on each layer, and sprinkle with freshly grated or prepared cocoanut.

CREAM CAKE.
Miss Bertha Dessey, Orange.

Five eggs, yolks and whites beaten separately; 1 tumbler sugar; 1 tumbler flour; 1 teaspoon cream tartar; ½ teaspoon soda. Bake in two layers in moderate oven.

When cold, whip a pint of cream; sweeten with ½ cup sugar, flavor with ¼ teaspoon pineapple extract, and spread on one layer; place the second layer on this; cut in the number of pieces required and spread the remaining cream over the top. Serve as a dessert or cake.

MOCHA CREAM CAKE.
Mrs. A. E. Goodrich.

One cup granulated sugar; ½ cup butter; ½ cup sweet milk; 1½ cups sifted flour; 1½ teaspoons Cleveland's baking powder; 3 eggs, whites only, beaten to stiff froth.

Cream the butter and sugar together; add the milk, then flour and baking powder; last, the whites of the eggs. Bake in three layers in a moderate oven.

Filling: Make a scant ½ cup of strong Mocha and Java coffee, reserving 2 tablespoons for the icing; to the remainder, add sweet milk to make one half pint; put this in a double

boiler and heat; when cool, stir in 1 teacup sugar; 2 tablespoons flour; yolks of 4 eggs, thoroughly beaten together.
Cook 15 minutes, stirring often; when lukewarm, beat in
slowly 2 tablespoons butter.   Spread between layers and
finish top with the following icing: Beat together 1 teacup
powdered sugar and white of one egg; add the two tablespoons coffee and beat till light and smooth.

CARAMEL CAKE
Mrs. John Beckwith.

One and one-half cups fine granulated sugar; ½ cup
butter; 1 cup sweet milk; 2 cups sifted flour; 1 large teaspoon
Cleveland's baking powder; 4 eggs, whites only, beaten light.

Work butter and sugar to a cream; add milk, then flour
with baking powder; slowly stir till smooth; add eggs lightly.
Flavor with vanilla, and bake in brisk oven, watching closely.

Caramel for cake: One cup morning's milk; 2 cups "C"
sugar.

Dissolve sugar in the milk, placing on stove to melt
slowly; when it is ready to boil, stir it constantly until it
ropes on the spoon;   then remove from the stove and add a
large spoon of butter, a teaspoon of vanilla and beat until it
grains, spread quickly on the cake, which should be in
two layers and cold.   The cup for measuring this cake should
be a large coffee cup.

CARAMEL CAKE
Mrs. H. T. Hazard.

One cup butter; 2 cups sugar; 5 eggs, whites only, well
beaten; 2 teaspoons Cleveland's baking powder; 1 cup sweet
milk; 1 cup corn starch; 1½ cups flour;   flavor with vanilla.

Stir well until smooth and bake in two long pans.

Filling for this cake: One cup sugar; ⅓ cup water; ¼
cup butter; 1 teaspoon vanilla.

Boil five minutes without stirring.   Remove from the fire
and stir until white and creamy, but not too hard.   Place
this filling between the two layers and on top of the cake,
smoothing it quickly in place.   Great haste must be made
in order to have this a success.

MACCAROONS
Mrs. John Beckwith.

One pint sugar; 1 pint flour; 1 pint almonds, or white of English walnuts, chopped fine; 4 eggs.

Drop on greased paper and bake a light brown. They will keep for a long time and are fine.

ALMOND CREAM CAKE
Mrs. George L. Arnold.

Two cups sugar; $\frac{1}{2}$ cup butter; $\frac{2}{3}$ cup sweet milk; 6 eggs, whites only; 3 cups flour; 3 teaspoons Cleveland's baking powder.

Line the tins with paper, and bake in three layers.

Cream for cake: Between the layers, spread a custard made as follows: One cup milk; $\frac{1}{2}$ cup sugar; let it come to a boil, and add 1 egg or two yolks and 1 tablespoon corn starch; flavor with bitter almonds; and add $\frac{1}{4}$ pound of blanched and chopped almonds.

For the top and sides, make a boiled frosting of $1\frac{1}{2}$ cups granulated sugar and the whites of two eggs and ornament the cake with $\frac{1}{4}$ pound of blanched almonds split in two.

BIRTHDAY CAKE
Mrs. J. E. Murray.

One-half cup butter; 2 cups sugar; 1 cup sweet milk; 3 cups sifted flour; 2 teaspoons Cleveland's baking powder; 4 eggs, whites and yolks beaten separately; whites to be added last. Flavor with lemon.

NO NAME CAKE
Mrs. W. W. Lord.

One cup butter; 3 cups sugar. Cream the butter and sugar together, then add $\frac{1}{2}$ cup sweet milk; $3\frac{1}{2}$ cups flour; $\frac{1}{2}$ teaspoon soda, in the milk; 1 teaspoon cream tartar, sifted in flour; whites of 10 eggs, put in mixture next to last; flour last.

VIOLET CAKE
Mrs. H. T. Hazard.

One cup butter creamed; 2 cups sugar; yolks of 3 eggs; 1 cup sweet milk; 3 cups flour; 1 teaspoon Cleveland's baking powder; whites of eggs.

Mix in the order given; divide the batter into four equal parts and bake in four layers. Color half the batter with violet paste (size of a pea). When baked; lay first a light layer, then a violet, then light, then violet. Put together with lemon jelly.

Lemon Jelly: Beat one egg; add 1 cup water, the grated rind and juice of 1 lemon; pour this slowly on 1 cup sugar, mixed with 1 tablespoon flour. Cook in double boiler until smooth like cream.

Frosting: Whites of 2 eggs beaten light with 20 teaspoons powdered sugar; flavor with violet extract; color with violet paste, and decorate with candied violets.

TRI-COLORED CAKE
Mrs. T. C. Griswold.

One and one half cups sugar; ⅔ cup butter; ⅔ cup milk; 1½ cups flour; ⅔ teaspoon soda; 1½ teaspoon cream tartar; whites of 7 eggs.

Take ⅔ of the batter and bake for white cake, and put pink coloring in remaining third. For yellow part, take 1 cup sugar; ½ cup butter; ½ cup milk; 1 cup flour; yelks of 5 eggs; 1 teaspoon cream tartar; ½ teaspoon soda.

Flavor with lemon. Put pink cake in center, white on each side and yellow top and bottom. Put together with custard or frosting.

LEOPARD CAKE
Mrs. L. M. Wheeler.

Six eggs, whites only; ¾ cup of milk; 2 cups powdered sugar; 3 scant cups of sifted flour; ½ cup butter; 2 teaspoons Cleveland's baking powder.

Flavor with lemon. Mix 1 cup of chopped raisins in ½ cup of the cake batter, and drop it into the cake in spoonfuls as it is put into the pans.

MARBLE CAKE
Mrs. F. H. Pieper.

Light part—1 cup butter; 2 cups sugar; 3 cups flour; ½ cup sweet milk; 1 teaspoon soda; 2 teaspoons cream tartar; whites of 7 eggs.

Dark part—1 cup butter; 1 cup molasses; 2 cups brown sugar; 1 cup sour milk; 5 cups flour; 2 tablespoons each cinnamon and spices; 1 tablespoon cloves and 1 nutmeg; 1 teaspoon soda; yelks of 7 eggs. If sweet milk is used in *dark part* add 2 teaspoons cream tartar.

GOLD AND SILVER CAKE
Mrs. D. M. Welch.

Silver part—½ cup butter; 1 cup sugar; 4 eggs, whites only; 1½ cups sifted flour; ½ cup sweet milk; 1½ teaspoons Cleveland's baking powder; ¼ teaspoon extract of bitter almond.

Gold cake—Make just the same as the silver, only use the yelks of 4 eggs and flavor with vanilla instead of bitter almond.

EXCELLENT CAKE
Miss Josie Kaiser.

Two cups sugar; 1 cup butter; 4 eggs, well beaten; ½ cup corn starch; 1 cup milk; 4 cups sifted flour; 2 teaspoons Cleveland's baking powder; 2 teaspoons lemon extract.

Beat sugar and butter to a cream, add eggs and corn starch, then milk and flour, baking powder and flavoring last.

BOSTON CREAM PUFFS
Mrs. W. T. Carter.

Puffs—1 quart water; 20 eggs; 12 ounces butter 1½ pounds flour, sifted.

Have water boiling, add butter, then the flour, stirring briskly. Remove from fire and let cool. When cold add eggs, one or two at a time, rubbing constantly until the mixture is perfectly smooth, then drop on well-buttered tins and glaze over with a little milk and yelk of egg. Bake in hot oven.

Cream—6 ounces pulverized sugar; 4 ounces corn starch; 3 eggs; 1 quart milk.

Beat eggs, sugar and corn starch together until perfectly smooth.   Heat the milk until it boils, then add eggs, sugar, etc., stirring very briskly to prevent scorching.   Let boil a few minutes then remove from fire. Flavor with lemon. Open puffs on one side and insert cream with teaspoon.   Sprinkle with sifted sugar and serve while fresh.   This makes a very large quantity.

PLAIN LOAF CAKE
Mrs. A. M. Whaley.

One and a half cups sugar; ½ cup butter; ¼ cup hot water; ½ cup cold water; 3 eggs, yelks and whites beaten separately; 2½ cups flour; 1 teaspoon Cleveland's baking powder.

Beat the butter and sugar to a cream and add the hot water.   Then add the other ingredients, the whites of eggs being last.

PLAIN CAKE
Mrs. A. D. Hall.

One cup sugar; 1 cup sweet milk; ½ cup melted butter; 1 egg; 2 teaspoons Cleveland's baking powder; 1 pint sifted flour. Bake ¾ of an hour.

CUP CAKE
Mrs. Alice Curtin.

One and a half cups flour; 1 cup sugar; ½ cup milk; 2 teaspoons Cleveland's baking powder; yelks of 3 eggs and white of 1, using whites of 2 for frosting.

MARGARET'S CAKE
Miss S. E. Smith, St. John, New Brunswick.

Two and a half cups powdered sugar; ¾ cup butter; 1 cup sweet milk; 3 cups flour; 1 lemon, juice and rind; 1 small teaspoon soda.

Bake in square or oblong tin and frost with whites of two eggs beaten stiff with powdered sugar.

COFFEE CAKES
Mrs. J. W. Hendricks.

One quart flour; 1 yeast cake, or 1 cup yeast; 2 eggs; 4 tablespoons sugar; 1 teaspoon cinnamon; 1 teaspoon lemon extract; ¼ pound butter.

Mix with sweet milk, and put in a warm place to rise. When light roll out quite thin and spread with melted butter; then sprinkle with sugar and cinnamon, currants, raisins and citron to suit the taste. Cut into squares, let them rise again and bake.

COFFEE CAKE
Mrs. D. S. Dickson.

One cup butter; 1 cup sugar; 1 cup molasses; 1 cup seeded raisins; 1 cup cold coffee; 3 cups flour; 2 eggs; small quantity citron, sliced very thin; 2 teaspoons soda; nutmeg and cinnamon to taste. Bake slowly 1½ hours.

BREAD CAKE
Mrs. George Segar, Riverside, Cal

One coffee cup bread sponge; 1½ coffee cups brown sugar; ½ pound raisins; ¼ pound currants; 1 cup butter, creamed with the sugar; 3 eggs; spices to taste; 1 teaspoon soda dissolved in hot water.

Beat whites and yelks separately. Mix thoroughly. Put fruit in last. Let it rise until light. Add a little flour if necessary to make a tolerably stiff batter. Bake in moderate oven.

BREAD CAKE
Mrs. W. M. Dickson.

Two cups bread dough; 1¼ cups sugar; ½ cup butter; 1 cup raisins; 2 eggs; ½ teaspoon each salt and soda.

Rub sugar and butter to a cream. Beat the eggs very light, and mix with the dough. Add a little spice if desired. Bake when light.

SPICED GINGER CAKE
Mrs Henry T. Lee.

One cup sugar; ½ cup butter, or drippings, or both together beaten to a cream; 1 cup molasses; 3 small cups flour; 1 cup very sour milk, 4 days old; 2 heaping tablespoons ginger; 2 small teaspoons soda, stirred in milk; 1½ tablespoons cloves; 1½ tablespoons cinnamon.

Stir all well together and add ½ pound of currants dipped in flour.

"When you have a cake or bread in the oven, do not slam the oven door, or walk heavily about the kitchen while it is baking. A fine cake will be irretrievably ruined by a slight jar at a certain stage of its baking."

GINGER BREAD—With Yolks of Eggs
Mrs. M. R. Sinsabaugh.

Seven eggs, yolks only; 1 saltspoon salt; 1 cup New Orleans molasses; 1 tablespoon lard or butter; 1 level teaspoon soda in ¾ cup hot water; 1 heaping teaspoon ginger, or about the same of cinnamon, cloves, allspice and ginger mixed, if preferred; ¾ cup brown sugar.

Use flour enough to make the batter of the same consistency as for ordinary loaf cake or muffins. Bake slowly 45 minutes or more if necessary.

OUR MOTHERS' GINGER CAKES
Mrs. Charlotte M. Wills.

Two quarts flour; 3 teaspoons baking soda, sifted with the flour; 1 pint New Orleans molasses; 2 eggs; ½ cup brown sugar; 1 cup lard; 1 cup milk; 3 teaspoons ground ginger; 1 teaspoon ground cinnamon and cloves.

Heat the molasses and lard. Mix with sugar, milk and beaten eggs. Stir the mixture well and it will foam. (Keep out one pint of the flour to roll the cakes in). Add flour and let it all become cool. Roll out as soft as possible. Cut with biscuit or fancy cutter and bake in pans in quick oven.

SOFT GINGER BREAD
Mrs. D. L. Whipple.

Four cups flour; 2 cups molasses; 2 cups buttermilk; 1 cup thick sour cream; ½ cup butter; 3 eggs; 1 teaspoon ginger; 1 teaspoon soda.

FINE SOFT GINGER CAKE
Mrs. J. E. Murray.

One cup butter; 1 cup boiling water; 1 cup sugar; 1 cup New Orleans molasses; 3 cups flour; 1 tablespoon ginger, cinnamon and allspice, mixed; 1 tablespoon soda, sifted in the flour; 4 eggs, beaten light and stirred in the last thing.

SOFT GINGER BREAD
Mrs. Vida A. Bixby.

. Half cup molasses; ½ cup sugar; 2 eggs; ¼ cup butter; ½ cup milk; 2 cups flour; 1 teaspoon Cleveland's baking powder; a sprinkle of cinnamon, cloves, ginger and nutmeg.

FAIRY GINGER BREAD—For the Little Ones
Mrs. T. W. Brotherton.

One cup butter; 2 cups sugar; 1 cup milk; 1 tablespoon ginger; ¾ teaspoon soda; 4 small cups flour, sifted.

Beat the butter and sugar together until light, dissolve the soda in the milk, mix, and add the sifted flour. Turn baking pans upside down, wipe very clean, butter well. Spread mixture upon them very thinly, bake in moderate oven until brown. While still hot cut into squares—with case knife. Slip carefully off.

GINGER BREAD
Mrs. Louisa C. Carran.

One cup molasses; 1 cup brown sugar; 3 cups flour; 3 eggs, well beaten; 1 large tablespoon ginger; 1 large tablespoon soda; 1 cup melted butter; 1 cup boiling water; a little cinnamon. Bake twenty minutes.

SPICE CAKE
Mrs Gerrard Irvine.

One cup sugar; 1 egg; 1 small teaspoon soda; ½ teaspoon salt; ½ cup sour cream; ½ cup buttermilk; ½ teaspoon ginger; ½ teaspoon cinnamon.

GINGER SNAPS
Mrs. J. W. Gillette.

Two cups molasses; 1 egg; 1 cup butter and lard mixed; 2 teaspoons soda; flour to roll.

Boil the molasses and shortening together five minutes, let it cool, then stir in the beaten egg and soda, ginger to taste. Mix soft as possible and roll thin. Will bake in a few minutes. These are excellent.

GINGER SNAPS
Mrs. Morrell, Albany, Texas.

One cup sugar; 1 cup New Orleans molasses; 1 cup butter or meat fryings; 1 tablespoon ginger; 1 teaspoon soda, dissolved in a little water; as much flour as can be stirred, not kneaded. Pinch off a piece the size of a marble and roll in the hands, and place in baking tin, leaving quite a space between to allow for spreading. Bake in a moderate oven and leave in the pan until they cool enough to snap. Keep the dough warm.

COOKIES
Mrs. Alex. Fawcett, Ohio.

Two cups sugar; 1 cup butter; 3 eggs; 1 teaspoon soda; 1 cup sour cream or milk; flour to mix soft. If cream is used ½ cup of butter is sufficient.

Take sifted flour and mix the butter with it the same as for pie crust, then add the sugar. Make a cup-shaped hole in this mixture, and break in the eggs, add the cream (or milk) in which the soda has been dissolved. If more flour is needed to roll the dough into thin cakes add what is necessary, but be careful not to make too stiff. Sprinkle the cakes with granulated sugar and roll gently in. Bake quickly.

COOKIES
Mrs. R. C. Hunt.

One cup butter; 1 cup sugar; ½ cup sweet milk; 4 eggs; 2 teaspoons Cleveland's baking powder; flour to mix quite soft.

If nut cookies are desired, mix finely chopped nuts into dough before rolling out.

JUMBLES
Mrs. Gerrard Irvine.

One and one-half cups white sugar; ¾ cup butter; 3 tablespoons sweet milk; 3 eggs; ½ teaspoon soda; 1 teaspoon cream tartar.

Mix with sufficient flour to roll.   Sprinkle with sugar, cut and bake in quick oven.

BACHELOR BUTTONS
Mrs. S. B. Caswell.

One cup white sugar; ½ cup butter; 1½ cups flour; 1 egg. Flavor with almond.   Roll into balls about the size of a small walnut, roll these in white sugar and place in buttered tins some distance apart to allow them room to spread.   Add a little more flour if they flatten too much.

This recipe should make between fifty and sixty of these little cakes.   They are very nice.

SAND TARTS
Mrs. C. C. Carpenter.

Two cups sugar; 1 cup butter; 3 cups flour; 2 eggs, leaving out the white of one.

Cream the butter and beat in the sugar and eggs well. Add flour.   Roll out very thin and cut in diamond shape. Spread the white of egg on top.   Sprinkle with sugar and cinnamon.   Press a blanched almond or raisin in the center of each.

FRUIT COOKIES
Mrs. George Segar, Riverside.

One coffee cup butter; 1 coffee cup brown sugar; ½ coffee cup molasses; ½ coffee cup sour milk or cream; 1 coffee cup raisins; ½ coffee cup currants; 3 eggs; 1 teaspoon soda; spices to taste; flour to make a soft dough.   Roll thick.   Bake in moderate oven.

CRULLERS
Mrs. Elizabeth Dickey.

Two cups sugar; ½ cup butter; 1 cup sour cream; 1 cup buttermilk; 3 eggs; 1 teaspoon soda; flavor, or not, to suit.

Beat the eggs well, then add all the ingredients together

and put in all the flour you can knead in.   Knead as long as it will take flour.   Now roll as thin as crust for pies, and cut any desired shape, and fry in hot lard.

The beauty of crullers consists in kneading hard, and rolling thin.   This amount will fill a three-gallon jar, and will keep well.

DOUGHNUTS
Mrs. D. L. Whipple.

Two cups sugar; 1 cup sweet milk; 3 eggs; butter size of walnut; 3 teaspoons Cleveland's baking powder.

Mix with as little flour as possible. Beat yelks of eggs and mix with milk.   Beat whites and mix with batter last.   Fry in hot lard.

DOUGHNUTS
Mrs. J. E. Murray.

One cup sugar; 1 cup sour milk; 1 egg; a very little butter; 1 teaspoon soda; ½ teaspoon cream tartar; 1 teaspoon salt; flour to mix soft.   Flavor with nutmeg.

RAISED DOUGHNUTS
Mrs. Converse Smith, Boston.

One pint milk; 1 teacup mashed potatoes; ½ cake of yeast dissolved in half cup warm water, (not hot) water.   Flour to make stiff batter.   Let it rise over night, in the morning add 1 cup sugar; 1 egg; 3 tablespoons melted butter, small piece of soda and little nutmeg.   Mold very soft and let rise again, then cut out or twist them and fry.

ORANGE ICING FOR CAKE
Mrs. H. G. Otis.

One cup sugar; 4 tablespoons water; 2 oranges, rind grated into juice; add sugar and water, then boil until syrup begins to string.   Beat the white of one egg to a foam, then pour syrup over it, stirring constantly, and put upon the cake while warm.

GELATINE FROSTING
Miss Farmer, Boston Cooking School.

Two and a half tablespoons hot water, (boiling); ¾ cup

confectioner's sugar; ⅓ level teaspoon granulated gelatine: ¼ teaspoon vanilla.

Add the granulated gelatine to the boiling water, and when it is thoroughly dissolved add the sugar, vanilla, or other flavoring if preferred, and beat until of the right consistency to spread.

This is a frosting quickly made, and does not require the whites of eggs. If the granulated gelatine cannot be procured. ordinary gelatine may be used by allowing one tablespoonful.

CHOCOLATE FROSTING
Miss Farmer.

Two squares Ghirardelli's chocolate: ¾ cup sugar; 3 tablespoons milk; 1 egg, yelk only.

Melt the chocolate and add the sugar and the milk, either hot or cold. Cook in double boiler until smooth and add the egg yelk. Cook for one minute and pour over the cake. Especially nice for layer cake.

BOILED FROSTING
Miss Ida Maynard, Colorado Springs.

One cup sugar; ⅓ cup water. Boil together until a thread will drop from the spoon, then pour this slowly on the beaten white of one egg, beating all the time. Add one teaspoon flavoring, and when slightly cool spread upon the cake.

ROYAL ICING
Mrs. W. T. Carter

This icing should be made of the finest sugar dust. If made from common pulverized sugar, it must be run through a lawn sieve. Work into a soft paste with the whites of eggs, and flavor with lemon or any essence you may prefer. Tint to any shade with vegetable colors, or leave plain. Work the icing with a wooden spatula, or paddle to such consistency that when withdrawn the point of icing left behind will stand erect, or lay like piping.

222 How We Cook in Los Angeles

MILK FROSTING
Mrs. D. S. Dickson.

Five tablespoons milk; 1 cup sugar. Boil until it will drop from a spoon like jelly, and cool.

MILK ICING
Mrs. Jerome Curtin.

One cup granulated sugar; 6 tablespoons milk or water. Put on stove and boil five minutes. Do not stir. Take off fire and stir briskly until cool. When nearly cold, or when commencing to thicken, add white of one egg, beaten stiff and flavored to taste.

PUDDINGS AND THEIR SAUCES

BOILED PUDDINGS

Miss K. R. Paxton.

Grease the mold very thoroughly and there will be no danger of sticking. Do not *fill* the mold as room must be allowed for the pudding to swell. Put the mold into a kettle of boiling water. It is not necessary for the water to cover the mold; half way to the top of mold is sufficient; when the water gets too low, replenish with boiling water. The kettle must be covered with a tight fitting lid to keep in steam. Put a flat-iron on the lid to keep it down tight. On no account, allow the water to stop boiling. If pudding is boiled in a bag, dip it in boiling water, wring, sprinkle with flour, tie up the pudding in the bag leaving room for it to swell.

Bavarian creams, gelatine, corn starch, or any pudding served in a form; wet mold with cold water; pour out water but do not wipe the mold; pour in pudding and put in cold place; when ready to serve, turn it out in dish.

PLUM PUDDING

Mrs. J. P. Widney.

One quart cracker crumbs; 1½ cups sugar; 1 large teaspoon cinnamon; 1 small teaspoon salt; ¾ pound currants; ¼ pound candied lemon or orange peel—chopped; 3 pints milk; ½ cup butter; 6 eggs; 1 nutmeg; 1 pound stoned raisins; ¼ pound citron—chopped fine.

Pour the milk over the cracker crumbs, beat the yelks of the eggs, sugar and butter until light, and add them. Stir in all the fruit, first adding to it a trifle of flour, to prevent its sticking. Add the beaten whites of eggs last. Butter a large mold, or two smaller ones, and put in pudding, leaving room for rising. Cover close and steam five hours. Serve with hot sauce, or cold hard sauce.

This has proved most excellent, and is enough for 18 persons.

ENGLISH RECIPE FOR PLUM PUDDING
Mrs. Mary O. Lerrigo.

Twelve eggs—well beaten; 2 pounds beef suet—chopped fine; 2 pounds bread crumbs; 1½ pounds flour; 2 pounds stoned raisins; 2 pounds currants; 1 pound sultana raisins; 1 pound sugar; ½ pound candied peel; 1 nutmeg and ½ ounce mixed spices; rinds of 2 lemons grated; 1 small teaspoon salt.

Mik well together and add the eggs. If not moist enough, add a little molasses and water. Put into buttered molds, tie up safely, put into boiling water, and keep boiling for six hours.

This will make 3 good-sized puddings.

ENGLISH FRUIT PUDDING
Mrs. H. E. Smith.

One cup chopped suet; 1 cup seeded raisins; 1 cup currants; 1 cup sour milk; ½ cup sugar; ½ cup molasses; ¼ pound citron; 1 teaspoon soda; small quantity each—nutmeg, cinnamon and cloves.

Steam three hours.

BLACK PUDDING
Mrs. E. D. Major.

Half pint molasses; ¼ cup sugar; ¼ cup sweet milk; ½ teaspoon cloves; ½ teaspoon cinnamon; ¼ cup butter; 1½ cups flour; 3 eggs; ½ teaspoon soda

Steam one hour.

MOLASSES PUDDING
Mrs. D. S. Dickson

Three cups flour; 1 cup cold water; 1 cup seeded raisins; 1 cup molasses; ½ cup butter; 1 teaspoon soda.

Steam 3 hours and then invite your friends to dinner.

BLACK PUDDING
Mrs. R. J. Widney.

Two eggs—yolks; ⅔ cup molasses; 2 cups flour; 1 teaspoon cinnamon; 1 teaspoon cloves; 1 cup cold water, and 1 even teaspoon soda—to be added at the last.

Put in an air-tight steamer, and cook for an hour. Serve with hard sauce.

PLAIN PLUM PUDDING
Mrs. Col. Mudge.

One cup crackers—rolled fine; 1 cup raisins—stoned; 1 cup molasses; ½ cup sugar; small piece of citron—sliced thin; 2 eggs—well beaten; 1 teaspoon cinnamon; ¼ teaspoon cloves; ¼ teaspoon allspice extract; 1 teaspoon lemon extract; ½ teaspoon vanilla.

Steam three hours.

SUET PUDDING
Mrs. J. M. Stewart.

One cup milk; 1 cup raisins; 1 cup syrup or brown sugar; ⅔ cup suet; 1 teaspoon soda; flour to make a stiff batter.

Boil steadily three hours. Serve with sauce.

NESSELRODE PUDDING
Miss Ruth Childs.

Three dozen chestnuts; 8 eggs—yolks; 1 pint cream; 2 sticks pounded vanilla; ½ pint pine apple syrup; little salt; 4 ounces quince citron; 6 ounces pine apple; 6 ounces dried cherries; 4 ounces Smyrna raisins; ½ pint whipped cream.

Boil the chestnuts in water; when done, peel, pound and rub through a sieve; put this pulp into a stewpan with the eggs, cream, vanilla, pineapple syrup, and a very little salt. Stir these ingredients over a stove fire until the eggs are sufficiently set in the custard, then rub the whole through a Tammy, and put into a basin. Cut the citron and pineapple, (previously simmered in the syrup above alluded to), and place these in a basin with the cherries and raisins. Allow the fruit to steep for several hours in two wine glasses cherry cordial. Place the chestnut cream in a freezing pot, immersed in rough ice, and freeze it in the usual manner; then add half pint whipped cream and the fruit. Mix the pudding, and continue working the freezing pot for a few minutes longer. When the pudding is set firm, put it into a mold, cover it down and immerse in ice until it is required to be sent to the table.

FRUIT JELLY PUDDING
Mrs. J. H. F. Peck.

One box gelatine; 1 pint cold water; 3 lemons; 1 pint boiling water; ½ pound white sugar; strawberries; peaches or bananas.

Put gelatine in a large pitcher, add cold water. Squeeze lemons into this and throw in the skins. Let all stand an hour, then add boiling water and white sugar. When dissolved, strain through a fine sieve or flannel bag. When this commences to thicken, put a layer of strawberries in a large dish or mold, then some of the jelly, then a layer of peaches or bananas, then the jelly again, and so on until the dish is full. Set away on ice. When ready to use, turn out of mold, and serve with whipped cream and powdered sugar.

CABINET PUDDING
Mrs. Emeline Childs.

Dried cherries; candied citron; slices of sponge cake; ratapas or macaroons; 8 eggs—yolks; 1 pint milk or cream; 6 ounces sugar; rind of 1 lemon; arrowroot sauce or custard.

Spread the inside of a plain mold with butter, and ornament the sides with the cherries and citron. Fill the mold with alternate layers of slices of sponge cakes, ratapas or macaroons; then fill up the mold with a lemon custard, made with the eggs, milk or cream, sugar, and the grated rind of a lemon. This custard must not be set, but merely mixed up. Steam the pudding in the usual way for about an hour and a half. When done, dish it up either with arrowroot sauce or a custard.

WALNUT PUDDING
Mrs. M. G. Moore.

Two cups flour; 1 cup sugar; ½ cup butter; ½ cup walnuts; ½ cup water or milk; 1½ teaspoons Cleveland's baking powder; 3 unbeaten eggs.

Bake and serve with sauce.

FIG PUDDING
Mrs. W. H. Workman.

One cup chopped, dried figs; 1 cup chopped suet; 1 cup brown sugar; 1 cup bread crumbs; 1 cup flour; ½ cup milk; 2 eggs; 1 heaping teaspoon Cleveland's baking powder; salt.

Steam four hours, and serve hot with any sauce desired.

PRUNE PUDDING
Miss M. E. McLellan.

Fifty prunes; 5 eggs—whites; sugar.

Soak prunes over night, then stew until thoroughly done, and there is but little water left. Rub through a colander. Sweeten to taste with powdered sugar. Add the whites of eggs beaten to a stiff froth, and bake 20 minutes. Turn on to a platter and serve with whipped cream, either as a hot or cold pudding.

PRUNE SHAPE
Mrs. C. H. Howland.

One quart prune juice; 1 pint stewed prunes; 1 box gelatine; ½ cup sugar, unless prunes are sweetened when boiling.

Stew the prunes until tender. Pour off the juice. Add to it the gelatine, previously soaked in a little water, then the sugar, and stir them all together on the stove until the gelatine is dissolved. Stir in the prunes. Pour into a wet mold, and when cold and firm serve with whipped cream.

PUFF PUDDING
Miss Mina Jevne.

One quart milk; 5 eggs; 5 tablespoons flour; a pinch of salt.

Whip separately the yolks and whites of the eggs. Pour the milk (boiling) on the flour and whipped yolks. Stir in the whipped whites and bake twenty minutes. Serve with hot sauce.

STEAMED PUDDING
Mrs. W. G. Whorton.

One cup sugar; 1 cup sweet milk; 1 tablespoon butter; 1

teaspoon Cleveland's baking powder; 1 egg; 1 pint flour; a little salt. Steam one hour. Eat with cream and sugar, or a nice pudding sauce. Very nice with any kind of fresh fruit *in it*, or stewed fruit *under it*.

QUEEN OF PUDDINGS
Mrs. W. J. Brown.

One pint bread crumbs; 1 quart milk; 1 cup sugar; butter —size of an egg; 4 eggs; 1 lemon.

Beat the yolks of eggs well, then add milk, sugar, bread crumbs, butter and the grated rind of lemon. Put in a pudding dish and bake ¾ hour. Beat the whites of the eggs to a stiff froth, adding a cup of powdered sugar and juice of the lemon. Spread this over the pudding when done, and replace in the oven and brown slightly. This is good cold; or, let the pudding get cold, then spread with a layer of currant jelly before putting on the frosting.

BREAD PUDDING
Marian Harland.

One scant teacup bread crumbs—bread dried in oven and rolled; 2 eggs; 1 pint milk; ¼ teaspoon soda—scant; 1 tablespoon melted butter. Flavor with nutmeg.

Soak crumbs in milk. Add butter and soda—dissolved in a little water, yolks and nutmeg; and last, the whites beaten stiff. Beat well together, and bake in buttered pan ½ hour. Serve with nutmeg sauce.

SWEET POTATO PUDDING
Mrs. A. M. Whaley.

One pound raw sweet potato—grated; 2 eggs; 2 tablespoons sugar; 1 teaspoon ginger; ½ teacup molasses; 1 tablespoon butter; milk to make thin batter; any other spice, if desired.

Mix the ingredients well together—the eggs well beaten— and bake one and one-half hours.

CARROT PUDDING
Mrs. G. G. O'Brien, Riverside,   Mrs Harriet J. Meakin, San Diego.

One cup grated carrot—raw; 1 cup grated potato—raw; 1 cup stoned raisins; 1 even teaspoon soda; ½ teaspoon nutmeg; 1 cup flour; 1 cup brown sugar; ½ cup suet or butter; ½ teaspoon cinnamon; ½ teaspoon cloves.

Mix soda with the grated potato and mix all together. Steam three hours. Serve with carrot pudding sauce.

SPONGE PUDDING
Mrs. E. R. Smith.

Three eggs; 4 tablespoons flour; 1½ pints milk; a little salt.

Stir the milk, (scalding hot), into the flour, then add the yolks, then the whites—beaten to a stiff froth, and bake immediately for one half hour. Serve as soon as baked with lemon sauce.

This is a favorite dessert at many tables.

ORANGE PUDDING
Mrs. Hancock M. Johnston.

Juice of 6 oranges; 5 eggs; 1 coffeecup sugar.

Beat yolks and whites separately. Add the other ingredients and stir well. Bake 20 to 30 minutes in a pan of water.

ORANGE PUDDING
Mrs. W. W. Widney.

Two and one half cups hot water; 1½ cups sugar; 3 eggs —yolks; 2 tablespoons corn starch; juice 4 oranges; rind of one; butter—size of a walnut; 1 teaspoon vanilla.

After this mixture has been well boiled, put into baking dish, and pour over it the whites of the eggs, well beaten, and mixed with two tablespoons sugar. Brown in oven.

ORANGE SPONGE
Mrs. G. W. Garcelon, Riverside.

One ounce gelatine; 1 pint water; 6 oranges; 1 lemon; 3 eggs, whites only; sugar to taste.

Dissolve gelatine in pan, let stand until almost cold. Mix

in the juice of the orange and lemon; add eggs and sugar. Whisk all together until it is white and spongy.   Put in molds   Will be ready for use the next day.

APPLE SAGO PUDDING
Mrs. C. G. Du Bois.

One cup sago; 6 cups water; 12 apples.

Put the sago in the water, and set in a warm place to swell.   Stew the apples and mix them with the swelled sago. Bake three quarters of an hour.   If apples cook quickly it is nice to put them in raw, with a little sugar.   Peaches are good used raw.   Serve with cream or sugar, or any sauce desired.

APPLE PUDDING
Miss M. E. McLellan.

Two large tart apples: ½ tablespoon butter; 2 eggs; sugar; ¼ cup fine bread crumbs.

Pare and quarter the apples.   Boil them in a very little water.   Strain them and add the butter with sugar to taste. Add the bread crumbs and the beaten yolks of eggs, and the white of one.   Bake about half an hour and cover with a méringue made of the white of the other egg, and 1 table-spoon sugar.   Brown the méringue. Serve warm or cold with cream.

A NEW APPLE PUDDING
Mrs. M. G. Moore.

Six tart apples; 1 pint flour; 1 teaspoon Cleveland's baking powder; 1 egg; 1 teacup sweet milk; a little salt.

Pare and core the apples, stew them in very little water until done.   Make a batter of the other ingredients.   Beat the stewed apples into it.   Bake in a buttered earthen dish. Serve with sugar and cream.

PLAIN APPLE PUDDING
Mrs. S. E. Smith, St. John, New Brunswick.

Three or four good-sized tart apples; 1 cup milk; 1 egg; 1 teaspoon cream tartar; ½ teaspoon soda: small piece butter; flour; salt to season.

Cut up apples in a pudding dish. Make a batter of the milk, egg and other ingredients. Add flour to make a rather thin batter. Pour this over the apples and steam or bake. Serve with sauce.

SNOW PUDDING
Mrs. M. Pickering.

One quart boiling water; 3 tablespoons corn starch; ½ cup sugar; 6 eggs; 1 pint sweet milk; lemon; 1 teaspoon butter.

Dissolve the corn starch in a little cold water with the sugar and butter, and pour into the boiling water. Add the whites of eggs, beaten very stiff. Stir fast until all is very light. Make a custard of the sweet milk, and the yolks of the eggs. Season with lemon, and when cold serve with the snow pudding.

SNOW PUDDING
Mrs. C. B. Woodhead.

Half box gelatine; ½ pint milk; ½ pint whipped cream; 5 eggs (whites only); 1 teaspoon vanilla; sugar to taste.

Soak gelatine in milk, place over stove and stir until gelatine is dissolved; then add cream, whites of eggs, well beaten, vanilla and sugar to taste. Mix all together well. Place on ice 12 hours.

SNOW PUDDING
Mrs. A. S. Baxter

Three cups milk; 3 tablespoons corn starch; 3 eggs, whites.

Sauce—One cup milk; 1 cup sugar; 3 eggs, yolks.

Pudding—Heat the milk and add the corn starch wet with a little milk, when this is thick take from the fire and stir in the whites of eggs, well beaten, and pour in a mold to cool.

Sauce—Heat milk, add sugar and beaten yolks. Cook until it thickens. Flavor to taste.

FROZEN RICE PUDDING
Mrs. Hancock Banning.

Half cup rice; 1 quart water; 1 saltspoon salt; 1 pint milk; 3 eggs; 1 cup sugar; ½ pint cream; ½ pint milk; vanilla.

Compote—1 pint granulated sugar; 1 pint water; 1 quart strawberries.

Boil for one-half hour, the rice in the water with the salt. Drain and put in double boiler, with 1 pint milk, and cook until milk is all absorbed.   Beat the eggs light, and just before removing from fire, add to the rice; with 1 cup of sugar. Flavor with vanilla and set away to cool.   When cold add ½ pint of cream and ½ pint milk, and freeze.

Compote for rice pudding—Dissolve the granulated sugar with the boiling water.   Do not stir, and take from fire just before it reaches the boiling point.   Pick, wash, and wipe dry the strawberries, and pour syrup over them.   Serve with the rice pudding.

CHOCOLATE PUDDING
Miss Frances Widney.

One pint milk; large ½ cup sugar; 2 heaping tablespoons Ghirardelli's grated chocolate; 1 heaping tablespoon corn starch; pinch of salt.

Let the milk come to a boil, then add the sugar and chocolate, well mixed, then the corn starch wet with two spoonsful of the milk.   Boil until it thickens, and turn into cups or mold.   Set it away to cool.   Serve with whipped cream well sweetened, or with plain cream and sugar flavored with vanilla.

DELICATE PUDDING
Mrs. J. E. Plater.

One cup water; 1 cup fruit juice; 3 tablespoons corn starch; ½ saltspoon salt; sugar to taste; 3 eggs.

Boil the water and fruit juice, wet the corn starch in a little cold water, stir into the boiling syrup and cook ten minutes.   Add the salt and sugar to taste; the quantity depending upon the fruit.   Beat the whites of eggs till foamy, and stir into the starch.   Turn at once into a mold.   Serve cold with boiled custard sauce made with the yolks of the eggs.

MOUNTAIN DEW PUDDING
Mrs. J. S. Chapman.

One pint milk; 2 eggs; 4 tablespoons cocoanut; ½ cup rolled crackers; 1 teaspoon lemon juice; 1 cup sugar. Mix the milk, yolks of eggs, well beaten, cocoanut, cracker and lemon juice together. Bake half an hour. When done cover with frosting made of the whites of the eggs and cup of sugar.

INDIAN PUDDING
Mrs. J. A. Gilchrist.

One pint milk; 5 tablespoons sifted Indian meal; ½ cup light molasses; 1 teaspoon salt; 1 teaspoon ginger; 1 teaspoon cinnamon; 1 egg; 1 pint milk used cold.

Put milk to scald, when it begins to simmer, stir in sifted Indian meal, wet with molasses. Cook a few minutes. Add salt, ginger and cinnamon. Put cold milk into which the well beaten egg has been added into a baking dish, (earthen preferred). Pour the mixture in, stirring but little. Bake slowly two or three hours. Serve with sauce.

BAKED INDIAN PUDDING
Mrs. Mary B. Welch.

One pint sweet milk; ½ pint Indian meal; 1 cup molasses; ½ cup butter; 3 well-beaten eggs; 1 cup cold sweet milk.

Boil the pint of milk in a double kettle and stir in the meal; let it stand on the back of the stove an hour; melt the butter and molasses together and add to the hot mixture, and leave for half hour. Then add eggs and cold milk. Bake ¾ of an hour. Serve with sauce.

HEAVENLY HASH
Mrs. L. W. Wheeler.

One pineapple, sliced thin; 4 oranges; sugar; 1 box strawberries; 6 bananas; lemon juice.

Put a layer of pineapple in a dish, cover with sugar, then a layer of berries, of orange and of bananas until all are used. Cover each layer of fruit with powdered sugar.

SIMPLY MADE DESSERT
Mrs. M. G. Moore.

Batter; fruit; 1 egg.

Make a common griddle-cake batter, add egg and some fruit. Fry in a little lard and serve with pudding sauce. If canned fruit is used, it should first be drained.

FRUIT FRITTERS
Mrs. C. C. McLean.

Two eggs, whites; 1 tablespoon flour; 1 tablespoon cold water; 1 tablespoon butter, or Howland's olive oil; apricots, peaches, and strawberries.

Make a batter with the beaten whites of the eggs, flour, cold water and butter or oil.   Mix thoroughly before putting in the whites.   Pare the apricots and peaches, and cut in quarters, strawberries used whole.   Dip each piece of fruit into the batter, and drop into the boiling fat.   Two minutes will cook them brown and crisp; then sugar them and serve hot.

FRUIT DUMPLINGS
Mrs. E. R. Smith.

One pint flour; fruit; a little salt; 2 teaspoons Cleveland's baking powder; milk to make a *very* soft dough.

Sift the salt, baking powder and flour together; mix with milk till very soft. Place in a steamer well greased cups.   Put in each a spoonful of batter, then one of fruit.   Cover with another of batter.   Steam twenty minutes.   Serve with whipped cream or lemon sauce.

PEACH ROLLS
Mrs. M. G. Moore.

Stew dried fruit; sweeten and flavor to taste. Make a good baking powder crust, roll very thin and spread with fruit, putting small pieces of butter on the fruit.   Roll up and place in a deep pan.   To 3 or 4 rolls add 1 cup sugar, and ½ cup butter, and pour over this hot water enough to cover.   Bake ½ hour.   Serve with sauce or cream and sugar.

BLACKBERRY MUSH
Mrs. M. G. Moore.

Two quarts ripe berries; 1½ pints boiling water; 1 pound sugar; 1 pint sifted flour.

To the berries add the boiling water and sugar; cook a few minutes, then stir in flour.   Boil until the flour is cooked. Serve hot or cold, with sweet cream or hard sauce.

FRIED BANANAS
Mrs. W. W. Ross.

Take medium sized, firm bananas; peel and slice length-wise. Fry in good salad oil, or sweet butter, (which has been previously heated), until the banana is a delicate brown. Serve with pudding sauce.

FRUIT FOR DESSERT
Mrs. C. C. McLean.

One egg, white; fruit; sugar.

Beat well the white of an egg, with a little water, dip the fruit in and roll it immediately in powdered sugar; place on a dish; leave it for five or six hours, then serve. A more beautiful, palatable and exquisite dessert than a plate of currants thus dressed, cannot be had.

SUGARED POMEGRANATES
Mrs. W. W. Ross.

Fill a glass dish with the red pomegranate seeds, sprinkle with pulverized sugar, and serve.

SAUCE FOR CHRISTMAS PUDDING
Mrs. Flanders.

One cup boiling water; 1 cup sugar; 1 cup butter; 5 eggs.

Cream the butter, sugar, and yolks. Beat in the whites, and pour in the water.

HARD SAUCE
Mrs. W. J. Brown.

One cup powdered sugar; ½ cup butter.

Beat the butter well, then stir in the sugar and beat to a cream, flavor to suit the taste.

STRAWBERRY SAUCE
Mrs. Helen W. Watson.

One large tablespoon butter; 1½ cups powdered sugar; white of one egg; 1 pint mashed strawberries.

Beat the butter to a cream, add gradually the sugar and the beaten white of the egg. Beat till very light, and just before serving add the mashed strawberries. Instead of the

butter and egg, one quart of the whipped cream may be added
to the strawberries and sugar. A generous half pint of cream
makes a quart when whipped.

CREAM SAUCE

One half cup butter; 1 cup sugar; ½ cup milk or cream;
1 teaspoon flavoring.

Cream the butter, add sugar gradually, beating all the
time; add milk or cream gradually, then flavoring. Beat until
very smooth and creamy. Serve.

CARROT PUDDING SAUCE
Mrs. G. G. O'Brien, Riverside.

One cup sugar; 1 egg; ½ cup boiling milk; juice of one
lemon.

Beat sugar and egg till foamy, pour gradually into milk,
add lemon juice. Cook in pan of boiling water, stirring constantly.

PUDDING SAUCE
Mrs. Alice Curtain.

One pint milk; ¼ cup sugar; 1 tablespoon flour, or corn
starch; 1 teaspoon butter; cinnamon or nutmeg.

Mix the flour in a little water till perfectly smooth. Scald
the milk, add the sugar, stir thoroughly, then add the thickening and butter. Cook 5 or 10 minutes. Flavor with a little cinnamon or nutmeg.

This sauce may be varied, by adding the yolk of one egg,
well beaten with the sugar, to the milk. Then add about ½
the thickening, and just before serving beat the white of egg
stiff, and stir in the sauce. Flavor with vanilla or almond
extract.

EVERY-DAY SAUCE
Mrs. A. M. Whaley.

Two tablespoons butter; 1 cup sugar; 1 tablespoon flour;
pinch of salt; 1 scant pint boiling water; 3 tablespoons cold
water.

Beat the sugar and butter to a cream, add the flour and

thoroughly mix. Then add the salt and cold water, then the boiling water, and let it boil a few minutes; after removing from the fire, flavor with vanilla or almond.

LEMON SAUCE

Mrs. E. R. Smith.

Three-quarters cup of sugar; 1 egg; ½ cup butter; 1 lemon; 1 teaspoon nutmeg, ½ cup boiling water.

Cream the butter and sugar and beat in the egg whipped light, then add the juice of the lemon and half the rind—grated; also the nutmeg. Beat hard, then add the water, put the sauce into a tin pail and set within the uncovered top of the tea-kettle—which must be boiling—until the sauce is very hot. Stir constantly.

NUTMEG SAUCE

Mrs. Geo. B. Dunham.

Half coffee cup sugar; butter, size of hickory nut; 1 tablespoon flour, rounded; few drops vanilla; ½ teaspoon nutmeg, scant.

Mix butter, flour, sugar, and nutmeg together. Dissolve with a little cold water, then pour on one pint boiling water. Stir well and cook about 10 minutes. Just before serving add vanilla.

ARROWROOT SAUCE FOR PLUM OR SUET PUDDING

One cup sugar; two teaspoons arrowroot; two tablespoons butter; juice of one lemon; one small teaspoon good extract vanilla; half cup cold water. Mix sugar and arrowroot, the lemon juice and water. Boil slowly until well-cooked and nice and clear. Take off and add butter. When nearly cold, put in the vanilla. If the butter does not make it sufficiently salt, a little salt may be added. If too thick, thin with warm water. To give it more of the lemon flavor, a little of the rind may be put in while cooking.

This is a most delicious sauce.

PIES

CHOPPED PASTE
Miss Ida G. Maynard, Colorado Springs.

One quart flour; 1 pint butter, or butter and lard mixed; ice water; 1 teaspoon salt.

Put flour into a chopping bowl. Add salt and butter, or butter and lard. Chop thoroughly. Mix into a stiff dough with ice water. Toss out onto a floured board. Pound and roll thin. Fold the sides so they will meet in the center. Fold the ends to meet. Then fold one half on to the other. Pound and roll again, and fold as before. Keep on ice until ready to use.

This is excellent for pastry and pies, and is very good for patties.

RICH SHORT CRUST
Mrs. B. C. Whiting.

Ten ounces flour; 1 egg—yolk; ½ pound butter; 2 ounces finely-sifted sugar; 2 tablespoons water.

Rub the butter, flour and sugar together. Beat up the egg with the water, then mix with the flour to a moderately soft paste. Roll it out twice.

GRAHAM PIE CRUST
Mrs. E. R. Smith.

Graham flour; sweet cream; butter; salt.

Sift the flour and rub into it a small piece of butter, a little salt, and use sweet cream to mix with. Roll out as you would other crust.

This is healthful as well as delicious.

CRUST FOR PUMPKIN PIE
Mrs. S. Speedy.

Butter your pie tin well, then take some dry corn meal and shake it around in the buttered tin; empty it out, leaving only what sticks to the tin. Have your pumpkin ready, the same as for any pie; pour it in your tin; set it in the oven and bake it. You will be surprised to see what a nice crust it will form.

PIE CRUST
Mrs. W. J. Brown.

Four cups flour; 1 cup lard, or half lard and half butter; white of 1 egg; 1 teaspoon salt, if lard is used.

Rub the shortening well into the flour, then add cold water to make it the consistency to roll out, then add white of egg beaten to a stiff froth.

FLAKEY CRUST WITHOUT BUTTER
Mrs. Carl Schutze.

Flour; lard; Highland evaporated milk; salt.

Use four parts flour to one part lard. Chop together. Add a little salt. Mix to a consistency to roll out with evaporated milk, or any other unsweetened variety.

This will be as flakey as real butter paste.

MINCE MEAT
Mrs. R. M. Widney.

Three pounds tender beef—chopped fine; 3 pounds cold, boiled tongue—chopped fine; 3 pounds beef suet, free from membrane, chopped fine; 4 pounds stoned raisins—soaked in one pint grape juice; 4 pounds pared, cored and chopped tart apples; 4 pounds CLEAN currants; 1 pound chopped citron; ¼ pound orange peel—candied; ¼ pound lemon peel —candied; 1 pound sweet almonds—blanched; 1 teaspoon ground pepper; 1 teaspoon ground all-pice; 1 teaspoon ground mace; 2 ounces bitter almonds—blanched; 4 lemons—juice and grated yellow rind; 4 oranges—juice only· 4 pounds coffee sugar; 2 level tablespoons salt; 1 teaspoon ground cloves; 1 teaspoon ground cinnamon; 2 nutmegs—grated.

See that the flavor is rich and even, adding more sugar or spices, if required; but not allowing any one flavor to predominate. Let the mixture stand at least over night before using it. It will be better if it is left in a cool place for a week or ten days. Will keep good all winter.

The above is Miss Juliet Corson's recipe for mince meat— omitting the wine and brandy which she uses. I use cider and grape juice, which have been boiled down from one gallon to one quart.   I often use also the rich juices of sweet pickles, such as peaches, plums, etc., also jellies—currant is especially nice—which have been left over.

MINCE MEAT—An English Recipe
Mrs. Mary O. Lerrigo.

One pound finely chopped kidney suet; 2 pounds raisins—chopped fine; 3 pounds currants—cleaned and dried; 3 pounds apples—chopped fine; 1 pound candied peel—chopped fine; 1 pound sugar; rinds of 3 lemons—grated; 1 small teaspoon salt; ½ ounce mixed spice; 1 pound lean meat.

Mince the lean meat very fine.   Mix all well together.

MOCK MINCE PIE
Mrs. J. S Van Doren.   Mrs. Baldwin.

Two eggs; 2 pounded crackers; ½ cup sugar; ½ cup boiling water; 1 teaspoon cinnamon; ½ teaspoon nutmeg; ½ cup molasses; ½ cup vinegar; ½ cup chopped and seeded raisins; ¼ teaspoon cloves; 1 teaspoon salt.

Boil all together 5 minutes.   Remove from fire.   Add piece of butter, half as large as an egg.   The well-beaten eggs.   Makes two pies.

EXCELLENT MINCE MEAT
Mrs. M. G. Moore

3 pints finely chopped meat; 5 pints chopped apples; 1 pint molasses; 4 pints brown sugar; 1 pint chopped suet; 2 pints raisins; 1 tablespoon salt; 1 tablespoon pepper; 1 pint currants; 1 pint vinegar; 1 pint chopped citron; 2 level table-spoons salt; 2 level tablespoons cinnamon; 2 level table-spoons ground nutmeg; juice and grated rinds of 3 lemons.

If anything seems lacking, add salt.

A CALIFORNIA PIONEER APPLE PIE—1852
Mrs. B. C. Whiting.

Break four soda crackers into an earthen bowl.   Pour over them a pint of cold water, made very tart with citric acid.   When soft, but not mashed, removed the soda crackers to your pie plate, with the under crust already on; then sift over two tablespoons of light brown sugar, and a little allspice and cinnamon to flavor. (The brown sugar and spice give the requisite color), after which put on a prettily perforated top crust, and bake in a very quick oven a few moments.

The deception was most complete and readily accepted. Apples at this early date were a dollar a pound, and we young people all craved a piece of mother's apple pie to appease our homesick feelings.

SQUASH PIE
Mrs. Wm. F. Marshall.

Two heaping tablespoons squash; ½ coffee cup sugar—granulated; 1 egg; scant ½ teaspoon level full of cinnamon; pinch of salt; 1 large teacup rich milk.

The Hubbard squash is best and should be steamed. Mash it through a colander. Beat the egg *thoroughly*, then add the sugar, salt, squash and cinnamon, and beat well together, then add the milk. Stir it in well. Bake with one crust. This makes one pie.

SQUASH PIE
Mrs. W. J. Brown.

Two teacups steamed or baked squash; ¾ cup sugar; 3 eggs; 2 tablespoons N. O. molasses; 1 tablespoon melted butter; 2 teaspoons ginger; 1 teaspoon cinnamon; 2 cups milk; a pinch of salt.

Mash the squash through a colander. Beat the eggs well, then add the sugar, molasses, butter, salt and spices, and stir together thoroughly, then add the milk and stir again. Bake with one crust. This will make two pies.

TO MAKE FRUIT PIE
Mrs. Wm. F. Marshall.

Line pie pan with crust; put in fruit; sprinkle sugar, flour and a few bits of butter over it. If apple, add a little cinnamon. If fruit is very juicy, no water will be needed; if not, add 1 large tablespoon water. Add more or less sugar, according to tartness of fruit. Cover with top crust, and bake about half an hour.

In making fruit pie, be careful to make, as a little friend used to say, "a fat pie."

LEMON PIE
Mrs. S. J. Peck.

One lemon; 1 cup sugar; 3 eggs; 1 cup sweet milk; 1 tablespoon corn starch; 1 teaspoon butter.

Cream the butter, sugar and starch. Add the milk and beaten yolks. Grate the yellow off the outside of the lemon, and use as flavoring. Squeeze out the juice and add it to the mixture. Beat whites of eggs to a stiff froth. Add these the last thing and stir well. This makes enough for two pies. Bake with bottom crust only.

LEMON PIE
Mrs. H. C. Austin.

Three-quarters cup sugar; ⅔ cup water; 1 lemon; 3 eggs; 1 tablespoon butter; 1 tablespoon flour. Cream butter and sugar; add flour, yolks 3 eggs—well beaten, water, 1 lemon, and piece of rind.

Beat the whites of the eggs very light, with a tablespoon of sugar to each egg, for a méringue; flavor this with lemon juice. Spread it over the pie when baked, and put it back in the oven until it is slightly browned. Use half the grated rind and all the juice of the lemon.

LEMON PIE
Mrs. Olive Storm.

One cup milk; two tablespoons flour; 1 cup sugar; 1 lemon; 3 eggs.

Put milk in double boiler. When it comes to boiling point, stir in flour, after it has been mixed to a smooth paste in a little cold milk; then add sugar and the juice of lemon.

Take the eggs, keeping the whites of 2 for the frosting, add the other with the yolks to the milk. Let cook a few minutes, then pour into the crust and bake. Frost after it is done and then brown.

LEMON PIE
Mrs. A. T. Tuttle.

One lemon; 1 cup water; 1 tablespoon corn starch; 1 cup sugar; 1 egg; butter—size of an egg; 1 cup boiling water.

Use juice and grated rind of the lemon. Dissolve the corn starch in the water. Pour the boiling water on the butter and sugar, and stir in the corn starch and cold water. Let it get cold and then add the egg and the juice and grated rind of the lemon. Bake with upper and under crust. This will make two pies.

ORANGE PIE
Mrs. W. G. Kerckhoff.

Two tablespoons butter; ½ cup sugar; 2 eggs; ½ cup milk; 1 cup flour; 1 teaspoon Cleveland's baking powder; rich cream.

Filling.—Two oranges—juice and grated peel; ½ cup sugar; 1 tablespoon flour; ¼ cup water.

Beat the butter and sugar to a cream, then add the yolks of the eggs, the milk, the beaten whites and flour. in which has been mixed the baking powder. Bake in deep jelly pan. When done, split in half with a sharp, broad bladed knife, and spread filling between. Serve with rich cream.

Filling.—Mix flour and sugar. Add juice and rind of oranges, then water. Boil five minutes.

APPLE CUSTARD PIE
Mrs. S. Speedy.

Sour apples; 3 eggs; ⅓ cup butter; ⅓ cup sugar; nutmeg.

Peel apples and stew until soft, with little water left in them. Rub through a sieve. Add eggs, butter and sugar. (If very sour, more sugar may be needed.) Season with nutmeg. Pour into crust and bake. When baked, cover with a méringue and season as for lemon pie.

CHOCOLATE PIE
Mrs. S. E. Bennett.

Three ounces Ghirardelli's chocolate; 1 cup boiling milk; 2 eggs; 1 small cup sugar; 6 or 8 drops vanilla extract.

Dissolve the chocolate in the milk. Stir until it is very smooth, then add the eggs—beaten separately, sugar and sufficient milk to make a large pie. Cook for about three minutes, stirring constantly. Bake in a moderate oven—otherwise, the custard will curdle.

Vanilla improves the pie greatly.

CUSTARD PIE
Mrs. W. J. Brown.

One egg; 1 pint milk; 3 tablespoons granulated sugar; nutmeg and a pinch of salt.

Beat the egg well, with one tablespoon sugar; then add the milk, the remaining sugar, nutmeg and salt. Bake in a moderate oven. Do not let it come to a boil. When the custard is set, remove from the oven carefully, and when cold you will have a delicious pie.

Very much depends on the baking.

REAL CREAM PIE
Mrs. J. H. F Peck.

Whites of 4 eggs; 1 teaspoon vanilla; 1 jelly-glass powdered sugar; ½ pint of cream.

Beat whites of eggs to a stiff froth. Add a little at a time the powdered sugar and vanilla. Bake, in a well-buttered pie plate in a slow oven, ten minutes. When this méringue is cold, whip the cream to a stiff froth; add two tablespoons powdered sugar, one teaspoon vanilla, and spread over the pie.

CREAM PIE
Mrs. Burdette Chandler.

Generous pint milk—scald; 3 generous tablespoons sugar; 1 tablespoon butter; 2 tablespoons corn starch; 3 eggs—yolks; 1 teaspoon vanilla, or other flavoring; pinch salt.

Beat all together with a little cold milk, and add to scalded milk. Let cook a minute or two. Bake crust before filling. Beat the whites of eggs with two tablespoons sugar, and spread on the top. Put in the oven and brown.

GREEN CORN PIE
Mrs. M. G. Moore.

Three ears raw corn grated; 1 even cup sugar; 1 pint sweet milk; 2 eggs; a little butter.

Boil milk and pour over the other ingredients.   Bake as
other custard pie.   This makes one deep pie.

STRAWBERRY SHORT CAKE
Mrs. Frank A. Miller, Riverside.

Make a crust with one-third more shortening than for
biscuit.   Roll it in two sheets; place one of them on a round
jelly cake tin and spread with butter;   place the other on top
and bake.

When baked, separate the layers and place mashed strawberries, sweetened, between and on top the layers.   Serve with
sweetened cream.   In the absence of sweet cream, cream
butter and sugar in the proportion of one cup sugar to one-
half cup butter, and mix with the strawberries before placing
between the layers.   Serve hot.

STRAWBERRY SHORT CAKE
Miss Frances Widuey.

One pint flour; 2 teaspoons Cleveland's baking powder; 2
level teaspoons butter; 1 level teaspoon lard.

Mix as for biscuits; bake quickly in a deep round pie pan
in one layer.   When done, cut the cake in three layers, butter
well, and spread liberally between and over the top with
mashed strawberries.   There should be at least one quart after
they are mashed, and sweetened with half pint of sugar.
Serve immediately with or without sweet cream.

CREAMS AND CUSTARDS

K. R. P.

Wherever we mention milk or cream in the following recipes, it is self-understood that we speak of the ordinary unprepared article. As, however, pure concentrated milk, commercially known as Highland Brand Evaporated Cream, is largely used in many families to the exclusion of all other forms of milk, owing to its uniform wholesome qualities, besides its convenience and economy, our book would not be complete without giving directions for its use.

As it is simply pure milk partially dessicated, the addition of about three parts of water to one part of Highland Evaporated Cream restores it to its original fluidity, and after thus diluting it, you may use it in precisely the same manner, for either cooking or drinking as ordinary milk.

For coffee or cocoa it may be used undiluted, about two teaspoons to the cup.

As a dressing for fruits, cereal foods, etc., it should be diluted with about two parts of water, which gives it the richness of cream.

A mixture of one part of Highland Evaporated Cream to about four parts of ordinary milk also answers instead of dairy cream for ice cream and other purposes.

GENERAL DIRECTIONS FOR ICE CREAM.
MISS K. R. PAXTON.

For the best ice cream only the best materials should be used. Good cream, granulated sugar, ripe fruit or the best flavoring extracts. Do not use milk, corn starch, gelatine or eggs, except for Neapolitan cream. Half the cream should be scalded, as it makes a smoother frozen cream. If extract is used dissolve the sugar in the scalding cream. If ripe fruit is used dissolve one-half sugar in the scalding cream and mix the other half with the fruit. Flavoring and fruit should be added when the cream is nearly frozen, that is, when it turns hard.

For a four-quart freezer about ten pounds of ice and four pounds of rock salt will be required. Chip the ice in a tub with an ice chipper, or else put it in a coarse sack and pound with a mallet. Mix the ice and salt. Place the freezing can in the tub being careful to put the ball of the can in the socket of the tub; put in dasher, pour in mixture (scalded cream and sugar dissolved in it, and the unscalded cream), put on cover, fasten on crank, then turn the handle to see if it works properly, then pack with the ice and salt, pounding it down solid. Turn slowly and steadily until it turns a little hard, take off cover and add flavoring or else the sweetened, strained fruit, cover, turn until you can turn it no longer, take out dasher, scrape it off and work the cream well with a wooden paddle for about ten minutes. Put on cover, put cork in dasher hole, repack with ice and salt, cover with a piece of old carpet, and let it stand an hour or two before using. If it is to be molded, fill the molds with cold water, pour out water but do not wipe. Pack in the frozen cream after you have worked it well—close the molds and bind with strips of muslin dipped in melted butter, then bury in ice and salt for an hour or more. When ready to serve wash off the molds with cold water, and the cream will soon slip out.

ICE CREAM
Miss Ida G. Maynard.

Half cup sugar; 1 saltspoon salt; 1 tablespoon flour; 1 unbeaten egg; 1 pint hot milk; 1 quart cream; flavor.

Mix sugar, salt and flour together; add egg; mix well. Pour slowly over this the hot milk, and cook in a double boiler twenty minutes, stirring often. When cold, add cream; strain and flavor; freeze, using three parts ice to one of salt.

RASPBERRY ICE CREAM
Miss K. R. Paxton.

One quart cream; 1½ pounds sugar; 3 pints raspberries; scald half the cream; add half the sugar and stir till dissolved.

Mash berries with remainder of sugar and let stand half hour, stirring often to dissolve sugar.   Mash berries and sugar through a sieve fine enough to prevent seeds from going through.   Add the remainder of cream to the cold scalded cream and freeze, when it turns hard add the berry mixture and finish as usual.

PINEAPPLE ICE CREAM
Miss K. R. Paxton.

One quart cream; 1 pound sugar; 1 pineapple; juice and ½ grated rind of 1 orange.

Scald half the cream, put in half the sugar and stir till dissolved.   Pare the pineapple, leaving the leaves at the top for a handle; cut out eyes, then either grate the pineapple, or with a silver fork tear it into small pieces.   Mix the remainder of the sugar with this, stirring often until sugar is dissolved. When the scalded cream is cold, put in the can with the remainder of the cream and freeze.   When it begins to turn hard, add the pineapple and sugar, to which has been added half the rind and juice of orange, finish freezing, remove dasher and beat according to directions.

SAGO CREAM
Mrs. A. S. Averill.

Two tablespoons sago; 1 pint milk; salt; 2 eggs, yelks; 3 tablespoons sugar; meringue; 2 eggs, whites; 1 tablespoon sugar.

Soak sago in half cup cold water for half hour; add milk and salt.   Place in a rice boiler over the fire.   When hot, add the well-beaten yelks of eggs and sugar.   Cook until it thickens.   Place in a mold.   Spread over the top the whites of eggs beaten to a stiff froth, to which has been added 1 tablespoon sugar.   Set in oven until a delicate brown.   Serve with whipped cream. Pearl tapioca may be used instead of sago.

COFFEE CREAM
Mrs. Emeline Childs.

One package Cox's gelatine; 1 pint strong coffee; 1 pint whipped cream; vanilla flavoring.

Divide the gelatine, leaving more for the coffee part, than for the cream. Dissolve part for cream in milk, and the part for coffee in cold water, for about an hour. Then make a pint of strong coffee, which, when clear, pour into the gelatine intended for the coffee part, and sweeten to taste.

Mix a pint of whipped cream with the cream part, and sweeten to taste, adding a little vanilla flavoring.

When all is ready, put alternately in a mold half cup of each, coffee, first; let each layer stand until cool. Then set it on ice, and when required serve with a sauce of whipped cream.

CHANTILLA CREAM
Mrs. W. W. Widney.

One pint sweet cream; 2 eggs, whites; 1 cup sugar; sponge cake.

Add to the cream beaten stiff, the well beaten whites, sugar, and flavoring to taste. Cut squares of sponge cake lay alternately in a dish with the cream.

BISCUIT TORTONI
Mrs. Frank Phillips.

One gallon whipped cream; 1 cup powdered sugar 2; tablespoons candied cherries; 2 tablespoons blanched almonds; ⅛ teaspoon extract almond; 1 cup water; yolks of 5 eggs; 4 tablespoons raspberry or strawberry syrup; ½ cup dried or powdered maccaroons.

Boil the sugar and water together 20 minutes. Add the beaten yolks and set the basin in another of boiling water for five minutes, stirring all the time. Then add the syrup and extract; then the cream, then the maccaroons and chopped almonds and cherries. Then pour in the mold or freezer. Take great care in packing the ice and salt.

BAVARIAN CREAM WITH PEACHES
Mrs. H. McLellan.

Eighteen fine peaches; ½ pound sugar; ½ package gelatine; 1 glass cream; 1 pint whipped cream.

Cut peaches into small pieces; boil them with the sugar.

When reduced to a marmalade, squeeze them through a sieve; add the gelatine and cream.   Stir it well to make smooth. When it is cold and about to form, add the whipped cream and mold.   Cut up fresh peaches and serve around the mold. The gelatine, should of course, be dissolved before used.

STRAWBERRY CREAM
Mrs. F. M. Hotchkis.

One quart ripe strawberries; ½ box gelatine: ½ cup hot water; 1 heaping cup sugar: 1 pint cream.

Stem the berries, then mash them, add sugar and let stand for half hour.   Cover the gelatine with cold water and let stand for an hour or more.   Whip the cream to a froth; strain the berries and sugar through a rather coarse strainer; dissolve the gelatine; add it to the berries.   Place berry mixture in a basin a tin one is preferable—and put in ice water and stir until it begins to thicken.   Then add whipped cream.   Turn into a mold and let harden. Serve with whipped cream. This will make two quarts.

HAMBURG CREAM
Mrs. M. B. Welch.

Two large lemons, juice and rind; 1 cup sugar; 8 eggs.

Stir together the juice, rind and sugar, add the well beaten yolks, put all in a tin pail and set in a pot of boiling water (if you have not a double boiler); stir for three minutes, take from the fire, add the well beaten whites of the eggs, serve when cold.

VELVET CREAM
Mrs. A. C. Goodrich.

One pint sweet cream; 2 tablespoons gelatine; 3 tablespoons sugar; any flavoring desired.

Dissolve the gelatine in a little warm water.   Put the sugar and flavoring in the cream, then whip stiff, and while whipping pour in the gelatine.   When whipped sufficiently pour in a mold and set away to cool.

TAPIOCA CREAM
Mrs. Burdette Chandler.

Three tablespoons tapioca; 1 quart milk; ⅔ cup sugar; 3 eggs.

Cover the tapioca over night with water. In the morning pour off the water, if any, and put tapioca into the milk. Put on the stove, and when it boils stir in yolks of eggs, sugar and a little salt. Stir until it begins to thicken. Make a frosting of the whites of the eggs, and spread over the top, sprinkle a little sugar over and brown in oven.

MOUSSÉS
Miss Parlon.

This dish is really a mossy froth. Whip cream and drain it, for if there is any liquid cream in the moussé it will not be perfect. Pack the mold in salt and ice, using five pints of salt for a gallon mold. Put the moussé preparation into the mold, cover and set away for four or six hours. Six hours is always best. If the mold be lined with white paper, the moussé will have a smoother and handsomer appearance when turned out on a dish, but it takes a little longer to freeze. It is a great improvement to line the bottom and sides of the mold with a sherbet that will combine with the flavor of the moussé.

PINEAPPLE SOUFFLÉ
Miss Farmer, Boston.

One large, ripe pineapple; 6 eggs; 1 pound sugar; 1 pint water.

Peel and chop the pineapple into little bits. Lay the pulp in a dish, sprinkling each layer with sugar. Set aside for several hours, then mash the pulp and strain. Put to one pint of pure fruit juice the pint of water and put in double boiler; add the eggs, well beaten with the sugar. Cook to a soft custard, strain and beat until cold. Freeze and serve either plain or with cream flavored with juice of the fruit.

CHARLOTTE RUSSE
Mrs. C. W. Blaisdell.

One quart thin cream; ½ box gelatine; sugar; lady fingers; flavoring.

Sweeten, flavor and then whip the cream until in a froth. Put gelatine in as little cold water as possible to soak. Set on the stove to melt. Let cool before putting into the cream. Line a dish with cake or lady fingers. Pour the cream into it and set on ice until ready for use.

CHARLOTTE RUSSE
Mrs. E. R. Smith.

Half pound of lady fingers; 2 boxes strawberries; 1 pint sweet cream; ½ cup sugar.

Fit the cakes neatly in the dessert bowl or platter; cover them with the berries and sprinkle over them the sugar. Pour over all the cream which has been lightly whipped, flavored and sweetened. This is a very delicate dessert. Other fruit can be used—raspberries, very ripe peaches, or pineapple.

RASPBERRY CHARLOTTE
Mrs. Augusta Robinson.

Butter and cover the bottom of a pudding dish with dry bread crumbs. Put on this a layer of ripe raspberries sprinkled with sugar. Proceed with layers of crumbs, berries and sugar, until the dish is full, the last layer being crumbs. Put bits of butter on the top and bake with a plate over it for ½ hour. Remove the plate and let it brown just before serving.

DELICIOUS APPLES FOR TEA
Mrs. M. G. Moore.

Two pounds apples; 1 pound white sugar; 3 lemons.

Pare, core and slice the apples into a pan. Add the sugar, the juice of the lemons, and the grated peel of one; boil two hours, turn into a mold. Serve cold, with custard or cream.

BAKED PEACHES
Mrs. J. H. Norton.

Peaches; brown sugar; flour; butter.

Peel the peaches, place them in a pan, sprinkling on each one, brown sugar, flour, and a bit of butter, add sufficient water to make a nice syrup. Bake until soft, and light brown in color.

APPLE SNOW
Mrs. H. McLellan.

Six tart apples; 3 eggs, whites only; sugar to taste; vanilla.

Pare, core and boil the apples in as little water as possible; cool and strain; beat thoroughly and add the eggs beaten thoroughly. Sweeten and beat until like snow. Serve on top of soft custard. The grated rind of a lemon may be used instead of vanilla, if preferred.

FRUTTI SNOW
Mrs. R. R. Glassell.

Six eggs; 6 tablespoons powdered sugar.

Beat the whites of eggs to a very stiff froth, then add gradually powdered sugar, beating not less than fifteen minutes. Place on ice, and just before serving, dot with preserved crab-apples, whole cherries, or bits of jelly. Place in large glass dish and surround with whipped cream.

COUSIN KATE
Mrs. James Foord.

Eight large apples, sweet; 1 coffee cup milk; 1 cup flour; 2 eggs.

Peel and core the apples. Make a batter of the milk, flour and eggs, beaten light. Add apples and bake in a shallow pan, well buttered, twenty-five minutes, in a hot oven. Serve with hard sauce or icing.

ORANGE SAGO
Mrs. J. P. Widney.

One cup sago; 2 cups cold water; 3 cups orange juice, equal to the juice of about 12 oranges; 2 cups sugar; pinch of salt.

Wash sago thoroughly. Soak in the water two hours. Add orange juice, sugar, and salt, and boil in a porcelain vessel until the sago is perfectly clear.   Turn into a bowl which has first been rinsed in cold water; then it will turn out in good shape.   Serve with sweet cream, or a delicate boiled custard.

ORANGE TRIFLE
Miss Ida G. Maynard.

Half box gelatine; ½ cup cold water; 1 cup boiling water; 1 cup sugar; 1 pint cream; 4 or 6 oranges; ½ lemon; 3 eggs; lady fingers.

Soak the gelatine in the cold water twenty minutes; add the boiling water, the juice of the oranges, the grated rind of one, and the juice of the half lemon.   Strain, add the yolks of the eggs, slightly beaten, cook until it thickens a little, then add the sugar, stir on ice, until thick.   Add the cream whipped, and turn it into a mold lined with lady fingers.   When ready to serve, turn out on a platter.

ORANGE CUSTARD
Mrs. H. G. Otis.

Juice of 10 large oranges; 1 pint cream; 1 teacup sifted sugar; yolks 12 eggs.

Sweeten the orange juice with the sugar and set it over the fire.   Stir constantly till hot, then skim it carefully, and set aside to cool.   When nearly cold add the yolks of eggs, beaten very light, and the cream.   Put all into a sauce pan and stir over a very slow fire until thick.   Pour into cups and serve cold. If desired, the whites of the eggs beaten stiff with a teacup of powdered sugar may be used.   A heaped tablespoonful on the top of each cup of the custard.

ORANGE CUSTARD
Mrs. Augusta Robinson.

Three or four oranges; ½ cup sugar. For custard—2 cups milk; 1 egg; a little sugar; 1 large tablespoon corn starch.

Peel carefully, and slice thinly across, the oranges; sprinkle the sugar over them and let them stand for about 1 hour, then pour over them the custard prepared as follows:

Put the milk on the stove in a double boiler. Beat together the egg, the corn starch and the sugar.   Pour this into the hot milk, stir till it thickens.   Pour over the oranges.   Serve cold.

WEST INDIAN FLOATING ISLAND
Mrs. T. Masac.

Make an ordinary custard for floating island, only beating up any preferred fruit jelly with the stiffly beaten whites of the eggs, thus giving them a pretty color and flavor.

LEMON SPONGE
Mrs. Cameron Thom.

Half package gelatine; 1¾ pints water; ¾ pound sifted sugar; juice six lemons; rind of 1 lemon; whites of 2 eggs.

Dissolve the gelatine in the water; then add the sugar, the juice, and rind of the lemon.   Boil the whole a few minutes, then let stand till quite cold, and just beginning to stiffen; then add the beaten whites of the eggs and whisk till it is quite white.   Wet a mold with cold water and pour the mixture in.

STRAWBERRY OR RASPBERRY SPONGE
Mrs. A. C. Doan.

One quart strawberries or raspberries; ¼ box gelatine; 1½ cups water; 1 cup sugar; juice of 1 lemon; 4 eggs, whites.

Soak the gelatine in ½ cup of the water.   Mash the berries, and add half the sugar to them.   Boil the remainder of the sugar and the cup of water gently 20 minutes.   Rub berries through a fine sieve.   Add gelatine to boiling syrup, take from the fire and add the berry juice.   Place the bowl in pan of ice water and beat with egg beater five minutes, then add lemon juice and the beaten whites, beat until it begins to thicken.   Pour into well wet molds and set on ice.   Serve with cream.   Delicious.

APRICOT SHERBET
Mrs. W. W. Ross.

Rub through a colander a sufficient quantity of ripe or canned apricots to make three quarts of the pulp.   Into that stir two pounds of sugar and a pint of water. Beat the whites of 4 eggs to a stiff froth, and stir thoroughly into fruit the last thing. Place in the freezer and stir constantly until frozen quite hard. Keep the freezer packed in ice until you wish to serve. Eggs can be omitted if desired.

ORANGE SHERBET
Mrs. Anna O'Melveny.

Six oranges; 2 lemons: 1 quart water; 1 pint sugar.

Cut a circle about 2 inches in diameter from the stem end of each orange and remove carefully to keep them unbroken. Scoop out the pulp neatly with a silver spoon, and set the skins in a refrigerator or in a pail surrounded with ice and salt. Put the water, sugar, and grated rind of two oranges over the fire and cook twenty minutes. When cool, add the juice of 6 oranges, 2 lemons, and freeze. Shortly before serving, fill the chilled orange skins with the sherbet and put on the covers of orange rind which have been previously decorated with narrow yellow ribbon, for handles. A circle of wavy green leaves will add to the effect of this dish, which may be served as a dessert, or just after the roast.

PINEAPPLE SHERBET
Mrs. S. S. Salisbury.

One heaping tablespoon gelatine; 2 pounds granulated sugar; 1 can grated pineapple; 1 pint cold water; 3 pints boiling water; juice of 7 lemons; white of one egg.

Put the gelatine in the cold water and let it stand until dissolved, then add the boiling water, sugar, juice of the lemons and the pineapple; put in the freezer, and when about half frozen add the well beaten white of the egg. This fills a six quart freezer, and will serve thirty-five people.

STRAWBERRY SHERBET
H. F. W.

Two quarts of berries; whites of 4 eggs; 2 pounds sugar; water.

Wash the berries, cover with the sugar, let them stand an

hour, then press out all the juice. Add as much cold water as there is juice. Freeze until slightly stiff. Then stir in the stiffly beaten whites, and freeze until hard.

PINEAPPLE ICE

Mrs. J. M. Johnston

Johnson's Bahama pineapple, 25 cents per can.

Strain juice from the fruit, then pour cold water over fruit, and strain off into juice. Add little less than quart of cold water. Take 2 tablespoons Cox's gelatine, soak it in just enough cold water to cover well, for half an hour, then add enough boiling water to dissolve; add to juice, sweeten to taste. Use about 3 cups sugar, then freeze. Flavor with oranges if preferred, one dozen oranges and three lemons.

BEVERAGES

DIRECTIONS FOR MAKING TEA
H. Jevne.

To make a perfect cup of tea, the water must be fresh and quickly boiled, and the teapot hot—an earthen one being preferable.

Put one teaspoonful of tea for each pint of water into the warm pot, pour in the boiling water and let stand from three to four minutes on the back part of the stove. Never allow to boil.

Serve tea from the first infusion, and, if a second cup is wanted, make fresh tea, unless you have transferred the liquid from the leaf before the tannin has had time to be extracted.

Tea is a healthful beverage, if made and used as above; but as commonly used by the majority, it can be properly called a soup made of tea leaves. There is also more danger of too large a quantity of leaf being used than too little. Very few people like a strong tea.

Avoid cheap teas, as one pound of good quality will go as far as two pounds of common, if used intelligently.

CARE OF COFFEE POT
Mrs. R. M. Widney.

Never allow cold coffee or grounds to remain in the coffee pot. Empty, wash thoroughly and dry well, as soon as the meal at which you have used coffee is over. If cold coffee remains, it can be used to wet the coffee for next time. A fruitful cause of poor coffee is a poorly-kept coffee pot.

CHURCH SOCIAL COFFEE
Mrs. W. J. Horner.

Half pound coffee; 1 gallon boiling water; 1 egg. Put coffee in a bag and boil three or four minutes.

COFFEE
Mrs. W. B. Abernethy.

Use a mixture of ⅔ Java and ⅓ Mocha, *finely* ground. Allow 1 heaping tablespoon of ground coffee for each cup, and for each four cups of coffee add ¼ teaspoon chicory. In the evening prepare the coffee for breakfast, by mixing the required quantity with the white of egg. Add enough cold water to cover and let stand till morning, in a closely-covered bowl. Put the mixture in the coffee pot which *must* be kept clean and dry. Add 1 cup cold water and let come to the boil, then pour in the required amount of boiling water, and put where it will keep very hot but not boil. If for dinner, mix six hours before the meal is served.

COFFEE
Mrs. I. R. Dunkelberger.

Equal weights of Mocha and Java make the best coffee. To make one quart coffee, grind one large cup of coffee. Put into pot with one egg, and sufficient cold water to moisten. Let it stand till the coffee swells; then pour on boiling water, and let it stay over fire till it reaches the boiling point; take off; let stand five minutes; turn off into another pot, and send to table to be served with boiled cream.

CHOCOLATE
H. F. W

One ounce unsweetened Ghirardelli's chocolate; ¾ cup sugar; ½ teaspoon corn starch; 1 pint boiling water; 1 pint milk; 1 egg.

Grate the chocolate, or cut in small bits. Mix with sugar and corn starch. Blend them over hot water; then add, slowly, boiling water. Simmer ten minutes and set it in a double boiler until ready for use. Beat the egg to a cream, pour the boiling chocolate over it and serve at once.

LEMONADE
H. F. W.

Five lemons; 1 orange; ½ pound loaf sugar; 1 pint water; 1 bottle (quart) Appolinaris water; ice.

Make a syrup of the sugar and water, add the lemon rinds

and let stand one hour; then remove the rinds. Add the strained juice of the lemons, the Appolinaris water, and the orange—cut in very thin slices—each slice quartered. Pour the lemonade into a bowl, having a block of ice in the center. Serve a piece of orange in each glass.

RASPBERRY VINEGAR
Mrs. E. F. Spence.

Three pounds raspberries to 1 quart white wine vinegar. Put in stone jar for three days. Strain through flannel bag. To each pint juice, one pound cube sugar. Place over a gentle fire. Boil ten minutes. Bottle, seal and keep in a cool place. Blackberry vinegar may be made in same way—allowing 5½ pounds sugar to 3 pints juice.

Mixed with ice-water makes a delicious drink for warm weather.

STRAWBERRY VINEGAR
Mrs. Wm. J. Robinson, Moncton, Canada.

Let one gallon strawberries stand 48 hours in one quart cider vinegar; then mash and strain, and add one pound sugar to every pound juice. Put it over the fire and let it simmer very slowly for half an hour. Skim well, bottle, and when cold, cork tight.

I have kept this for two years.

SPANISH MENUS

A. Sepulveda de Mott

— ‒

BREAKFAST	ALMUERZO
Omelet with fine Herbs	Tortilla de Hierbas finas
Boiled Trout	Trucha Cocida
Stewed Rabbit	Conejo Guisado
Fried Artichokes	Alcachofas fritas
Dessert	Posties

DINNER	COMIDA
Julienne Soup	Sopa Juliana
Garvanzo Pottage	Potage de Garvanzo
Cod with Potatoes	Bacalao con Patatas
Veal à la Mode	Ternera Estofada
Salmon Spanish Style	Salmon à la Espanola
Roasted Turkey	Pava en Asador
Lobster Salad	Ensalada do Langosta
Dessert	Posties

SPANISH DEPARTMENT

JULIENNE SOUP
A. Sepulveda de Mott.

Take same amount of carrots, celery, lettuce, sorrel, green peas and French beans.   Put them in butter, with a few cuts of onion.   Add boiling broth, boil on slow fire and add some thin slices of bread.

SOUP 'a la CATALANA
Mrs. Juan Foster.

Six ounces beef; 6 ounces mutton; ¼ chicken; Spanish peas; salt; a large pot, ⅔ full of spring water.

When the water boils, put in the meat, chicken and peas, with salt to taste.   Boil slowly, skimming carefully.   When the meat is done, remove it.   This stock can be used for rice, noodle, macaroni, or bread soup.

SOPA ESPANOLA
Reliable.

Four pounds lean veal; ½ pound salt pork; 2 turnips; 1 onion; 1 beet; 4 tablespoons oat meal; ½ nutmeg; 1 teacup cream; ½ teaspoon allspice.

Put the veal in a stew pan, cover with cold water, and let it simmer four hours.   Mince the pork, fry to a light brown, and add it to the veal.   One hour before serving, add the sliced turnips, onion, carrot, and beet.   Cook slowly forty minutes.   Strain through a colander, return the broth to the pan.   Add the oatmeal, cook twenty minutes, add cream, spices, pepper and salt. Pour into a tureen, over toasted bread cut in dice.   Serve hot.

PURSLAINE SALAD
Mrs. A. F. Coronel.

Purslaine; lard, or butter; onions; oil; vinegar.

Wash well, and boil in salted water, when cooked, drain. Fry some onions in lard, or butter, then fry the purslaine. When well fried, place in a dish, and add oil, vinegar, and a raw onion cut fine.

TROUT à la CASCARA
Mrs. Juan Foster.

Trout; salt; lard; flour; 1 onion, 1 head garlic, parsley, peppermint, cloves, thyme, sweet basil.

Clean the trout, cover with salt for an hour. Wash and boil them (over a quick fire), with sufficient water to cover. add all the other ingredients. When done, take out the onion, garlic, and thyme, and serve.

BOILED TROUT
A. Sepulveda de Mott.

Boil the trout, after cleaning them, in boiling water with a few pieces of parsley. After boiled pour on a little more fluid, and on top of that a little powdered pepper.

SALMON SPANISH STYLE
A. Sepulveda de Mott.

Boil with leeks and pepper in white broth, and serve with the leeks, or else with parsley and onions chopped, covering lightly with pepper.

COD WITH POTATOES
A. Sepulveda de Mott.

Keep the cod in water for some time, then cut it in pieces and fry it in oil; when it is a golden color add some water and some potatoes; crush some fried garlic, parsley, and pepper, with which make a sauce and thicken with crumbs of bread, and pour over cod and potatoes.

ROASTED TURKEY
A. Sepulveda de Mott.

Dress turkey; cover it with a coat of sliced bacon, if it is very fat; and if not fat, lard it, (or stuff) with small strips of bacon well cooked, and cover the whole with a greased paper, which will be removed when it is half cooked, so as to take a fine color. Serve sprinkled with gravy.

BROILED CHICKEN
Mrs. A. F. Coronel.

Cut the chicken open on the back. Salt it, inside and out, rub it with butter or lard. Broil over coals, keeping it well covered with butter or lard.

CHICKEN DRESSING
Maria de los Dominguez de Francis.

Grated bread crumbs; 5 soda crackers, wet; 1 large table-spoon butter; 1 onion; ½ cup raisins, seeded; ½ cup olives; salt, pepper, grated nutmeg.

Fry the onion in the butter, (not too brown). Mix with the bread crumbs and crackers, add the raisins and olives, half of which may be left whole, the other half slice. Season with salt, pepper, and nutmeg, if desired. This quantity is sufficient for one chicken.

STEWED PARTRIDGES
Mrs. Juan Foster.

The partridges after being dressed, are put over a slow fire in a round earthen pot (olla), with fried bacon cut in squares, onions quartered, (plenty of them), two heads of garlic, all kinds of spices, salt and lard. Let the whole boil slowly, covered with another smaller round earthen pot (olla), full of water, putting between the two pots a piece of wrapping paper.

CROQUETTES OF CHICKEN AND PORK
Senorita Epitasia Bustamente.

One pound each of fresh white pork and white meat of chicken, grind as for sausage. Season to taste with salt, pepper, mint, garlic, onion, and tomato—the last three ground fine. Mix two eggs with cup dry bread crumbs, and two tablespoons cold water, and work into the ground meat. Make into balls the size of walnuts, and cook in soup or salted boiling water. Take out with ladle and serve on fried bread crumbs. The balls should almost double in size in cooking.

DRESSING FOR SMALL BIRDS
Mrs. A. F. Coronel.

Chop equal quantities of walnuts and almonds. Mix with bread soaked in vinegar, fry in oil, season with salt. Serve with any small birds, putting over all green peppers, and olives chopped together.

FRIED RABBIT

Mrs. A. F. Coronel.

Wash the rabbit, fry it in oil, seasoning with salt and vinegar. Just before serving add thyme and chopped olives. Green peppers cut open are placed on the dish. On them is served the rabbit.

STEWED RABBIT

A. Sepulveda de Mott.

Prepare it, without wetting it, then cut in slices and put in the "olla" with cooking oil, parsley, garlic and pepper, and keep it over a slow fire; then add some hot water, and when it is half cooked put in a few leaves of laurel, cloves and pulverized cinnamon.

RABBITS CALADONIAN STYLE

Mrs. Juan Foster.

As rabbits, wild or tame. have a strong odor, it is best to lay them in a pan and rub them with oil and salt before cooking; then cut them in pieces; put the pieces in a kettle with oil and bacon. Turn them, several times, add water and a small piece of bacon. When they are half cooked put them in the following sauce: Put into a mortar a piece of laurel leaf, some wild marjoram, sage, and a piece of lemon peel, add a little toasted bread, if you have any; take a piece of bacon from the kettle, pound it up with the rest. Pour boiling water on this, strain it through a sieve, pour it on the rabbit, and cook till done over a very slow fire. Rabbits are very nice cooked with onions or mushrooms and chestnuts, truffles or artichokes, olives and capers and with other kinds of vegetables.

HARES AFRICAN STYLE

Mrs. Juan Foster.

Take the bones out of two partridges and one hare; lard the latter with large pieces of pork heavily seasoned with all sorts of spices and aromatic herbs. The sauce is made from the livers of the hare and the partridges, garlic and sliced onions, thyme, green mint, black pepper, salt, and two laurel leaves. Put the pieces of meat in a stewpan in layers, mixed with this sauce, and arrange them in the form of a roll. Wrap all well in a light paste of flour and lard; put it in the oven until the cover is golden brown and cracked on the outside. This is a sign that the dish is ready to be served.

SPANISH STEAK
Mrs. E. A. Pruess.

One and one-half pounds round steak; 6 red chilis; 1 table spoon flour; 2 cloves; garlic; a little thyme, lard.

Vein, and seed the chilis, cover them with boiling water, soak until tender, then scrape the pulp into the water. Cut the steak in small pieces, fry it brown in hot lard, add the flour and brown it, cover with the chili water, add garlic, and thyme. Simmer until the meat is tender, and the gravy of the right consistency.

VEAL a la MODE
A. Sepulveda de Mott.

Cut in small pieces the veal. Fry some bacon, and in this fry the veal; then put in the olla. Fry some onion, well-chopped, and put on the meat: also, a little vinegar, two heads crushed garlic, salt, sprig parsley, and a few leaves of laurel. Put the whole over a slow fire, covered by a paper, on the top of which set a cup of water, to prevent evaporation. Let it boil two hours.

SPANISH STEW
Mrs. Vida A. Bixby.

Cold cooked meat: 1 tablespoon lard or beef drippings; 1 onion; 1 chili; 4 ripe tomatoes.

Heat the lard, or drippings, in a skillet. Add the meat cut fine. Fry it a few minutes, then add the chopped onions, chili and tomatoes. Cover and let simmer twenty minutes, or more.

This is a good way to serve up odd bits of steak, roast or stew.

FINE BRAINS
Senorita Epitasia Bustamente.

Soak a set of brains an hour, vein and prepare thoroughly. Beat till fine and foaming like omelet, 1 egg; tablespoon dried bread crumbs, salt, pepper and taste of grated onion, add to brains. Take eight slices fresh bread, spread with preparation of brains in a dripping pan, and bake in a hot oven about ten minutes. Take out and set bread in a spider of hot fat, and fry carefully, so that the bread is a light brown color on the underside. Serve immediately.

Spanish rice is proper accompaniment.

TONGUE PIQUANTE
Senorita Epitasia Bustamente.

Boil a beef tongue till tender; skin and cut, like lyonnaise potatoes.

Sauce.—Seed and vein 15 chili peppers. Boil half an hour with a little salt, changing water three times. Take out chilis and mash to a red pulp. Add one pint cold water.

Roast one pound pumpkin seed ten minutes in a hot oven; skin and run them through a coffee mill. Add ½ pint cold water, and run through strainer. Mix with chilis. Add one tablespoon pork fat, tablespoon flour, and tablespoon salt. Boil, stirring carefully. Add the prepared tongue and cook for half an hour.

ESTAFADO
Mrs. J. G. Downey.

Two pounds beef, ribs or mutton; 1 spoon lard; onions; green peppers; black pepper; thyme; garlic; vinegar; raisins; olives; tomatoes; 4 slices toast.

Heat the lard in a saucepan. Put in all the ingredients. (Leave the peppers whole, mince the garlic.) Cover close and stew. Serve on the toast.

CHILI CON CARNI
Mrs. J. L. Slaughter.

Beefsteak—round; 1 tablespoon hot fat; 2 tablespoons rice; 1 cup boiling water; 2 large red peppers--dry; ½ pint boiling water; salt; onions; flour.

Cut the steak in small pieces. Put in frying pan with the fat, hot water and rice. Cover closely and cook slowly until tender. Remove the seeds and part of the veins from the peppers. Cover with half pint of boiling water, and let them stand until cool, then squeeze them in the hand until the water is thick and red. If not thick enough, add a little flour. Season with salt and a little onion, if desired. Pour the sauce on the meat and serve.

DRIED BEEF WITH PEPPERS
Mrs. W. S. Moore.

Two pounds jerked, dried beef; 2 ounces lard; 1 onion; 6 red peppers; brown flour.

Place the beef in pan in hot oven ten minutes, then shred. Place in a frying pan with lard and onion, and fry for five minutes. Pour boiling water over the peppers. Pass them through a sieve, and mix with the beef. Thicken with brown flour. Season to taste. Cook twenty minutes, and serve piping hot.

JAMBALAZA
Mrs. W. J. Elderkin.

One pound of rice; 1 pound sausage; 1 pound ham; 2 onions; 2 large tomatoes; a small piece of red pepper; a sprig of parsley; 1 heaping tablespoon lard; 1 pint boiling water; a little salt.

Wash the rice and soak it one hour. Cut up the sausage, tomatoes, onions, parsley, pepper and ham. Fry these in the lard, then add the water. Stir in the rice gradually. Cover the pot and set it where it can cook slowly. Serve while hot.

Jambalaza is very nice made with oysters, shrimp or chicken substituted for sausage.

OMELET WITH FINE HERBS—Breakfast
A. Sepulveda de Mott.

Beat some fresh eggs, add a little milk, and then add some fine herbs, well chopped, and make the omelet as required.

SPANISH OMELET
Mrs. E. M. Ross.

One tablespoon butter; 1 finely-chopped onion; 1 pint tomatoes; 1 tablespoon sliced mushrooms; 1 tablespoon capers; salt; pepper; 4 eggs; 4 tablespoons milk.

Melt the butter, add onion, and cook till yellow; then add tomatoes, and cook till nearly dry, when the mushrooms, capers, ¼ teaspoon salt, and ½ saltspoon pepper should be added. Beat the eggs slightly, add ½ teaspoon salt, ½ saltspoon pepper, and the milk. Butter an omelet pan and pour in the mixture. When creamy throughout, let it brown on the bottom. Pour some of the tomato on one side, fold over, and turn out on a platter; pour the rest of the tomato sauce around the omelet and serve. The addition of a green pepper is a help in seasoning—about a tablespoon being sufficient. Both onion and pepper should be chopped very fine. The tomato mixture should cook very slowly, and until it is quite dry.

Stir with a wooden spoon.

SALZA
Mrs. J. J. Mellus.

Three large tomatoes; 1 small onion; 5 *hot* green peppers; ½ teaspoon salt; *2 tablespoons vinegar*.

Lay the peppers on coals, turning them until blistered. Throw them into cold water, then remove the skins and seeds. Skin the tomatoes and chop all together until quite fine. Strain off the juice, and add the salt and vinegar.

To be served with soups or roasts as a relish.

SALZA
Mrs. W. H. Workman.

Six ripe tomatoes; 4 green peppers; salt; raw onion.

Scald and skin the tomatoes. Squeeze out part of thin juice. Roast the peppers on coals, or in an oven, until a light brown. Then throw them into cold water. Skin and chop them with the tomatoes quite fine, strain off the water, add salt and a little finely-chopped onion. To be eaten with all kinds of meat. It will keep several days.

ARTICHOKES
Mrs. Juan Foster.

This is a most delicious tuber. Mash and peel the artichokes. Cut in pieces. Scald and cook them. Remove them from the soup in which they have been cooked. Put them in a saucepan with oil and fried garlic. Add some of the soup in which the artichokes were cooked and all kinds of spices, and let them boil. If you desire some soup also, season what remains of the water in which the artichokes were boiled, as you would a meat soup. It will be so good that you will doubt whether it is a meat or fish soup.

FRIED ARTICHOKES
A. Sepulveda de Mott.

Select the tenderest. Cut them in pieces, after washing and drying them. Put them in a paste made with flour, two eggs, a little vinegar, and same amount of oil. Season with salt and pepper. Fry them and serve with fried parsley.

STEW—Catalonian Style
Mrs. Juan Foster.

Cut the beef in small squares. Put it in a stew pan with a small piece of bacon, and the right amount of salt. Add some fried onion and a few pieces of garlic. Cover the stew-pan with packing paper, and set over an iron kettle containing water. Put the whole over a slow fire, and shake occasionally, so that it will not burn. In this way you avoid adding water.

GARVANZO POTTAGE
A. Sepulveda de Mott.

After the garvanzos are well boiled, with onion, cook them with oil, in which must have been fried garlic and chili. Put in beaten eggs, and a little cloves and pepper.

FRIJOLES CON QUESO—Beans with Cheese
Mrs. W. S. Moore.

One quart red beans; 4 tablespoons lard; salt; pinch of cayenne; ½ pound good cheese.

Boil the beans until soft, then drain and turn into a fry-ingpan with the lard. Salt to taste. Pepper and cheese grated. Stir until cheese dissolves and thoroughly blends. Serve hot.

FRIJOLES

E. Benton Fremont.

One cup beans; 1 long red pepper; ½ clove garlic; 1 small thin slice bacon.

Soak the beans over night. Cook slowly from eight to ten hours, as big hominy is cooked.

Like hominy, they are even better the next day.

STUFFED CHILIS

Mrs. Vida A. Bixby.

Six green chilis; 2 pounds meat; 2 onions; 1 large ripe tomato; 2 slices bread; 1 pound raisins; 1 pound olives; 1 tablespoon vinegar; salt; pepper; 1 tablespoon sugar; 2 eggs; lard; flour.

Remove stems and seeds from the peppers. Boil the meat until tender. Chop fine. Add onions, tomato and bread—chopped fine. Add raisins, olives, vinegar and salt, sugar and pepper to taste. Fry all together in a little lard. Remove from the fire and stuff the chilis. Beat the eggs to a stiff froth. Add enough flour to make a batter. Dip chilis in the batter and fry in hot lard.

STUFFED CHILIS

Mrs. Carrie Schumacher.

Green chilis; yellow cheese; ½ tablespoon flour; 2 eggs; butter, lard, milk.

Roast the chilis, so that the skins can be easily removed; seed and fill with cheese finely minced, dip them in a batter made of the flour, milk, and beaten eggs, and fry a nice brown, in a little butter and lard mixed. Serve with tomato sauce.

TOMATO SAUCE
Mrs. E. A. Pruess.

One tablespoon lard; ½ teaspoon flour; 4 large tomatoes, chopped; 2 small chilis, chopped. Cook all together until done.

STUFFED PEPPERS
Mrs. J. G. Downey.

One dozen large peppers; 1 onion; ½ cup grated corn; 1 cup meat or chicken; 1 tablespoon lard or butter.

Remove the seeds from the peppers, then throw them upon a bed of live coals, turning them constantly until they are of a light brown; then take them up, throw them into cold water, and remove the skins. Heat the lard or butter in a saucepan, and add the minced onion; when this is hot, add the tomato, and grated corn, with pepper and salt. Let it simmer fifteen minutes, stirring occasionally to prevent burning. Remove from the fire. Add the minced meat or chicken. (A small slice of ham or bacon improves the flavor.) Mix well, stuff the peppers, and fry a light brown.

Sauce for the peppers.—One spoon butter; 1 spoon flour; 1 onion; 1 tomato; green pepper; 2 apples.

Chop the pepper, slice the onion and tomato. Add a few raisins and olives, and sufficient water to make a sauce. Boil until the apples are soft. Put the peppers in this sauce. Simmer a moment, then serve.

GREEN PEPPERS
Spanish Lady.

Beefsteak; green peppers; tomatoes; eggs; apples; raisins; sugar; vinegar; onions; thyme; pepper; salt.

Roast the peppers on hot coals, remove the skins and stuff them.

Stuffing—Boil and chop a steak fine, as for hash, fry chopped onions, one green pepper, one tomato, a little thyme, vinegar, pepper and salt to taste. When stuffed, roll them in flour, dip in beaten egg, and fry in hot fat.

Gravy—Make gravy by frying onions, peppers, tomatoes, a few raisins; slices of apple, thyme, vinegar, and a little sugar.

STUFFED POTATOES (PERU AND BOLIVIA)
Chas. F. Lummis.

Mashed potato; salt, black pepper, raisins, olives; cloves; beef; hard-boiled egg.

Make a dough of the mashed potato, season with salt, pepper. Mince the cooked lean beef fine, and mold it to egg shape, with raisins—stoned, a little ground clove, minced egg and stoned olives. Cover this with the potato dough, and fry the roll, (which should be the size of a large goose egg), in hot lard, taking care not to burn, but only to give it a bright golden brown.

MACARONI
Mrs. Carrie Schumacher.

Macaroni; ham; tomatoes; cheese.

Boil the macaroni in salted water until tender, then drain. Fry some small pieces of ham, add a few tomatoes. Simmer a little while, then add the macaroni, and quite a large piece of cheese, finely minced. Cook until the tomatoes are done, and the cheese melted.

GREEN CORN TAMALES
Maria de los Reyes Dominguez de Francis.

Two dozen ears sweet corn; 1 tablespoon fresh lard; a little salt.

Grate the corn, (saving the inside husks), beat it smooth with the lard, and salt. Put a tablespoon of the mixture into a husk and double it over. Put some of the cobs in a kettle with sufficient hot water to cover them. Lay the tamales on the cobs, with a plate on top to keep them in place. Cover the kettle, and steam them half an hour. Serve hot, with butter.

CHICKEN TAMALES
S. Machado de Bernard.

Take two quarts yellow dried corn, boil in water mixed with ½ teacup lime. Let it boil till well cooked, then wash thoroughly and grind on the *metata*, three times till it becomes very fine.

Take two full-grown chickens and boil in water enough to cover them; season with a little salt; let boil till quite tender, then remove and let cool; then cut in small pieces. Mix with the corn, (which has been rolled on the *metata*) enough of the water in which the chickens were boiled, to make it soft, and add about two cups lard. Season with a little salt, and knead thoroughly.

After this take three dozen red chilis, remove seeds—then roast in a moderate oven for a few seconds. Take out and place in tepid water, then grind on the *metata* several times, together with almost a head of garlic, then strain well.

In a stewing pot place some lard, and when hot drop in one onion, cut fine, and about a spoon of flour, let cook a little while, then drop in the chili; let come to a boil, then add the cut chicken, a cupful raisins, a cupful of olives, about a teaspoon of sugar, a little salt and pepper, and let come to a boil again, then take away from the fire. Let soak in cold water, dry corn leaves. When well soaked, shake them well and apply a thin layer of the corn dough on the half of each leaf, then put a spoon of the stew on the prepared leaf, and cover with the prepared leaves, tie the ends with strings made of the same leaf.

If liked, boiled eggs cut in halves may be placed in each spoon of stew. When the tamales are finished, place them in a large pot with a little boiling water and boil one hour. Any other meat can be used if desired. The *metatas* can be purchased at any Mexican store.

A NICE WAY TO COOK SQUASH.
Mrs. Carrie Schumacher.

Cut the squash, and a little onion. Fry it a light brown in hot lard, then stew until tender, in a little water.

STUFFED SQUASH, BAKED
Mrs. W. S. Moore.

Six young scalloped summer squash; 2 pounds lean veal, minced; 6 tomatoes; 3 green peppers; 1 onion.

Season the above with salt and white pepper, and stuff the squash. Bake in hot oven one hour. Serve in baking dish, hot.

SPANISH RICE
Senorita Epitasia Bustamente.

Into tablespoon boiling salt pork fat, put cupful well washed rice. mixed with teaspoon chopped onion, salt, pepper and taste of mint, fry about five minutes, stirring carefully. Add one quart of cold water, and cook on back of range for one hour.

When serving, use a layer of rice on platter, and a layer of sauce, such as given in Pipian de Leugua, till it is thoroughly seasoned. The sauce must redden the outside.

RICE á la VALENCIA
Mrs. Juan Foster.

Put the rice, with sweet oil, chopped onions, garlic, parsley and tomatoes in a pot, and fry all for awhile. Add water and rice in the proportion of five of water to one of rice, and let it boil until the water is absorbed by the rice. Let it cool and if it is done properly you will find the grains of rice entirely dry and separate from each other.

FRIED RICE
Mrs. A. F. Coronel.

Rice, lard, onions, garlic, salt, black pepper, hot water, tomatoes.

Wash the rice, brown it in hot lard, then add onions, tomatoes, garlic. Cover the whole with hot water. Season with salt and pepper. Let the rice cook thoroughly, adding water as needed, but do not stir it.

TORTILLA
Spanish Lady.

One quart flour; 1 cup milk; salt; 2 tablespoons lard.

Make a dough and knead thoroughly. Take pieces of the dough and pat between the hands until it makes a large round cake, and cook on griddle until brown.

SPANISH BUN
Mrs. A. C. Goodrich.

Two eggs; 1 cup brown sugar; ½ cup butter; ½ cup sweet milk; 1½ cups sifted flour; 1½ teaspoons Cleveland's baking powder.

Bake in a thin cake.

Icing—White of one egg, 1 cup brown sugar. Beat until light, then spread on the cake and set in the oven for a few minutes.

RECIPE FOR PRESERVING ORANGES
Sister Immanuel.

Five dozen oranges; 10 gallons water; 2 pounds common salt.

The oranges should be of good size—thick skinned, and not too ripe. Grate the surface lightly. Place them in a shallow vessel, so that they are not crowded, and let them come to a boil in the water and salt. Take out carefully, and throw them into fresh cold water. Set them in a cool place, changing the water every two hours, for three days. The second day remove the seeds and juice, but not the pulp. This can be done by making an incission in one end of the oranges. Continue to change the water every two hours, wiping each orange dry with a coarse towel, and pressing out the water after each change. Do this gently. Prepare a syrup as follows:

Syrup—first day. Five gallons water; ½ pound white sugar to one pound fruit. Boil over a slow fire three hours, then take out the fruit and let it drip.

Second day—Make a new syrup. Five gallons water; one pound sugar to one pound fruit. The oranges must be put in the syrup when it is cold, then brought to a boil. (If fruit is put in hot syrup, the surface is toughened like leather). Take out fruit and let drip.

Third day—Make a new syrup. Pound for pound, boil to the consistency of thick molasses. When cold put in the oranges. They are now ready for use or for jars.

Lemons and citrons are prepared in the same way.

How to Make Crystallized Chinese Oranges.
Mrs. Juan Foster.

Take oranges not quite ripe, cut off the colored part of the rind carefully with a sharp knife; cut a hole where the stem has been, sufficiently large to take out all the inside. Be careful not to change the form of the orange. When they are clean inside and outside, cover them with water and salt for 24 hours. Then change the water, but this time omit the salt. Do this for five or six days, or until all the bitterness has disappeared. Then put them in boiling water and boil for twenty minutes; then put them immediately in cold water; then allow them to drain while preparing the syrup. The syrup is made by putting equal quantities by weight of sugar and fruit in enough water to give the consistency of ordinary syrup. Boil the fruit in the syrup over a slow fire until the syrup attains the consistency of honey. Take the fruit out and let it dry in a convenient place.

Small lemons or limes are crystallized by the same process, except that they are simply cut in two before being placed in the brine.

LEMON PRESERVES
Maria de los Dominguez de Francis.

Ten pounds fruit; 10 pounds sugar; ½ gallon water.

Grate the lemons well. Make an incision in one end. Put them in water, with two pounds of salt, and boil them a few minutes. Then throw them immediately into cold water. Wash, and squeeze them slightly. Keep them in cold water two days, changing the water twelve times each day, so that the juice and seeds will come out—the last time—squeeze them again, drain, and dry on a towel. The day before they are to be cooked, prepare the syrup, boil, skim, and cool it over night. In the morning, put the lemons which have been drained and dried, into the cold syrup, and boil them seven or eight hours.

PRESERVE OF ORANGE OR LEMON FLOWERS
According to the Formula of Don Diego Granada, Chief Cook of His Majesty, the King Don Felipe III.

Take the flowers from the tree when they are well opened;

wash them, boil them for a little while; change the water and boil them again until they are very tender. Take them out of this last water and when the flowers are cool, open them one by one as you would a book. Put them in a vessel (olla) with their weight of sugar and a little musk. Stir them up with the sugar, slowly; put them over a slow fire until the sugar thickens, spread them on a marble table, separate the flowers one from another as rapidly as possible, and allow to dry.

TO PRESERVE FIGS WHOLE
Marie de la Domingues de Francis.

One-half cup lime; 1 bucket water; syrup for 10 ℔s figs made of 10 ℔s sugar; 1 gal. water, cold.

Use half ripe figs, prick them twice with a fork. Stand them in the lime water over night, in the morning wash, and throw them into cold water, drain them. When the syrup has boiled and been well skimmed, put over the figs and cook them very slowly seven or eight hours.

PRESERVE OF MUSKMELON
Mrs. Juan Foster.

Take a melon not quite ripe, cut it into longitudinal pieces; cut away the rind and the white nearest to the rind and throw away; soak what is left for three days in salted water. Then put them in clear water for six days, changing the water every day. Then boil them until they are tender, rub them in cold water, drain them until all the superfluous moisture has disappeared. Then put them in a round earthen vessel (olla), cover them with clarified sugar (common syrup), and leave them for eight days, so as to absorb the syrup. After this boil them in the syrup for about one hour over a slow fire and keep them in a proper place. If you wish you can put any kind of essence you prefer, or none at all.

TO CURE OLIVES
Mrs. Isabel del Valle, of Camulos.

Cut the olives from the tree when they are not over-ripe. Put them in fresh water and change it every third day until the bitterness is removed. Prepare a lye of wood ashes and if possible let it be the ashes of grape vines, as experience has taught that this is the best. They should remain in this lye twenty-four hours. Take them from it and put them in salt water and keep for use.

HOW TO MAKE OIL FROM OLIVES
Mrs. Juan Foster.

Cut the olives from the tree when quite ripe; keep them for three weeks in the dark, mill them; put the paste in sacks, strong but porous; press them and you have oil of the best quality. To have a second grade of oil put the paste, after being pressed, in hot water, and press it again. This water mixed with the oil should be put in jars or pans, and when the oil comes to the top it must be taken off and filtered and put in bottles.

If you add a little salt to the oil before filtering you will be repaid for the trouble.

CHILI SAUCE
Mrs. W. H. Workman.

Dry red peppers; onions; salt.

Remove the seeds from the peppers; soak them in boiling water until soft; remove the skins by rubbing them through a coarse sieve; season with salt, and a small quantity of finely chopped onions. If too thick add water. Use as a sauce, or in gravies, and stews.

CHILI COLOROW
Mrs. Kenyon Cox, Long Beach.

Eight quarts ripe tomatoes; 1 quart onions; 1 quart strong green peppers; 1 quart strong vinegar; 1 cup sugar; 6 tablespoons salt.

The tomatoes should be measured after peeling, and mashing; the onions and peppers chopped very fine. Boil until thick, bottle and seal.

SPANISH CATSUP

One-half gal. green cucumbers; ½ gal. cabbage; 1 quart tomatoes; 1 pint beans; 1 dozen onions; 1 dozen ears of green corn; 2 teacups white mustard seed; 1 teacup ground mustard; 1 ℔. sugar; 3 tablespoons tumeric; 2 tablespoons grated horseradish; 3 tablespoons celery seed; 2 tablespoons Howland's olive oil; 1 tablespoon mace; 1 tablespoon cinnamon; 1 tablespoon cayenne pepper.

Peel, and slice the cucumbers, sprinkle with salt, and let them stand six hours. Prepare the cabbage in the same way. Chop the onions, let them stand in boiling water half an hour; chop the tomatoes, beans, and corn, scald and drain. Mix all the other ingredients, place in a jar; with the prepared vegetables, and cover with boiling vinegar.

GERMAN MENUS

MRS. J. G. MOSSIN

BREAKFAST
Coffee or Chocolate
Rolls, Kuchen

DINNER
Klœsse   Soup
Raddish   Caviar with Rye Bread
Blue Trout
Roast Young Pig
Red Cabbage   Rice
Fried Goose Liver
Green Peas and Young Carrots
Fricassee Squab
Noodles
Celery Salad
Omelet with Raspberry
Peach Ice
Crackers   Cheese
Coffee

SUPPER
Cold Roast Ham
Pickled Trout
Herring Salad
Rye Bread
Pickled Goose
Pickled Mushroom
Spiced Peaches
Schwartz Brod Torte

AFTERNOON COFFEE

Rye Bread   Unsalted Butter
Jelly   Preserved Fruit
Chocolate Cake
Leb Kuchen
Apfel Kuchen
Pfeffer Nusse
Blitz Kuchen
Zimmet Sterne

GERMAN DEPARTMENT

SOUP STOCK
Mrs. John G. Mossin.

Three quarts water; 4 ℔s. beef; 1½ ℔s mutton; veal knuckle; 1 red pepper; 1 turnip; 1 carrot; 1 onion; salt, pepper.

Boil slowly five hours, strain, cool; when ready to use, take off the fat.

MILK SOUP WITH PRUNES
Mrs. J. Johansen.

Boil 1 ℔ dried prunes, until soft, in a pan; put in with them 1 quart of milk (less a little to stir the flour). Let come to a boil, then stir in a tablespoon of flour mixed with the reserved milk, a little of the yellow rind of a lemon and sweeten to taste; let boil up, then turn into a tureen, sprinkle sugar over it, and serve.

BUTTERMILK SOUP
Mrs. J. Johansen.

Take 1 cup rice, pearl barley or sago, and boil until soft, in water with some currants, raisins, a stick of cinnamon, and a little grated lemon peel (the yellow, not the white). When the above ingredients are well cooked, add the buttermilk, stirring rapidly to prevent its being grainy.

FISH SOUP
Mrs. J. Johansen.

Take carp or codfish, cut up and roll in flour. Toast some bread, butter well, then place the fish between the pieces of toast. Boil some carrots, cut in cubes, in some bullion until tender; season with parsley, mash well and strain. Steam the fish and toast while boiling the bullion; then mash fine and add to the bullion; salt to taste. Serve with toast well browned in butter; cut in cubes and put in the soup.

DUMPLINGS FOR ANY KIND OF SOUP
Mrs. J. Johansen.

One and one-fourth ℔s cold boiled potatoes; ¼ ℔ butter; 2 whole eggs; yolks of 2 more; 1 tablespoon flour.

Grate the potatoes and put in frying pan with the butter, and thicken with grated bread; stir well but do not let it brown; turn it into a dish to cool. Take the two whole eggs and the two yolks beaten separately, stir in the flour and a pinch of salt. Mix all the ingredients together with a spoon and drop into the soup; slip the spoon into the soup every time you put in a dumpling. Boil them about three minutes

MEAT DUMPLINGS FOR MEAT SOUP
Mrs. J. Johansen.

Take a porterhouse steak and scrape it with a sharp knife, and sprinkle with salt. For an ordinary-sized family, take 2 eggs and mix with the meat; add bread crumbs or crackers, season with salt. Make into balls the size of a walnut and drop into the soup; boil about five minutes.

EGG DUMPLINGS OR CLÖSE
Mrs. J. G. Mossin.

Three eggs; 3 tablespoons butter; 4½ soda crackers, crumbed.

Cream butter, add eggs, then cracker crumbs. Mix one hour before using. Roll in small balls and cook fifteen minutes. Be sure your soup is boiling before adding dumplings.

BAKED PICKEREL
Mrs. J. G. Mossin.

Fish; salt; bread crumbs; butter; 1 cup sour cream; 1 tablespoon vinegar; lemon; parsley.

Prepare the fish, place in a baking pan; rub with salt and bread crumbs; baste with butter. When nearly done, mix the vinegar with the sour cream, turn into the pan and let it boil. Serve very hot, and garnish with parsley and slices of lemon.

FRIED SMELT
Mrs. J. G. Mossin.

Smelt; milk; salt; bread crumbs; flour; lard.

Soak the fish in milk two hours, then dry thoroughly; rub with salt; roll in bread crumbs and flour; fry in hot lard.

FISH, TROUT
Mrs. J. G. Mossin.

Fish, weighing 4 ℔s; onion; bay leaves; vinegar; pepper; salt; lemon; parsley.

Clean the fish, leaving on head and fins ; put in a pan with a few slices of onion and a few bay leaves, half cover with boiling vinegar, (if vinegar is very sharp, dilute with water); add salt and pepper; simmer gently fifteen minutes. Cover with blotting paper; set aside to cool. When ready to serve, garnish with parsley and sliced lemon. Oil may be added.

HERRING SALAD
Mrs. A. Knoch.

Six herring; 3 ℔s roast veal; 6 pickles; 6 beets; 3 apples; 3 hard boiled eggs; 2 tablespoons Howland's olive oil; salt; pepper; mustard; vinegar.

Scale and soak the herring over night in water or sour milk. In the morning, bone and cut into small squares; cut veal, pickles, boiled beets, and green apples in the same way. Mix these ingredients thoroughly, being careful not to mash them. Make dressing of the yolks of eggs creamed with olive oil; adding salt; pepper, vinegar and mustard to taste. Garnish with chopped beets, pickles, parsley and hard boiled eggs.

STEWED CHICKEN
Mrs. Carrie Schumacher.

Cut the chicken in pieces; fry very brown, turning it frequently with a large spoon; season with salt and pepper. Brown a little minced onion; before the chicken is brown enough, sprinkle over it with a little browned flour; add water. Stew until tender.

FRICASSEED VEAL
Mrs. A. Knoch.

Four lbs veal (breast preferred); butter, size of a hen's egg; salt; pepper; 1 medium sized onion; mace; lemon peel; 1 tablespoon flour.

Cut the veal into pieces, two or three inches square; wash in cold water; then scald in hot water; sprinkle with salt and pepper and put in a stew pan containing the heated butter. Turn meat, being careful not to brown it; add the onion, mace, the peel of half a lemon (the yellow only) and water sufficient to cover. Cook until tender, keeping the pan covered. Mix the flour with enough water to make a creamy mixture. Add this when the veal is done; boil three minutes. The juice of a lemon added just before the thickening is a great improvement.

FRICASEED CHICKEN
Mrs. A. Knoch.

Same as fricasseed veal, except the chicken is cut at the joints. Care should be taken to avoid crushing the bones. Instead of sprinkling with pepper, add ½ teaspoon of pepper corns; also 3 or 4 mushrooms. The gizzard should not be put in until the meat is half done.

PIGEONS STEWED
Mrs. Carrie Shumacher.

Stew like chickens, and serve on toast. Very nice.

DRESSING FOR PIGEONS
Mrs. J. G. Mossin.

Chop the livers and hearts of six pigeons; use enough calf's liver to make a teacupful; one cup bread crumbs; two eggs; chop a little parsley; small piece of onion; ¼ cup currants.

Then fill the pigeons. Take a spoonful of butter, one of lard, half an onion. Let them brown. Lay in your pigeons. Fry them brown, then add a cup of soup stock. Let them simmer gently until tender. Add a tablespoon flour, ¾ cup sweet cream, 1 tablespoon catsup; for gravy.

ROAST DUCK, A SWEDISH RECIPE
Mrs. Carl Schutze.

One duck; 1 medium-sized lemon; 2 small apples; ¾ cup
sultana raisins; 1 teaspoon flour.

Rub duck well with salt, and pepper inside and out.
Thicken the juice of the lemon with flour, and slice the
apples into the batter thus made, until every piece is coated.
Wash sultanas and remove stems. Put a few raisins in the
duck, then a few slices of apple, until moderately well filled.
Sew with a cord. Cut off the neck, so as to leave the skin
long enough to tie over the end neatly. Bind wings to the
sides. Roast two hours in a moderate oven.

ROAST DUCK DRESSING
Mrs. J. G. Mossin.

Two hard-boiled eggs; 3 cups bread crumbs; 1 cup sausage meat; ½ cup shredded olives; ¼ cup raisins; salt;
pepper; a little thyme.

If too dry, moisten with a very little milk.

PICKLED GOOSE
Mrs. J. G. Mossin.

Goose; boiling water; 2 teaspoons whole cloves; 2 teaspoons whole pepper; 6 bay leaves; 1 cup vinegar.

Cut the goose as for fricassee, remove all fat, cover with
boiling water, and cook tender. Remove the meat from the
stock, skim off all fat, return stock to the kettle, boil until
there is only enough to cover the meat. While boiling—add
cloves, pepper, bay leaves, and vinegar. Pour this over the
meat. To be eaten cold.

GERMAN RELISH

One goose; 1 pint cider vinegar; pepper; salt.

Remove the loose fat from a nice goose. Season with salt
and pepper. Boil until nearly done in as little water as possible, then add the vinegar, and cook until very tender; then,
leaving in the bones, pack in a stone jar. Sliced cold,
this is a dainty dish.

Turkey and chicken may be prepared in the same way.

DRESSING FOR ROAST
Mrs. J. G Mossin.

Half pound sausage meat; 2 eggs; 1 small onion; 2 cups bread crumbs; ½ nutmeg; 2 tablespoons chopped parsley; 1 apple; 1 handful raisins; pepper; salt. Mix well.

Pig six weeks old.

BEEF CUTLETS
Mrs. W. W. Holt.

Take four parts of beef and one part of suet. Chop both fine. Season with salt and pepper. Form into pats. Beat one egg, add a little cloves and nutmeg, then dip the pats into the egg, roll in cracker crumbs and fry in butter.

MEAT ROLLS
Mrs. W. W. Holt.

Take several kinds, or one kind, of boiled meat, and chop fine. Fry one good-sized onion in butter, and add 1 teaspoon flour. Add the meat and two eggs—beaten, a little nutmeg, salt and pepper, and cook a few minutes. Bake an omelet and spread the above mixture over the omelet and roll, then cut in slices, dip them in egg, roll in cracker crumbs and fry till brown in butter.

MEAT BALLS
Mrs. W. W. Holt.

Chop fine some beef, or veal, with a little raw ham. Beat the yolks of two eggs, add 1 tablespoon sour cream, four crackers, rolled fine, a little grated lemon peel and nutmeg. Beat the whites of the eggs to a stiff froth, and add to the above mixture with the meat. Beat all well together, and drop off a spoon into hot lard and fry.

THE LEAVINGS OF SOUP MEATS
Mrs. W. W. Holt.

Slice the meat and lay it in vinegar over night, then dip it in a beaten egg, season with nutmeg, roll in cracker crumbs and fry in butter.

POTATO DUMPLINGS
Mrs. J. G. Mossin.

Six potatoes (good size); 1 tablespoon salt; 1 cup flour; 4 eggs; 1 slice bread; butter.

Boil the potatoes, and when cold, grate them, and mix with the salt, flour, eggs and bread—cut in small squares, and fried in butter—mold into balls like croquettes, put in boiling water, and boil fifteen or twenty minutes, or they can be steamed half an hour.

To be eaten with meat gravy.

ASPARAGUS
Mrs. George Kerckhoff.

Boil the asparagus in salt water until soft—from forty-five minutes to an hour and a half, and serve with either of the following sauces:

Egg Sauce.—Two whole eggs, or the yolks of three; 1 teaspoon flour; 2 tablespoons sweet cream; ½ cup asparagus water; a pinch of nutmeg; butter—the size of an egg; vinegar to taste.

Stir over the fire until it comes to the boiling point, then add a small piece of butter, and serve immediately.

Browned Cracker Sauce.—Two tablespoons butter; 1 tablespoon rolled cracker.

Brown the butter, then add the crumbs. When well-browned take up quickly.

CABBAGE
Mrs. Carrie Shumacher.

One cabbage; 1 tablespoon lard; flour; milk; nutmeg.

Boil the cabbage until tender, drain and chop fine. Have the lard very hot, put the cabbage in it, sprinkle it with a little flour, add milk—when it comes to a boil, grate in a little nutmeg, if liked, and serve.

RED CABBAGE
Mrs. J. F. Ellis.

Red cabbage; roast pork drippings; onions; flour; vinegar; salt; butter; sugar; pepper.

Halve the cabbage, remove the coarse leaves and large leaf ribs, and cut in fine long strips. Boil in just enough water to prevent burning, add the drippings and some chopped onions; put in the cabbage gradually, boil it briskly in an uncovered vessel a quarter of an hour; then cover closely and boil it from a half to three quarters of an hour; add salt very carefully. When the cabbage is cooked (not too tender), stir in a little flour, being careful that the liquid is neither too thick nor too thin; put a small piece of butter on top, and stir in a little vinegar and one or two teaspoons of sugar. Red cabbage should be cooked in granite ware; iron or tin dis· colors it.

BOILED SPINACH
Mrs. A. Knoch.

Spinach; butter; 1 tablespoon flour; milk; salt; pepper: nutmeg; hard boiled eggs; fried bread.

Carefully pick over and wash the spinach; boil until tender in enough salted water to cover; drain in a colander; chop fine on a chopping board. Heat a piece of butter in a skillet; stir in the flour, add milk sufficient to make a thick gravy; season with salt, pepper, and nutmeg. Put in the spinach and boil two or three minutes. Boil eggs five minutes, cut lengthwise and spread over the top of the dish. Bread cut in strips half an inch wide by two inches long, fried in butter, may be added, sticking them upright between the eggs.

RYE BREAD
Mrs. J. G. Mossin

Two tablespoons salt; 1 cake Magic yeast; 1 pint lukewarm water; ½ cake compressed yeast; 1 cup sour cream; 1 quart warm milk; rye flour; wheat flour.

At night, make a stiff batter with the warm water rye flour, and Magic yeast. In the morning, add the compressd yeast, cream and milk, and equal parts of rye and white flour sufficient to knead well. Bake in hot oven.

NOODLES
Mrs. J. G. Mossin.

Th ee eggs; enough flour to make stiff dough, knead as

for bread, roll very thin; let them dry about an hour, then roll as for jelly cake; slice very thin with a sharp knife. Boil in a quart of water with salt to season; boil fifteen minutes then drain in colander. Brown cracker crumbs in butter, two tablespoons butter, same of cracker crumbs. Put noodles on a platter covering with the brown crumbs.

NOODLES
Mrs. E. A. Preuss.

One cup flour; 1 egg; salt.

This quantity makes one dish of noodles. Mix into a stiff dough; roll very thin; spread on a cloth until dry enough to fold without sticking. Roll into a long roll, cut it fine crosswise, then toss them until they are separated into long narrow strips. Put them into boiling salted water; boil five minutes, drain. Brown a large piece of butter, add some bread crumbs and pour it over the noodles. These noodles make a nice dish.

A NICE LUNCHEON DISH
Mrs. E. A. Preuss.

Fry cold noodles in hot butter until brown, and beat in three or four eggs.

FLY AWAY
Mrs. E. A. Preuss.

Cut noodle dough into squares; fry in very hot lard; sprinkle sugar over them while hot. They will be deliciously crisp.

GERMAN PANCAKES
Mary Roach.

One pint flour; 6 eggs; 1 teaspoon salt; 2 cups sweet milk.

Make a batter of milk, flour and salt; beat it thoroughly; add the beaten yolks, beat again; then the frothed whites. Fry on hot griddle with plenty of rendered butter.

GERMAN PANCAKES
Mrs. J. Johansen.

Three to 5 eggs; ½ cup flour; ¾ pint milk.

Beat the eggs separately then add the milk and flour and pinch of salt. Take a large frying pan well greased with

butter and lard; pour the batter in and fry till brown, and
turn them over.   Serve with butter and cinnamon.

POTATO CAKES
Mrs. J. G. Mossin.

Four raw potatoes; 2 slices bread; 3 eggs; 1 cup boiling
milk.

Grate, and drain the potatoes; pour the boiling milk on
the bread; when cold, add potatoes, and eggs; fry like pan-
cakes, on a griddle.   Serve any kind of pickles with them, or
preserved fruits.

RICE CAKES
Mrs. J G. Mossin.

One cup rice; 1 tablespoon butter; 2 tablespoons flour; 3
eggs; salt; cinnamon; powdered sugar.

Boil the rice, adding salt, when the rice is done add the
butter and cook, then add eggs, and flour.   Fry in hot lard,
sprinkle with powdered sugar, and cinnamon.   Serve with
maple, or raspberry syrup.   Some prefer powdered sugar, and
lemon juice.

SPÄTZLE
Mrs. T. Masac.

One cup flour; 1 egg; a little water and salt.

To each cup of flour, take one egg, a very little water and
salt.   Beat up till light.   Drip through a colander with holes
about ½ inch in diameter into boiling salt water.   The
spätzle will rise almost immediately to the surface and are
ready to be drained.   Fry for a few minutes in butter and add
a few fried onions.   Serve with stew.

BRIOCHE
Miss Ruth Childs.

Dissolve ½ cake compressed yeast in one cup lukewarm
water.   Stir in ½ pound flour, and let it rise in a moderately
warm place, twice as high and fall again.   Stir up in another
bowl ½ ℔ butter and 8 eggs, one after the other; mix with
the other dough and add 1 teaspoon salt and 2 tablespoons sugar with ½ ℔ more flour.   Let it rise again and

set in the ice box for twelve hours, very near the ice. Take out, shape as you wish and let rise again. Bake in a moderate oven for three-fourths of an hour.

APFEL STRUDEL
Mrs. T. Masac.

One ℔. flour; ½ ℔. butter; ½ ℔. leaf lard tried out; 2 cups bread crumbs, butter, sugar, cinnamon, to taste; a little finely-chopped lemon rind; currants; finely-sliced apple.

Shortening and flour to be equal weight, the shortening to be kept on ice. Rub the flour and lard thoroughly together, add sufficient ice water to make the dough of the proper consistency to roll out. Sprinkle flour on pie-board, the dough rolled out to the thickness of about one-sixteenth of an inch, then scatter thin slices of ice cold butter over it, fold the dough over and again roll out, and repeat the process until all the butter is used. Keep on ice until used. Next fry the bread crumbs in butter seasoned with sugar and ground cinnamon to taste; a little finely-chopped lemon rind may be added. Take the dough, roll out on a tablecloth sprinkled with flour, stretch it as thin as possible with the hands. Sprinkle over this surface all of the fried bread crumbs, currants to taste, and a liberal share of apple. Roll up the strudel, pinch the ends together, put in a buttered pan, cover with a well-buttered paper, and bake in a hot oven, until quite brown. Good hot or cold, or sliced and fried the next day.

GERMAN PIE CRUST FOR BANANA TURNOVERS
Mrs. J. G. Mossin.

Seven ounces butter and lard mixed in equal parts; 1 egg; 1 teaspoon sugar; ½ teaspoon cinnamon; rind of 1 lemon, grated; 1 pint sifted flour; 3 tablespoons milk.

Roll thin as cooky dough. Peel bananas and cover the crust as for turnovers; bake for fifteen minutes. Use for dessert or for an afternoon coffee. This crust can be used for any fruit; can be used after standing in ice box.

KUCHEN WITH BAKING POWDER
Mrs. J. G. Mossin.

Two cups flour; ½ cup milk; 2 eggs; 11 tablespoons butter; 2 tablespoons sugar; 1 teaspoon Cleveland's baking powder; granulated sugar; cinnamon or grated almonds.

Mix, and spread thin in a buttered pan; melt a teaspoon of butter and spread it over the top; sprinkle with granulated sugar and cinnamon. Bake fifteen minutes. Grated almonds can be used instead of cinnamon, or apples cut very fine can be put on top with sugar and cinnamon.

KUCHEN WITH YEAST
Mrs. J. G. Mossin.

One-half cake compressed yeast; 1 tablespoon sugar; 1 cup lukewarm milk; 1½ cups flour; 1 cup butter; 4 eggs; 1 cup sugar; 1 cup flour; ½ cup seeded raisins; 1 tablespoon finely sliced citron.

Dissolve yeast and tablespoon sugar in the warm milk; mix with one and one-half cups flour. Let it rise one hour; then add one cup flour, butter, sugar, eggs, and fruit. Stir one hour. Butter a deep cake mold; pour in the batter, and let it rise two hours. Bake three quarters of an hour.

BROWN LEB KUCHEN
Miss Ruth Childs.

One quart honey; 1 ℔ sugar; 2 ℔s flour; 1 ℔ almonds; ¼ ℔ orange peel; ¼ ℔ citron; 2 oz. cinnamon; rind of 1 lemon; ½ teaspoon soda.

Warm the honey; chop the other ingredients; mix all together, and let stand one half hour. Roll out a quarter of an inch thick and cut into squares; let them stand over night in a warm room. Bake in a slow oven. Use boiled icing.

COFFEE CAKE
Mrs. E. F. C. Klokke.

One quart flour; 1 pint warm milk; ½ cake compressed yeast; 1 teaspoon salt; ½ cup sugar; ½ cup butter; ½ lemon; 2 eggs; flour; cinnamon; cracker or bread crumbs.

Stir the flour, milk and yeast to a smooth batter; when

light and spongy, add the salt, eggs, sugar, butter, lemon,
and flour to make it stiff enough to roll. Roll it an inch in
thickness; lay in a pan; spread warm butter over it, and
sprinkle with sugar, cinnamon, and either cracker or bread
crumbs.

LOAF COFFEE CAKE
Mrs. Rutz.

One ℔ flour; 1 pint warm milk; ½ yeast cake; ½ ℔
butter, beaten to a cream; 1 cup sugar; 4 eggs.

Mix flour, milk and yeast cake, and put in a moderately
warm place to rise. When light, add the butter, sugar and
eggs; beat for one half hour. Put in a well-buttered mold
and let it rise to the top. Bake in a moderate oven.

LIGHTNING COOKIES
Mrs. J. G. Mossin.

One-half ℔ butter, ½ ℔ sugar; 1 ℔ flour; ¼ ℔ almonds;
4 eggs; grated rind of ½ lemon; cinnamon.

Cream the butter; add eggs, sugar and lemon, stirring
constantly, then the flour. Spread the dough as thin as a
wafer on greased tins; sprinkle with sugar, cinnamon and
shaved almonds. Soon as baked, cut in diagonal squares and
remove from the tins.

CHOCOLATE COOKIES
Mrs. J. G. Mossin.

One-fourth ℔ brown sugar; ½ ℔ white sugar; 1 tablespoon
butter; 2 eggs; 7 oz. Ghirardelli's chocolate (grated); 7 oz.
flour; 1 lemon rind; 1 tablespoon chopped citron; ½ teaspoon
cinnamon; ¼ teaspoon cloves. Let stand one hour; then roll,
cut and bake.

SPONGE CAKE WITH SWEET ALMOND MILK
M. Bandini de Winston.

One-half gallon milk; 1½ ℔s ground sweet almonds; a
few sticks of cinnamon; sugar to taste.

Boil to the consistency of molasses, and let it cool. Divide
the sponge cake into squares, then horizontally into half
squares; place a layer of cake on a platter; cover with the
almond milk; put some fruit jelly over the milk, and over

the jelly another layer of cake; and so on, until it is of the desired thickness.   Cover with the milk; ornament with raisins and ground cinnamon.

MACCAROONS
Mrs. Rutz.

One-half ℔ almonds; 1 ℔ pulverized sugar; whites of 3 eggs; juice of 1 lemon and part of the grated peel.

Mix thoroughly the almonds (which have been blanched and pounded with the white of one egg) with the sugar, whites of two eggs and lemon juice and peel.   Stir this mixture constantly and quickly over the fire until it loosens readily from the stewpan.   Turn into another vessel; make into small cakes; put on a baking tin; spread over with paper or wafer; place in a partially cooled oven and bake slowly to a reddish yellow color.

CHOCOLATE CAKE
Mrs. J. G. Mossin.

Two cups sugar; 1 cup butter; 4 eggs; 4 sticks Ghirardelli's chocolate; ½ cup milk; 1 cup chopped almonds; ½ cup mashed potato; 2 cups flour; 2 teaspoons Cleveland's baking powder; 1 teaspoon cinnamon; 1 nutmeg; 1 teaspoon cloves.

ORANGE KALTSCHALE
Mrs. Rutz.

Grate the rind of a few oranges on sugar; peel them and cut in eight parts; dip them in powdered sugar and lay them in a tureen, and let stand one hour; then add as much water as you require.   Serve with lady fingers or sponge cake.

TUTTI FRUTTI
Mrs. George Kerchhoff.

One quart milk; ¾ cup starch; ½ cup sugar; yolks 6 eggs; vanilla or lemon peeling.

Make into a custard and let it come to the boiling point. Put in a glass dish a thick layer of any kind of fruit, or mixture of fruits, fresh or stewed.   When the custard is cold pour it over the fruit, and cover,the whole with the beaten whites of eggs. Heat an iron shovel and hold over the eggs until they color a light brown.

TO MAKE COFFEE
Mrs. J. Johansen.

Have the coffee ground fine (Mocha and Java) and add a little chiccory. Put the required amount of coffee in a cotton flannel bag, and pour the required amount of boiling water over it quickly; cover it and let it steam five minutes.

GERMAN WAY OF MAKING COFFEE
Mrs. E. A. Preuss.

Have a cone-shaped perforated tin (holes not too small). About an inch from the top should be a band to rest on the coffee pot. A bag of flannel or cheese cloth large enough to overlap the funnel. Put the coffee in the bag and pour boiling water over it; (the water must be *boiling*), and let it drip—the water runs through quickly. The coffee is delicious.

PICKLED MUSHROOMS
Mrs. J. G. Mossin.

One spoon butter; 1 can mushrooms; vinegar or lemon juice.

Stew the mushrooms in the butter very gently for a few minutes; add lemon juice or vinegar sufficient to cover; put them in a glass jar lightly covered; place in a kettle of boiling water and boil fifteen minutes. When cold; they are fit to serve.

PICKLED CUCUMBERS
Mrs. Rutz.

Cucumbers; salt; small white onions; peppers, red and green; bay leaves; horse radish; allspice; white mustard seed; whole black pepper; vinegar.

Peel ripe cucumbers; cut in two, lengthwise; remove the seeds; rub with salt, and lay upon platters for twenty-four hours. Then wipe them dry; cut in pieces to suit. Pack in glass jars alternating layers of cucumbers with layers of spices. Fill the jars with boiled vinegar.

FRENCH DEPARTMENT

BOUILLON
Mme. V. Chevallier.

One pound beef; 1 carrot; 1 onion; 1 spoon lard; ½ glass water; *1 pint boiling water;* salt.

Cut the beef in small pieces, put in a sauce pan with the carrot, onion, lard and half glass water. Simmer quarter of an hour, until it begins to stick to the pan, then, pour on the boiling water, salt, and boil it three quarters of an hour. Strain and serve.

LOBSTER `a la CREOLE
Mrs. E. A. Preuss.

One large, or two small lobsters; 3 tomatoes; ½ a green pepper; 1 cup cream; a good sized piece of butter; a little flour; toast.

Cut the lobsters in small pieces. Cook and strain the tomatoes and pepper. Melt the butter, add the flour, cream, and strained tomatoes. Cook a little while. Serve on toast.

STUFFED PIGEONS
Mrs. C. Ducommun.

Mince the hearts and livers of the pigeons, and some meat. Soak milk bread in hot milk, squeeze dry, and mix it with the meat. Add parsley, marjoram, pepper, salt, and a little bacon. Fill the pigeons and sew them up. Fry them in butter. When done remove the butter, and replace it with good broth. Add a little vinegar and spices. Thicken the sauce with a piece of butter rolled in flour.

CHICKEN FRICASSEE
Mme. V. Chevallier.

One chicken; butter; 1 spoon flour; glass water; salt, pepper; parsley; 3 egg yolks; 1 lemon.

Pluck, clean, and singe the fowl. Cut in pieces, and soak half an hour in tepid water to whiten the flesh, drain. Stir the flour and a piece of butter in a sauce pan until the butter is melted. Add water, salt, pepper, parsley. Put in chicken and boil an hour and a half. Take the chicken out, stir into the gravy, the yolks and the juice of the lemon.

Mushrooms are an excellent addition.

CHESTNUT FILLING FOR POULTRY
Mrs. C. Ducommun.

Three dozen chestnuts, boiled; milk bread; hot milk, pepper, salt, liver and heart of a fowl; 1 egg; lemon peel, 1 onion; butter.

Peel and pound the chestnuts fine in a mortar. Soak a few slices of bread in the milk, then squeeze it dry. Season with salt and pepper, and a little lemon peel, finely cut. Mince the heart and liver. Mix all with the white of an egg. Fry the chopped onion in butter, then add the other ingredients. Stir until it is thoroughly mixed and heated, then fill the fowl.

BEEF `a la MODE
Mme. V. Chevallier.

Beef; lard; ½ a calf's foot; 1 onion; 1 carrot; 1 laurel leaf; 1 small clove of garlic; a few cloves; salt, pepper, water.

Tie a layer of lard on top of the roast. Place in saucepan with a spoon of lard, calf's foot, onion, carrot, laurel, thyme, garlic, salt and pepper. Pour over this a glass of water. Cook until the meat is very tender. Strain the gravy before serving. Time four hours. Slow fire and pan well covered.

FILET de BOEUF
Mrs. C. Ducommun

Cut pieces of tenderloin the thickness of a finger; beat them well. Season with salt, pepper, and a few drops of sweet oil. Lay one upon another, and set them aside. Fry each piece on both sides in hot butter. Lay them in a hot dish and keep it warm. Remove the fat from the gravy, and add to it some broth, a lump of butter mixed with flour, herbs cut fine; cook a few minutes, then pour over the meat and serve, or the meat can be heated for a few minutes in the gravy, and then served.

CALF'S FEET
Mrs. C. Ducommuu.

Boil the feet three hours in four quarts water, remove the large bones, split and lay them in a sauce pan. Mix a little flour with two ounces of butter. Add it with pepper, salt, mace, and a little vinegar, to two cups of the liquor in which the feet were boiled. Simmer this ten minutes, garnish with sliced lemon. Serve very hot. The remainder of the jelly may be used as jelly.

MEAT BALLS
Mrs. C. Ducommun.

Two pounds veal; ½ pound bacon; 3 eggs, whites; milk bread; salt; pepper; nutmeg; fine herbs; lemon peel.

Mince the veal and bacon very fine. Add all the other ingredients. Mix thoroughly. Form into balls the size of a walnut. Cook in boiling water. When done, they rise to the surface. Place on a platter, and pour over them a white sauce, made of butter and flour, seasoned with a few drops of vinegar.

FOIE ä le POULETTE
Mrs. C. Ducommuu.

One calf's liver; 1 onion, good size; flour; butter· pepper; salt; broth; vinegar.

Cut the liver in thin slices, dredge with flour, mince the onion and fry it in butter, then the liver. Cook a little, then add the other articles, a few drops of vinegar, a piece of butter. Stir until well mixed and serve.

FRESH PEAS
Mrs. C. Ducommun.

Put the peas over a brisk fire, with a piece of butter and a teaspoon flour. Stir until the butter is melted and well mixed. Then add a little boiling water. Cook half an hour, then season with salt, very little pepper, and a little sugar if liked, and they are ready to serve.

SQUASH AND CORN
Mrs. C. Ducommun.

Three ears corn; 3 squashes; 1 spoon lard or butter; 1 onion, minced fine; 1 tomato, cut fine; 1 green pepper, cut fine; salt to taste.

Heat the lard or butter in a saucepan. When very hot, fry the onion a little, then add all the other vegetables. Cover closely, and stir frequently to prevent scorching.

MACARONI
Mrs. Carrie Schumacher.

Put the macaroni in salted boiling water. Cook until tender, then drain. Fry small pieces of ham. Add a few tomatoes. Simmer a little while, then add macaroni and quite a large piece of cheese, minced fine. Cook until the cheese is melted, and tomatoes done.

BATTER PUDDING
Mrs. C. Ducommun.

Three tablespoons sifted flour, heaped; 2 cups milk; 6 eggs.

Beat whites and yolks separately, very light. Mix the milk and flour. Add the yolks, the whites last, bake immediately. Serve with sauce.

RUSSIAN DEPARTMENT

RUSSIAN BEET SOUP
Mrs. P. A. Demens.

Take 3 lbs fat beef or pork; 1 or 2 bay leaves and 5 or 10 grains pepper. Boil about two hours or until tender, then add some cut-up cabbage and two tablespoons vinegar. Carefully wash, but not cut before boiling, five or six beets, and boil until tender; slip off the outside and cut into thin slices. Add a heaping teaspoon of flour to soup, mix well; season with salt, put the boiled beets into the soup and boil twice. Serve with sliced meat.

CABBAGE SOUP
Mrs. P. A. Demens.

Three lbs fat beef; 2 carrots; 2 onions; 1 turnip; 1 bay leaf; 5 to 10 grains pepper; ½ head cabbage; 1 tablespoon flour; parsley.

Cook, and strain the stock, add to it the cabbage, cut into twenty pieces, stir in the flour, boil twice; when about to serve, add some parsley and a little pepper.

RUSSIAN SALAD
Mrs. E. R. Smith.

Clean and boil in separate kettles red beets, carrots, and potatoes. Cut them in good slices and season each with salt, pepper, and butter. Garnish a platter with fresh lettuce, arranging the slices of potatoes, then the beets, more potatoes, and the carrots to finish. Serve with salad dressing. This makes a very showy dish if arranged with care.

Sweet Sauce for Pudding, Cauliflower, Asparagus, etc.
Mrs. P. A. Demens.

Six lumps sugar; 6 eggs, yolks; 1 dinner glass water; 1 slices lemon.

Beat the eggs; powder the sugar; add water and lemon. Put over a slow fire, stirring constantly, and when high and frothy, pour over pudding.

CRANBERRY PUDDING
Mrs. P. A. Demens.

Two cups cranberries; 1 cup sugar; ½ cup cornstarch; 1 glass water; cinnamon.

Of the cranberries make six or seven cups of juice, add the sugar, cinnamon, and cornstarch mixed with water. Stir well, serve hot. Boil in porcelain dish.

FARINA PUDDING
Mrs. P. A. Demens.

Five cups cream; 1⅛ cups farina; 1 cup sugar; ½ lb ground almonds; 1 teaspoon vanilla; bread crumbs; a little water.

Boil all together, then turn into a porcelain bowl, sprinkle with bread crumbs and bake.

APPLE SOUFFÉ
Mrs. P. A Demens.

Six baked apples; 6 whites of eggs; ¾ cup powdered sugar; cream.

Mash the apples; beat the whites; mix them, adding gradually half a cup of sugar. Place in a porcelain platter, set it in the oven for about ten minutes to brown. Serve at once with cream.

RAISIN MAKING IN CALIFORNIA

JAMES BOYD, Riverside, Cal.

Our best table raisins are made from a white grape called the Muscat of Alexandria, and by some the Muscatel.   Our seedless raisins come from the large clusters of raisins picked off in packing, also from the broken clusters when putting them through the stemmer preparatory to assorting and packing. There is also a seedless grape called the Sultana, which makes a very excellent raisin for cakes, etc.   The Sultana, as well as a new variety of seedless grapes called the Thompson's Seed-less, do well in California.   The Zante currant which is made from a small, seedless black grape, has not so far been success-fully grown in California.   These varieties of grapes, which are natives of Europe, do not succeed in the States beyond the Rocky mountains, for climatic reasons.

Our California grapes are grown in the same way that the native grape is grown in the Eastern States, except that we do not trellis them or need to protect them in winter, and in pruning, which is done every spring, they are cut back so that they look like a row of dry stumps until they start growing in the spring when the vineyards look beautiful in their rich green.

The grapes begin to ripen in August, but for raisin making they have to be very ripe, and are not fit to make into raisins until they are rich and full of sugar.   Grapes that are fit to make into raisins require to be very solid and fleshy, unlike wine grapes, that require plenty of juice.   When picking, which is usually well along in September and early in October, all imperfect berries are removed from the clusters and the bunches are then laid on trays, which are made of thin lumber the size being usually two feet by three feet.   They are left in the sun for the curing process, until the exposed surfaces begin to shrivel, which happens generally in ten days or two weeks, when they are turned by simply placing an empty tray on top of a full one and reversing the two, when the fresh surface is left exposed to the sun for about two weeks longer, or until they are properly cured, when they are slidden off the trays into large boxes called sweat boxes; where they are kept until the moisture is equalized through the whole and the stems get tough, when they are ready for packing.

The packing is usually done in large packing houses by firms who make a business of packing and marketing the fruit. The packing is usually done by women and girls for all choice fruit, but for loose raisins which are generally shipped in sacks; machinery is much used for stemming and cleaning, and men usually do this part of the work.

In the early years of raisin making everything was packed in boxes, but now much of the fruit is put in sacks to save expense for boxes and packing.

The process of raisin making is clean and agreeable all through. The production has increased so within the last five years, that California furnishes nearly enough to supply the whole of the United States. Owing to lack of co-operation among the growers, the business is not as remunerative as in former years, but steps are being taken to remedy the evil complained of.

DRIED FIGS

As Prepared by D. H. BURNHAM, Riverside, Contributed by
MRS. IOLA M. COLBURN.

Use White Smyrna, or some thin-skinned variety of white
fig, thoroughly ripe when picked, and must be dried quickly.
Use raisin trays for drying. All trays filled during the day
are placed that night in the bleaching house and subjected to
the fumes of a little burning brimstone; other nights, if
there is any dampness at all, they should be covered.   In the
morning they are placed in the sun.   When partially cured
turn in trays, same as raisins.   Only a few days is required
to dry them if the weather is good.   Watch carefully so as
not to let them get too dry, as that spoils them. Go over the
trays and pick them out as soon as cured.   The better the fig
the sooner it is cured.   When taken from trays they are put in
large sacks of cotton cloth like flour sacks, and put in a cool
place to sweat.   While still moist and pliable from sweating
they should be packed in boxes and pressed. The main
points to be considered are, 1, The quality of the fresh fig.   2,
Its thorough ripeness. 3, Bright, perfectly dry weather.   4,
The care which does not allow them to get too dry.

Figs cured in this way are excellent without the bleaching process, and are preferred by many for their own use.

While in the business, Mr. Burnham took the first pre-
mium for several years at the Riverside Citrus Fairs, on his
cured figs.

SMALL FRUITS

F. Edward Gray, Alhambra

They who possess a home in Southern California, be it city lot, suburban acre or extensive ranch, naturally aim to make it attractive.

Not the least among the means of making it such, within or without, is a well maintained small fruit garden.

With straw, black and raspberries properly cared for, growing within the home enclosure, the good housekeeper always has the wherewithal at hand to brighten up her table and please the taste of her most fastidious guest.

THE BLACKBERRY

Although dark of hue this branch is by no means the black sheep of the berry family. It keeps you at a respectable distance with its vicious thorns, but after careful persistency you will find it as attractive and beautiful as any of its kin.

There is one thing about the blackberry, the most decided ill treatment will not kill it. Once plant it in your garden, it will remain there forever, and a day.

It requires a sunny place, succeeding best in a light soil, possibly not so rich as the raspberry as it has a tendency to rankness.

Set out as early in winter as possible. If you need more than one row, allow six feet between each row, with plants three feet apart in the rows. They require more room than the raspberry, and should have support. Stakes at the ends of the rows with wires stretched from end to end will sustain them nicely.

Keep the growth down to three feet, if possible, more can be done with the thumb and finger at the right time than with pruning shears after neglect. Pinch back the green canes in early May and June with a result that you will have better shaped plants and a greater abundance of fruit.

Two varieties is all that is necessary and will give you more than you and your neighbors' children will need.

Crandall's Early is not only an excellent berry and prolific bearer but will ripen three weeks earlier than any other and last some times as late as December, but this is not desirable as it is not the berry for preserving and canning, as is the Kittatinny, for under good culture this latter variety is very large, sweet, rich and melting when fully ripe. It reaches its best condition if allowed to ripen on the vines.

THE STRAWBERRY

To make a success of your strawberry patch, the ground should be thoroughly cultivated and pulverized; properly deepened and enriched. A sandy loam will give the most satisfactory results. No shade, and an abundance of moisture are some of the chief needs of the strawberry.

Two hundred plants will be sufficient for an ordinary family. Procure *young* plants; set them out in the fall or winter just before the first rains, and you will get quick returns of the luscious fruit.

Select equal proportions of the "Monarch and "Sharpless" varieties and you will have berries every month in the year.

Prepare the ground in ridges, say from twelve to fifteen inches apart, according to the volume of water at your command. Set the plants one foot apart on top of the ridge. In planting, excavate a place for each plant sufficiently large to put the roots, *spread out*, down their whole length; fill and press earth firmly; be careful that crown of plant does not go below the surface.

Set a new bed *every* year with thrifty *young* plants. Pull up old plants after two years' bearing.

· THE RASPBERRY

To succeed with this crimson, melting berry, prepare the

ground as thoroughly and in same manner as for the strawberry, using care not to overfertilize.

Establish your row of plants where they will have partial shade, along a fence or hedge, if possible. Plant them out as early as possible in the winter to receive the full benefit of the rains, cutting back the old canes six inches from the surface.

Keep the ground level, don't let it bank up against the plants, mulch well with hay or long grass to preserve the moisture. Support the plants with stakes. Be liberal with water and you will have fruit every day—and for Christmas.

As for variety, none will give such general satisfaction as the Cuthbert, deservedly known as the "Queen of the Market." The berries are of the largest size; very firm; deep rich crimson; flavor excellent and very prolific.

Don't waste time and space in planting out the the Black Cap varieties; they will not do well in this climate and only produce sour fruit and bitter disappointment.

FRUITS

Mrs. W. J. Brown

Fruit should be carefully selected for canning or preserving and should be used as soon as possible after it is picked. Berries should be preserved the same day they are picked. Pears, peaches and apricots should be firm but not fully ripe as they then retain their shape and have a better flavor. Use only the best granulated sugar for putting up fruit or making jellies. To prevent fruit from fading or being injured by the chemical action of the light through the glass jar, wrap two or three thicknesses of paper around jars. The most satis-factory way of canning fruit after it is prepared is to place it with care in glass jars, until they are full, then fill to about an inch of the top with rather hot syrup prepared with the right quantity of sugar as given in the general directions which follow; fasten on the covers tight enough to lift by, but not air tight, then place several thicknesses of cloth on the bottom of the boiler to prevent the jars breaking; set the jars in and fill to about two or three inches of the tops of the jars with tepid water, and boil the required length of time accord-ing to general directions—that is after the water commences to boil rapidly in the boiler. When cooked, take out, being careful to cover the jar that the air may not strike it, or it will break; set on a folded towel wet with cold water, remove the cover and fill with hot syrup, or if the required amount of sugar has been used, fill with boiling water; see that there are no air bubbles in the jar, fasten on the cover securely, invert the jar and and let it stand twenty-four hours. If the fruit is sufficiently cooked, the rubbers good, and the jars air tight, your fruit will keep indefinitely.

As jellies and jams grow dark by cooking after the sugar is added, boil the fruit or juice well before adding the sugar, which should be heated in the oven but not allowed to brown.

When the jelly is ready to remove from the fire, have ready a heated pitcher with a piece of cheese cloth, wet with hot water, over the top; pour the jelly through the strainer; and if the cloth is wrung out of hot water, there will be no waste of jelly. Have the glasses standing in a pan of hot water; take them out and drain a moment and turn the jelly in from the pitcher; or if a silver teaspoon is placed in the glass and then the jelly poured in, there will be no danger of the glass cracking.

It is thought by some that fruit must be sweetened in order to keep from spoiling, but such is not the case. Fruit properly cooked, put up while boiling hot in air tight jars will keep just as well as the sweetened; and is preferable when intended for pie-making.

The fruit closet should be cool and dry; if too warm, the fruit may spoil; if too damp. it will mold. Jars of fruit should be examined two or three days after filling; if any of the syrup leaks out, they should be opened and the fruit used for jam, as it will have lost its delicacy of color and flavor—an item so desirable in canned fruits.

GENERAL DIRECTIONS FOR CANNING FRUIT

Amount of sugar for a quart jar and time for cooking:

			min.			oz.
Boil blackberries	moderately	about	6 min.	Amt. sugar,	6 oz.
" raspberries	"	"	6 "	" "	6 "
" strawberries	"	"	8 "	" "	8 "
" Bartlett pears in halves	"	20 "	" "	6 "
" peaches, halves moderately "	8 "	" "	6 "
" peaches, whole	"	"	15 "	" "	6 "
" plums	"	"	10 "	" "	8 "
" apricots	"	"	8 "	" "	8 "
" nectarines	"	"	8 "	" "	8 "
" crab apples, whole "	"	25 "	" "	8 "
" pine-apple, sliced "	"	15 "	" "	6 "
" ripe currants	"	"	6 "	" "	10 "
" pie-plant, sliced	"	"	10 "	" "	10 "
" cherries	"	"	8 "	" "	6 "
" sour apples, quar'd "	"	10 "	"	6 to 8 "
" grapes	"	"	10 "	"	6 to 8 "
" quinces, quartered "	"	20 "	"	8 to 10 "

CANNED BLACKBERRIES AND RASPBERRIES
Mrs. W. J. Brown.

Look over the fruit carefully, drop into a pan of cold water; remove from water with the hands, let drain, then fill the jars; add the syrup and follow the preceeding "General Directions."

FOR CANNING BLACKBERRIES
Mrs. S. H. Fairchild.

Put the berries in a vessel with a little water to create steam and sufficient to boil; add one teacup sugar to every two lbs of berries. Make a batter of one tablespoon flour and a little water to every quart of fruit, after being cooked, beat thoroughly until it is perfectly free from lumps; when berries come to a boil, stir in batter very gently to avoid mashing them. Use care at this point to prevent burning; when they are of the thickness of syrup, can immediately. Berries put up in this way keep better and have a more natural flavor than when put up in any other way. Raspberries and ripe currants may be canned in the same manner with equal success—currants requiring more sugar.

CANNED STRAWBERRIES AND GOOSEBERRIES
Mrs. W. J. Brown.

Look over the fruit, remove the stems and blows; drop them into a pan of cold water, remove carefully with the hands; fill the jars, add the syrup and follow the preceeding "General Directions."

STEWED CRANBERRIES
Miss Frances Widney.

One quart cranberries; 1 pint granulated sugar; 1 cup water.

Look over the berries carefully, wash and put in a granite stew pan; add the water and sugar; cover and let boil about ten minutes. Remove the scum but do not stir them. When cold, they will jelly and the skins will be tender.

CANNED PEACHES
Mrs. W. J. Brown.

Select peaches that are ripe but not soft. Pare, remove the stones, place the fruit in the jar; adding three peach stones (cracked) to each jar; prepare the syrup and cook according to preceeding "General Directions."

CANNED APRICOTS AND NECTARINES
Mrs. W. J. Brown.

Use the fruit before it is soft. Pare, remove the stones and place in the jars with three of the cracked stones; add the syrup and follow preceeding "General Directions."

CANNED PEARS OR QUINCES
Mrs. W. J. Brown.

Pare, cut in quarters or the pears in halves; place them in the jars, add the hot syrup and proceed according to preceeding "General Directions."

CANNED PLUMS
Mrs. W. J. Brown.

Plums should be thoroughly ripe. Remove the stems, fill the jars, add the syrup and follow the preceeding "General Directions."

CANNED TOMATOES
Mrs. W. J. Brown.

Use firm, ripe, medium-sized tomatoes; scald slightly; remove the skin and cook without breaking, by putting them into the jars carefully, filling with hot water, and cook according to general directions.

CANNED SWEET CORN
O. G. M.

Take fresh, sweet corn, when tender, and cut from the cob before cooking; put in glass jars and pack it tight; when full, fasten covers sufficiently to keep out the water. Place several thicknesses of cloth on bottom of boiler; pack in the jars, one over the other, and cover them with cold water. Watch carefully, and when it commences to boil, boil three hours, take out, fasten the covers air-tight. When cool, put in a cool place and the corn will be as fresh as in summer.

Peas can be canned in same way.

BLACKBERRY JAM
Mrs. S. S. Salisbury.

To 6 pounds blackberries allow 9 pounds sugar and boil twenty minutes.

BLACKBERRY JAM
Mrs. W. J. Brown.

Select fresh, ripe berries, removing all imperfect ones; mash well in in an earthen dish and add 1 pound best granulated sugar to each pound or pint of fruit. Put the berries in a porcelain or granite preserving kettle and *boil* fifteen minutes, add the sugar, (which should be heated in the oven) and *boil* fifteen minutes longer, stirring often to prevent burning. If the fruit is very juicy, it may require to boil ¾ of an hour. Put in jelly glasses or fruit jars.

STRAWBERRY JAM, No. 1
Mrs. R. M. Widney.

Wash, hull and weigh the berries. Mash them in a preserving kettle, (granite or porcelain), add ¾ pound sugar to each pound of fruit. Cook for about 30 minutess stirring constantly with a silver or wooden spoon. Dip into fruit jars and seal while hot.

STRAWBERRY JAM, No. 2
Mrs. R. M. Widney.

Four pounds fresh strawberries; 1 pint currant juice; 5 pounds sugar.

Mash the strawberries, add the currant juice and boil 10 minutes. Skim, add the sugar, and boil 10 or 15 minutes longer, or until it is sufficiently thick. Put in glass jars or jelly glasses, cover closely with paper, brushed over with white of egg.

RASPBERRY JAM
Mrs. R. M. Widney.

Made as directed for Strawberry Jam, No. 1.

PINE APPLE JAM
Mrs. W. J. Brown.

Pare the pine apple carefully; grate it, and add ¾ pound granulated sugar to a pound of fruit. Boil about fifteen minutes and seal in glass jars.

CURRANT JAM
A. C. B.

Remove the currants from the stems, crush them and boil fifteen minutes. Add the same quantity of sugar heated and cook but fifteen minutes longer, being careful not to burn.

PEACH BUTTER
Mrs. Wm. F. Marshall.

Use thoroughly-ripe peaches; pare them; remove the stones and take pound for pound of peaches and sugar. Cook the peaches until they are soft, then add half the sugar and boil half an hour; then add the remainder of the sugar, and boil an hour and a half, stirring constantly to prevent burning. If the flavor of the peach stone is desired, crack some of the stones, boil a few minutes in a small quantity of water, and add to the fruit, or season with cinnamon and cloves, if preferred.

APPLE AND PEAR BUTTER
Mrs. M. G. Moore.

One peck each apples and pears; ½ dozen quinces; 5 pounds lightest brown sugar.

Pare, core and cut into pieces the apples and pears; add the quinces and boil, stirring often till smooth and rich in coloring, then add the sugar and stir constantly till the bubbles gather in the middle and cook outwardly. Put in earthen jars and keep in a cool, dry place. The sun must not be allowed to fall upon it.

APPLE BUTTER
Mrs. R. W. Widney.

Ten gallons cider; 1 bushel apples.

The day before making the butter, boil the cider down one-half. The apples should be peeled, cored, and put in the boiled-down cider, as rapidly as possible in the early morning of the day in which the butter is made. At first it will be necessary to stir only every few moments; later on, as the apples are dissolved, the butter should be stirred constantly.

In the absence of the great copper kettles that our grandmothers used, I usually get a large new, tin wash-boiler. The butter should be cooked until when taken out the cider will not separate, but the whole be a thick, smooth substance—a butter indeed. The cooking requires a full day. The butter burns or scorches so easily that it is necessary to constantly stir, so as to scrape the entire surface of the bottom of the kettle.

APPLE AND QUINCE CHEESE
Mrs. C. C. Thomas.

Six pounds quinces; 3 pounds apples; 4 pounds white sugar.

Prepare as for preserving. Cook the quinces first in enough water to cover. When tender, add the apples and cook till done, then add the sugar and boil a few minutes as for jelly. Pour into shallow tin pans; when cold, cover with white paper dipped in white of egg. Cut into thin slices or cubes, and serve for lunch.

LEMON BUTTER
Mrs. T. F. McCamant.

One cup sugar; 1 cup boiling water; 1 tablespoon flour; 1 tablespoon butter; 1 egg; 1 lemon.

Mix together the sugar, butter, flour, egg—well beaten, and the juice of the lemon, with a little of the grated rind. Pour this into the boiling water and cook slowly. Stir well to prevent burning.

ORANGE MARMALADE
Mrs. G. W. White.

Slice very thin twelve oranges and five lemons, using the entire fruit, but removing all the seeds carefully. To every pound of fruit add one quart of water. Set away for twenty-four hours.

Second Morning.—Boil the fruit till tender. Set away twenty-four hours.

Third Morning.—To each pound of the boiled fruit add one pound of sugar. Boil until the liquid makes a jelly.

ORANGE MARMALADE—English Recipe
Mrs. Henry Smith.

One dozen oranges; 4 good sized lemons; 1½ pints water to each pound sliced fruit; 1 pound and 2 ounces sugar to each pound fruit.

Slice the oranges and lemons very thin, and take out the seeds, then add the water and let stand 24 hours.   Then boil till the peel is tender, (about 1 hour), let this stand till quite cold, take out the fruit and weigh it, and to every pound allow 1 pound 2 ounces sugar.   Boil this one hour, taking great care it does not burn.   Stir well with wooden or agate spoon.   When done put in glasses and seal while hot.   It is best not to boil too long in one pan, as it is very quick to burn.

ORANGE MARMALADE
Miss Eloise Forman.

Four dozen oranges; 4 lemons; ¾ pounds granulated sugar to every pound of oranges after the peel is removed. Less sugar for very sweet fruit.   Peel two dozen removing as little of the white lining as possible. Cut the peel into narrow strips about an inch long, with the scissors. Put in cold water and let it come to a boil.   Change the water three times and boil peel until tender.   Extract all the juice from these oranges.   Carefully remove white skin, stringy part and seeds from remaining oranges, (2 dozen), and cut the pulp into small pieces.   Put juice, pulp and sugar into a porcelain kettle; add the lemon juice and boil twenty minutes. Skim carefully, add the orange peel, which has been thoroughly drained after boiling; the sliced peel of the four lemons and boil the mixture until clear; from one half to one hour.   Put into jelly glasses when cold.   Cover and set away for one month.   This makes a dozen glasses of very rich marmalade.

ORANGE MARMALADE
Mrs. W. J. Brown.

Use as many oranges as desired, reserving the very thin peel, (yellow part only), of 3 oranges out of 12. Cut the peel in fine shreds with a pair of scissors, and soak in salt water over night. In the morning drain off the water, rinse the peel, and put on the stove in clear cold water; boil till tender, drain off the water and add to the pulp of the oranges, prepared as follows:

Remove every particle of the peel, white skin and seeds, from the oranges, cut the pulp or segments into small pieces, measure the peel and pulp of oranges, and use one pint of best granulated sugar to each pint of prepared fruit. Drain off some of the juice of the oranges into a preserving kettle, add the sugar, boil up and skim, then add the peel and pulp; boil about thirty minutes, or until sufficiently thick, remove from stove, and put in glass jars or jelly glasses.

ORANGE FLOWER SYRUP
Miss E. Benton Fremont.

One pint fresh white orange petals; 1 quart rich syrup, made of granulated sugar and water.

Select, and wash without bruising, the white petals of the orange flowers. While the petals drain on a cloth, prepare a rich syrup of granulated sugar and water, allowing one quart for each pint of blossoms. After skimming the syrup carefully, drop in the petals and simmer only two minutes, stir gently, strain and bottle; seal while hot. It will be a delicate sea green color, retaining all the fragrance of the flower and reminding one when opened, of an orange grove in Spring. A teaspoonful added to a glass of water makes a most delicious drink, and is regarded by the Floridians as a nerve tonic. This is also a very agreeable flavoring for custards, icing or pudding sauces.

PRESERVED BLACKBERRIES
A. C. B.

Look over, wash, and weigh the fruit, using pound for

pound of fruit and sugar.   Put the berries and sugar on the stove, and let it come to a boil slowly, then cook about an hour, being careful not to let it burn, pour into glass jars and seal while hot.

PRESERVED STRAWBERRIES
A. C. B.

Use one pound best granulated sugar to each pound of berries; place them in the kettle on back of stove until the sugar is dissolved, then boil slowly until the berries are clear, skim out the berries carefully and boil the syrup until thick, then carefully put the berries in the hot syrup and let them boil up, then put in glass jars and seal.

PRESERVED PEACHES
Mrs. W. J. Brown.

Use peaches before they are perfectly ripe.   Select them of even size, pare, remove the stones, weigh the fruit and allow a pound of sugar to each pound of fruit. Use just enough water to dissolve the sugar.   When boiling hot put in one layer of the prepared fruit, and three peach stones to each quart, simmer slowly about ten minutes, then turn each piece over carefully and simmer until the fruit is clear, then put in jars carefully and seal.   If the syrup is not all needed to fill the jar, add the sugar to it for the next jar and cook as before. A low, broad granite pan is best to use.

PRESERVED PEARS
Mrs. Helen W. Watson.

Bartlett pears are best for preserving.   Use them before they become soft.   Pare, cut in halves or quarters, and use a pound of sugar to each pound of fruit.   Put the sugar in the preserving kettle with just enough water to dissolve it.   Let it boil slowly until the required color is obtained. If you prefer to have them white, remove the fruit as soon as it becomes clear, boil down the syrup, drop in the pears, let them come to a boil, then put in jars and seal.   By cooking them slowly several hours they will become a rich, dark color.

PRESERVED QUINCES
Mrs. Frank Miller.

Select quinces of even size. As you peel and core them throw into cold water. Make a syrup of 1 pint water and 1 pound granulated sugar to every pound of fruit. Bring the syrup to a boiling point, drain the fruit from the cold water, and add to the boiling syrup. Boil slowly until they become the desired color.

GRAPE PRESERVES
Mrs. W. J. Brown.

Use muscat, or raisin grapes. Cut the grapes open with a knife, remove the seeds, and to each pound of fruit allow one pound best granulated sugar. Cook slowly for thirty minutes or until the grapes are perfectly clear. Put in glass jars and seal. Delicious.

FIG PRESERVES
Mrs. M. R. Sinsabaugh.

Select figs that are not over ripe; White Smyrna preferred. Pare them, and use as many pounds of sugar as fruit. Cover fruit with sugar and set in refrigerator over night. Pour off the syrup thus formed in a preserving kettle and heat it. Place enough figs to cover bottom of kettle and boil until a light amber color, and dip out and place in the jar. Keep adding and dipping out as fast as done, until all are cooked, and then pour hot syrup over figs and seal.

PRESERVED FIGS
Mrs. S. C. Hubbell.

Select fine, large, white figs, of equal ripeness. Peel, and weigh them. Cover with water, boil slowly until tender, but not broken. Take them out with care and lay on platter. Prepare a thick syrup of sugar—as many pounds as of fruit— boil, and skim it, then put in the figs, and cook slowly until transparent. When nearly done, add a few slices of lemon. Put in glass jars. Many persons add a little ginger also.

PRESERVED FIGS
Mrs. C. H. Haas.

Use white figs, picked the day before preserving. Peel and weigh them, and use ¾ pound sugar to one pound fruit. Sprinkle the sugar over the figs and let them stand over night. Pour the syrup off and boil it down. When thick put the figs in and cook gently until clear, then drain through a sieve and boil the syrup down again. Put the figs in and boil slowly 1 hour. Use 1 lemon sliced, to every 3 pounds of figs.

LOQUOT PRESERVE
Mrs. Alice Cooper.

Remove skins and stones from the loquots. Allow one pound of granulated sugar to one pound of fruit. Boil until clear, and seal in glass jars. A little of this preserve used in making fruit cake adds to its richness.

ORANGE PRESERVE
Mrs. J. C. Joplin, Orange Co.

Use ripe navel oranges, peel them carefully, be sure to remove all the white, also the end and stem running through the center, using great care not to break the orange. Throw in cold water a few hours, when you can remove more of the white, then drop them into boiling water. Have ready a syrup made of 1½ pounds granulated sugar to one pound of fruit. Lift the oranges out of the water with a skimmer, drain well and drop them into the boiling syrup, and cook till they are clear. When done put in glass jars and seal while boiling hot. If you do not remove all the white, the preserve will be bitter.

ORANGE PEEL PRESERVE
Mrs. J. C. Joplin, Orange Co.

Soak the peel in strong salt water nine days, changing the water every three days, then dry on a sieve. Make a syrup of one pound sugar to one quart water. Put the peel in and simmer until transparent. This is nice to put in with the preserved oranges. If the peel is cut in halves it is nice to put a preserved orange into the peel when served. If careful in placing; it makes a very pretty, as well as palatable dish.

PRESERVED CITRON
Mrs. C. H. Haas.

Remove the inside, cut in quarters, peel and put in a jar of strong brine and let stand three days. Drain off and put in a new brine three days. Drain second water off and put in third brine three days, then drain and soak three days in fresh water. The twelfth day make a syrup of ½ pound sugar to 1 pound fruit. Put in the citron and cook till clear. Orange or lemon peel can be preserved in the same way.

GREEN ALMOND PRESERVES
Miss E. Benton Fremont.

The shell of the almond must be soft; pierce them through in several places with a strong, coarse needle. Then lay them for five days in cold water, changing the water each morning. On the fifth day put the almonds in boiling water and cook until they are easily pierced by a thin, pointed sliver of wood. Take them out and drain off the water and sprinkle with granulated sugar; ¾ pound sugar to 1 pound almonds; cover with a clean cloth and let stand all night. Next morning pour off the syrup, boil the almonds again for a few moments and repeat the sprinkling of sugar as before. Do this three or four times in all, depending on the tenderness of the almonds. Then to the syrup which has been each morning drained off from the almonds, add sugar in the proportion of ¼ pound to each ¾ pound already used. Boil to a syrup, skim carefully, then drop in the almonds and let them boil a few minutes. When they are cooled, put in air-tight jars, and set in a cool but dry place.

BLACKBERRY JELLY
A. C. B.

Wash the fruit and let drain. Put into the preserving kettle with a cup of water. Heat slowly, until the juice begins to separate. Then boil until the berries are very soft: then

pour them into a jelly bag and let drain.   Measure the juice
and use 1 pint of sugar to each pint of the juice.   Boil the
juice rapidly 20 minutes, then add the heated sugar and boil
from 15 to 20 minutes, or until it thickens.

STRAWBERRY JELLY No. 1
Mrs. Z. L. Parmelee.

Put the fruit in a preserving kettle on back of stove, when
the juice separates from the berries let it come to the boiling
point.   Then turn into a jelly bag and drain.   Measure the
juice and allow ¾ pound granulated sugar to one pint juice.
Heat the sugar thoroughly, stirring often to prevent burning.
Boil the juice rapidly for 25 minutes.   Add the sugar and
stir until dissolved.   Boil from 2 to 5 minutes.   Then remove
from stove and pour into jelly glasses.   Set away a day or
two, then cover with paper, brushed over with white of egg,
and keep in a dark, dry, cool place.

STRAWBERRY JELLY No. 2

Mrs. J. M. Johnston.

Boil currants and strain out the juice, likewise strawberries.

To 1 cup currant and 2 cups berry juice, use 3 cups sugar.
Boil in a medium-sized kettle five minutes, and then pour into
glasses.   Apples may be used instead of currants if preferred.

RASPBERRY JELLY

Mrs. Z. L. Parmelee.

Make same as strawberry jelly No. 1.

RASPBERRY AND CURRANT JELLY

Mrs. W. J. Brown.

Use equal parts of each and make according to directions
for currant jelly.

CURRANT JELLY, No. 1

Mrs. W. J. Brown.

The best jelly is made from currants when they first ripen,
before they are thoroughly ripe.

Pick the currants from the stems, crush them in an earthen dish, put the pulp in a jelly bag to drain, but do not squeeze as it will make the jelly cloudy. To 1 pint of juice, use one pint of best granulated sugar. Put the sugar in the oven to heat, stirring it often to prevent burning. Boil the juice rapidly twenty minutes in a porcelain or granite kettle, skimming well, add the sugar that has been heated and let it come to a boil, then strain into glasses. When cold, cover it with paper cut to fit the glass, and brush over with the white of egg. Tie paper over the glass and set in a cool, dark, dry place.

By squeezing the fruit after it has been drained, one can make a jelly that will not be as clear, but it will answer for some purposes.

CURRANT JELLY, No. 2

Look over the fruit, remove all the imperfect currants, put over the fire and scald; drain in a jelly bag, boil the juice fifteen minutes. Skim well, add the heated sugar and boil five minutes, turn into glasses and cover as directed in No. 1.

GOOSEBERRY JELLY
A. C. B.

Boil 6 lbs green gooseberries in 6 pints of water until they are thoroughly cooked, but not broken too much, then pour them into a jelly bag and let drip until the pulp is dry. To every pint of juice, use one pound of granulated sugar; heat the sugar in the oven, and boil the juice rapidly half an hour; skim it, then add the sugar and boil half an hour longer.

TOKAY GRAPE JELLY
Mrs. Guy Smith, Tustin.

Wash and clean the grapes carefully. Boil slowly one hour, stirring frequently. Strain through a colander and then through a fine bag; do not squeeze. Measure juice and boil twenty minutes; then add one pint of sugar to each pint of juice and boil five minutes longer. Put in glasses and cover with paper dipped in alcohol to prevent moulding.

GRAPE JELLY
Mrs. Frank Miller.

Use the grapes before they are fully ripe. Wash and drain them, removing all imperfect ones; put them into a kettle, mash and cook them until their skins are broken, then strain through a flannel bag; and to each pint of juice use one pound of sugar. Boil the juice rapidly fifteen minutes, then add the sugar and boil from five to ten minutes longer.

LOQUOT JELLY
Mrs. G. L. Arnold.

One ℔ sugar to 1 pint juice.

Wash the fruit and put in water enough to half cover. Boil slowly until the juice is extracted, strain and add sugar in the above proportion. Boil until it will jelly, then fill the glasses.

LOQUOT JELLY
Mrs. W. H. Barnard.

Cut off blossom end of loquot. Boil in water until soft; squeeze out and strain through a jelly bag. Use ¾ ℔ of sugar to 1 ℔ of fruit, weighing both before boiling.

PLUM JELLY
Mrs. R. M. Widney.

Remove the stems, wash, put in the preserving kettle, cover with water and boil until well done; pour in jelly bag and drain. To each pint of juice allow one pint sugar; put on the stove and boil rapidly twenty minutes; skim, add heated sugar and boil from ten to fifteen minutes; remove from stove and put in glasses. Red plums make beautiful jelly.

PEACH JELLY
Mrs. A. W. Bessey, Orange Co.

Put the peaches in the preserving kettle with a little water, cover. Heat slowly and cook until the peaches will mash readily, then turn into a jelly bag and drip until the pulp is dry. Boil the juice rapidly twenty minutes, skimming it often. Remove it from the fire, measure and return it to the fire; as soon as it boils again, add as many pounds of sugar as you have pounds of juice, and boil until it jellies. Pour into tumblers, and stand aside two or three days; then cover with paper and put in a cool, dry place.

Apricot jelly is made much the same way; but be sure to use fruit that is not too ripe. A beautiful jelly is made by using half apricot and half blackberry juice.

GUAVA JELLY
Mrs. E. R. Smith.

After washing the fruit, put it into the fruit kettle, putting more than enough water to cover the fruit; cook until soft, run through a fruit strainer and add the same quantity of sugar as there is juice, boiling and testing as in other fruit jelly. Guavas require more water than any other jelly fruit. The late guavas are the best for jelly.

PINEAPPLE JELLY
Mrs. J. J. Ayers.

One and one-half quarts of wetting all together (scant measure); a scant pint sugar; white and shell of one egg; an ounce box of Cox's gelatine; juice of one lemon. Soak gelatine in ½ pint of water, an hour or so. Open a can of pineapple; strain off the juice, cut pineapple in small pieces; put into porcelain saucepan, pour on boiling water and simmer twenty minutes, then skim out the pineapple; add sugar, gelatine, lemon, pineapple juice and white and shell of the egg to the mixture. Let this boil up once and then set back for twenty minutes where it will keep hot but not boil. Strain through a napkin into molds, and set away to cool; when cold, keep it upon ice until hard. To be eaten fresh.

CRAB APPLE JELLY
Mrs. Helen W. Watson.

Wash the fruit clean, remove stems, put into the preserving kettle and cover with water; boil until soft; then pour into a jelly bag and let it drain; do not press the fruit through. Allow 1 cup sugar for every cup of juice. Put sugar in the oven to heat; put on the juice letting it boil 20 minutes, then add the sugar and boil 5 minutes. Remove from the stove and pour into jelly glasses which are set on a folded cloth, wet in cold water, to avoid their breaking. If you desire a darker colored jelly, boil the sugar with the juice for 25 minutes.

BANANA JELLY
Mrs. A. S. Baldwin.

Half box gelatine; ½ pint cold water; ½ pint boiling water; ½ cup sugar; 2 bananas.

Soak the gelatine in the cold water till soft, then add the boiling water and sugar. Stir thoroughly and strain into molds wet with cold water. When partly cold, stir in the bananas sliced thin.

ORANGE JELLY
Mrs. J. P. Widney.

Wash the oranges and, with a silver spoon, remove the pulp. (If a flavor of the peel is desired, squeeze a few of the oranges with a lemon squeezer. This will give sufficient flavor without making the jelly bitter). Boil quickly in a porcelain or granite kettle. Drain through a jelly bag, without squeezing. Add one pound of sugar to a pint of juice, and boil rapidly for 20 minutes. If managed rightly, the jelly will be of a clear, amber color and delicious.

ORANGE JELLY
Mrs. A. S. Baldwin.

Half box Cox's gelatine; ½ pint cold water; 1 cup sugar; ¾ pint orange juice.

Soak the gelatine in the cold water for ten minutes, then put it over the fire and stir until thoroughly dissolved, then add the sugar and orange juice and let it boil up once. Put in glasses and cover with manilla paper wet in white of egg.

LEMON JELLY
Mrs. M. J. Danison.

One box Cox's gelatine; 1 pint tepid water; 2 pints sugar; 3 pints boiling water; juice of 4 lemons.

Dissolve the gelatine in the pint of tepid water. It will need to stand two or three hours; then add the three pints of boiling water, sugar, and lemon juice. Strain and cool in molds, and keep in a cool place all the while—otherwise, it will not harden.   ½ of this recipe may be used.

I think for this kind of jelly, it is unsurpassed.

SPICED CURRANTS
Mrs. G. I. Cochran.

Five pounds currants; 4 pounds brown sugar; 2 tablespoons ground cloves; 2 tablespoons cinnamon; 1 pint vinegar.

Boil two hours.

SPICED GOOSEBERRIES
Mrs. C. G. Dubois.

Five pounds gooseberries; 2½ pounds brown sugar; 1 pint vinegar; 1½ ounces cloves; 1 ounce cinnamon.

Boil from two to three hours.   Add the vinegar and spices half an hour before it is done.   Stir while cooking.

SPICED GRAPES
Mrs. A. S. Marshall.

Seven pounds muscat grapes; 3½ pounds sugar; 1¼ pints vinegar; 1 teaspoon each ground cinnamon, mace and cloves, tied in a bag.

Boil the sugar, spice and vinegar and pour over the grapes. The next day pour off the syrup, boil it and pour over the grapes again. The next day pour off the syrup, and when it boils, put in the grapes and cook them until tender.

SPICED PEACHES
Mrs. S. C. Hubbell.

Nine pounds peaches; 4½ pounds sugar; 1 pint vinegar; ½ cup cloves; ½ cup cinnamon.

Pare and halve the peaches, and put them in a jar. Tie the spices in separate cloths, boil them with the vinegar and sugar a few moments and pour over the peaches boiling hot. Let them stand over night.   In the morning, put them in a kettle and boil ten minutes, then take out the peaches, leaving the spices. Boil the vinegar until it begins to thicken, then pour on the peaches.

CRAB APPLE PICKLE
Mrs. Augusta Robinson.

Eight pounds apples; 4 pounds sugar; vinegar to cover them; 1 tablespoon each cinnamon and cloves and a *little* cayenne pepper.

Put the vinegar, sugar and spices together, put in the crab apples and cook them slowly until tender.

SWEET PICKLE APRICOTS
Mrs. C. C. Thomas.

Seven pounds sugar; 1 pint cider vinegar; ½ teacup cayenne pepper; 1 dozen cloves—no more.

When the syrup boils, drop in the fruit. Cook until clear —but not soft. Seal while hot in glass jars.

Excellent with any meat, cold or hot.

FIG PICKLE
Mrs. J. C. Joplin, Orange County.

One quart vinegar; 4 pounds brown sugar; ½ ounce each cinnamon, cloves and mace.

Take ripe but firm figs with stems on. Let them stand over night in salt water; next day put them into fresh water for one hour, then put them into the hot syrup, made by boiling the vinegar, sugar and spices and boil ten minutes. Remove them from the fire and let them stand over night. Repeat the boiling the third time, letting them stand over night the second night, and the third time they boil put into glass jars and seal.

GINGERED FIGS
Mrs. J. C. Joplin, Orange County.

Take ripe but firm figs with stems on. Let them stand over night in salt water; next morning put them in fresh water for one hour, then put them into weak alum water for a few minutes to make them firm, then put them into a strong ginger tea—made of best white ginger root mashed and boiled. Cook the figs in this until they are clear, then put them into a boiling syrup, made with a pound of best white sugar to each pound of fruit, and ¼ pound of mashed ginger root to 10 pounds of sugar. Let them stand in the syrup over night; in the morning let them come to a boil and seal in glass jars.

PICKLED LIMES—Reliable

Limes, vinegar, salt, allspice, cloves, white mustard and horseradish.

Cut the limes, fill with salt, and lay them in the sun to dry. When dry, wash off the salt, and pack them in jars in alternate layers with the spices, and fill the jars with hot vinegar. They will be fit for use in four weeks.

SWEET PEAR PICKLES
Mrs. R. M. Widney.

Nine pounds fruit; 1 pint vinegar; 4½ pounds brown sugar; ½ pound stick cinnamon; ½ pound cloves.

Tie the spices in small bags, and boil them with the sugar and vinegar until a good syrup is formed. Then put in the pears, (Bartlett or Seckel). Place on the back of the stove, and cook very slowly until they can be pierced with a straw.

GOOSEBERRY CATSUP
Mrs. J. F. Conroy.

Nine pounds gooseberries; 6 pounds brown sugar; 1 pint vinegar; 1 tablespoon each of cloves, mace and cinnamon tied in a cloth.

Use the gooseberries before they turn ripe, add the vinegar, sugar and spices and cook four hours, and seal in bottles. Splendid.

GOOSEBERRY CATSUP
Mrs. H. L. Powell.

Ten pounds ripe gooseberries; 5 pounds sugar; 2 tablespoons pepper; 2 tablespoons each allspice, cloves and cinnamon; 1 quart vinegar.

Boil the berries and vinegar to a pulp, add the sugar and spice, and boil five minutes, then seal in glass jars.

GRAPE CATSUP
Mrs. J. F. Conroy.

Ten pounds grapes; 2½ pounds sugar; 1 quart vinegar; 2 tablespoons cinnamon; 2 tablespoons cloves and spice, mixed; 2 tablespoons each salt, pepper and cloves.

Boil the grapes and run through a sieve, then add the sugar, vinegar and spices, and boil until catsup is a little thick.

To Prepare Fruit (Glasé) for Family Use
Mrs. C. C. Thomas.

The fruit used must be preserved in thick syrup—if one year old, all the better. Drain the fruit from the syrup and lay in the sun for one or two days, then sprinkle with granulated sugar. Pears, crab apples, figs, cherries or any fruit of which the juice jellies when exposed, make fine dishes, when prepared by the above directions; and one quart jar at a time is enough.

OLIVE CULTURE IN CALIFORNIA

J. L. HOWLAND, Pomona

Little attention has been paid to the cultivation of the olive until the past few years, and the only variety known here formerly was the Mission, brought by the Spanish pádres from Spain, and planted at the old missions. Some of these trees are still standing, though planted a century ago—mostly neglected, or at best slightly cultivated. This proves the longevity and tenacity of life of the olive, and that when once rooted it will hold its own even under adverse circumstances. We have authentic records of its living to be over three hundred years old, so when we plant an olive orchard we are not planting merely for our own benefit, but for future generations.

The olive, because of the moderate care which it requires and the copiousness and value of its product, may be considered one of the most valuable of trees. Though it is limited in its possible extension, the Italian growers already look forward with dread to its being cultivated in other countries, and now California seems likely to prove a formidable rival. But the fear would seem to be unfounded, as the only source of supply for olives pickled, and pure olive oil in the United States is limited to this State.

The demand for the pure article is constantly growing, both abroad and at home, and it is doubtful if the production abroad will any more than supply the European market.

The growth of the olive is to be, it seems to me, one of the leading and most permanent industries of Southern California. It will give us what is nearly impossible to buy now, pure olive oil, in place of the cottonseed and lard mixture in common use. It is a most wholesome and palatable article of food.

The experiments have gone far enough to show that the

industry is remunerative. * *   A mature olive grove in good bearing is a fortune.   I feel sure that within twenty-five years this will be one of the most profitable industries of California, and that the demand for pure olive oil and edible fruit in the United States will drive out the adulterated and inferior commercial products.   But California can easily ruin its reputation by adopting the European systems of adulteration.

In regard to soil suitable for the olive, it will live in any soil except a dry and compact or wet one.   It is safe to say that the olive prefers a soft, friable, moderately cool soil, and one rich in lime and potash; a soil that the roots can extend through in all directions, and that will admit of the free circulation of air and moisture.   The olive will flourish wherever its roots will penetrate easily and there is plenty of lime and alkali, such as a loose soil of rocky clay, or sand, of granite or volcanic formation.

I consider the best age at which to plant the olive to be two or three years, for the reason that the one-year old plants and roots are apt to be soft and sappy, and the loss will be much greater in transplanting them from the nursery to the orchard than the older trees which have their roots and stems hardened.

The proper distance at which to plant olive trees is from twenty to thirty feet, as they need a great amount of sun and light to bring the fruit to perfection.   If planted closer, in a few years every other tree will have to be taken up, and that will leave too much vacant space.

The olive should be planted as early in the winter as the land can be suitably prepared, (of course that will depend on how early the rains come), and especially on dry lands they must be planted as early as possible so as to get all the benefit of the winter rains.

It is a great mistake not to take good care of olive trees when they are first planted.   The olive is rather a difficult tree to transplant, and should be given the same care as the orange tree until it gets started; after that there is no fruit tree which will stand so much abuse.

In the first place the ground should be plowed good and deep, say twelve inches, and the clods mashed. The holes should be from eighteen inches to two feet deep, and as wide. As soon as the trees are planted they should be thoroughly irrigated, and again in about a week (if it does not rain), after that in two weeks, and then in a month. After they once get started, give them about the same water you would a deciduous orchard. On dry lands the trees should be given about two pailfuls of water when planted, and the same amount three or four times during the first summer.

KINDS TO PLANT:

The following list has been made up from my own experience for the last eight years and are all varieties I would plant for myself:

For pickles—Regalis, Columella, Polymorpha, Manzanillo.

For oil—Rubra, Pendulina, Uvaria, Nevadillo Blanco, Oblongo.

Oil and pickles—Columella, Pendulina, Mission.

USES OF OLIVE OIL AS A FOOD

Olive oil is an excellent substitute for lard for frying certain articles of food. The use of oil dates back to the patriarchal epoch in Jewish history, from which it has come down almost without change to the Arabs of to-day, who make various kinds of cakes by frying or boiling mixtures of flour or meat in olive oil.

In Spain and Italy, where olive oil enters most generally into the cuisine of the people, it almost entirely replaces butter and lard. It is used for salads, for seasoning all kinds of vegetables, and for frying vegetables, fish and meats.

LOCATIONS FOR GROWING SUPERIOR OLIVES

ELWOOD COOPER, SANTA BARBARA

I have purchased the olives grown in the San Fernando Valley for two or three years. One of the parties had the Old Mission orchard, another had a young orchard grown not far from the Mission. These were the finest and largest olives I have ever seen grown in California. Just across the mountains, north, the olives grown are also very fine. The San Fernando olives I used in making oil, as I did not keep them separate from my own, I, of course, cannot tell how they compared in quantity and quality of oil. I suspect that the trees were irrigated, and hence the larger size of the berries.

It has been stated that by irrigation the fruit is larger, which is important for pickling, but that the crop will not yield more oil; but I am satisfied that with the average rainfall of 17 inches which falls in Santa Barbara, Ventura and Los Angeles Counties, that there is no better olive district on the face of the earth. Of course, there are conditions of heat in certain localities that is not the best for olives, but I have never seen anything on this side of the tunnel that would indicate too much heat for any of our fruits. The olive crops that I bought were in successive years and demonstrated beyond doubt the adaptility of the valley for olive growing.

PICKLES

PICKLING OLIVES
J. L. Howland, Pomona.

For the purpose of pickling, the olives must be picked just as they commence to turn red, about one month before maturity. Each berry should be picked carefully by hand and placed gently in a basket or can of water; they are then placed in vats and covered with water, to which is added a solution of American lye of one pound to every ten gallons of olives. The solution should be drawn off and poured over the olives every hour or so, till the lye has penetrated to the pit—or very nearly so—which can be told by cutting an olive open with a knife. It should be turned to a yellowish color to the pit. The lye should then be drawn off and fresh water poured on the olives, and changed every few hours for the first day. After that it should be changed every twenty-four hours for a week or ten days, till all the lye has been washed out and the olives are perfectly fresh. Then put them in a weak solution of salt for a week, after which time this should be drawn off and a stronger solution of 14 ounces of salt to a gallon of water should be poured over them. The salt should be first dissolved in hot water, then strained and water added till it is of the right strength. The olives should, also, be kept out of the sunlight.

TO CURE OLIVES
Mrs. Flora M. Kimball, National City.

Take 1 ℔ concentrated lye ; 10 gallons olives. Water sufficent to cover them.

Stir them from the bottom daily, and change the lye when the strength seems exhausted. Taste frequently to ascertain when the bitterness is extracted from the fruit. It requires from one to two weeks to accomplish this, as there is a difference in the strength of the lye. When free from the bitter taste add clear water and change it every day until the water runs off clear. Then put it in a weak brine.

PICKLED OLIVES

Mrs. E. F. C. Klokke.

Take the olives from the tree when they are ripe, dark brown or black. Prick each one with a silver fork in three or four places. Place them in fresh water, without salt, for a week, changing the water every twenty-four hours. After that, put them in salt and water, and change the same every forty-eight hours till they are good to eat.

OLIVE PICKLING.

Mrs. Guy Smith, Tustin.

Carefully pick the olives, keeping those of a color to gether. All green, all red, or turning red, or black—small green ones are *not* ripe enough to be good. To four gallons of olives, take one ℔ of concentrated lye and four gallons of water. Dissolve the lye in a small quantity of boiling water. Keep the olives all *under* the water, and stir *several times* each day. Keep the olives in the lye three days, when the bitterness should be out; soak in fresh water four days, changing the water at least twice each day. When no taste of bitterness, or of lye, is left, cover with brine; one pint of salt to one gallon of water. Keep every olive under the brine. Black and ripe olives need more salt to keep them.

PICKLING OLIVES

J. C. M. Rainbow, San Diego, Cal.

Dissolve 1 pound of American concentrated lye in 12 gallons of water, put in the olives and let them stand three days and nights, stirring frequently. Draw off the water and add a new lye of the same strength as the first, and let it stand 3 days, do this the third time, or till the. bitterness is taken out, then soak in fresh water, changing it till free of lye, then place them in brine for use.

Directions for making oil can be found in Spanish Department.

CHOWDER
Mrs. C. G. Dubois.

One peck green tomatoes; 1 dozen green peppers; 2 table-spoons cloves; 4 tablespoons white mustard seed; 3 table-spoons cinnamon; 1 tablespoon black pepper.

Chop the tomatoes fine, sprinkle with salt, and let them stand over night, then press out the juice. Add the peppers chopped, and the horseradish. Cover with weak vinegar. Let it come to a boil, then drain off the liquid, add the spices, pack in jars, and cover with fresh vinegar. Chopped onions can be added, if liked.

CHOW CHOW
Mrs. D. I. Whipple.

Two heads cauliflower; 1 peck green tomatoes; 6 green peppers; 6 large onions; 1 cup salt; 2 quarts vinegar; 1 tea-cup grated horseradish; ½ teacup sugar; 1 teaspoon ground cloves; 1 tea-spoon cinnamon; 1 teaspoon allspice.

Cut the cauliflower; slice the tomatoes, peppers and onions. Sprinkle with salt. Let them stand over night, then drain and chop them. Add vinegar, sugar, horseradish and spices. Stew slowly three hours, then add—½ cup white mustard seed; ½ cup French mustard; ½ package white celery seed.

CHOW CHOW
Mrs. A. L. Frasher.

One large cabbage; 3 large onions; 3 peppers—green; 1 peck green tomatoes; 3 quarts vinegar; 2 cups sugar; 1 cup mustard; 1 tablespoon cloves; 1 tablespoon cinnamon; 1 tablespoon allspice; 3 tablespoons salt.

Chop together tomatoes, peppers and onions. Boil in vinegar, then drain. To 3 quarts of scalding vinegar, add sugar, mustard, salt and spices, pouring it while hot over the chopped cabbage, peppers and onions. The mustard may be omitted, and the tomatoes may be scalded the first time in their own juice.

TOMATO CHOW CHOW
H. G. W.

Half bushel green tomatoes; 1 dozen onions; 1 dozen green peppers; 1 pint salt; 1 pint vinegar.

Chop fine, sprinkle with salt, let stand over night; in the morning, drain off the brine, cover with vinegar, and cook one hour slowly, then drain, and pack the chow chow in a jar. Heat the following ingredients and pour over it when boiling—2 pounds brown sugar, 1 pint vinegar, ½ pint horseradish—grated, 2 tablespoons cinnamon, 1 tablespoon ground cloves, 1 tablespoon allspice, 1 tablespoon pepper. Mix well, and cover immediately. It will keep for months.

TOMATO PICKLE
Mrs. A. D. Hall.

Ten pounds green tomatoes; 3½ pounds brown sugar; 1 tablespoon whole cloves; 1 pint strong vinegar; salt; 3 sticks cinnamon.

Wash and slice the tomatoes, then in a jar put a layer of tomatoes, then a light layer of salt, and so continue until the tomatoes are all used. Put a weight on them and let stand for twenty-four hours. Drain off the brine and rinse with cold water. To the vinegar add the sugar, cloves and cinnamon, and boil for thirty-five minutes. Pour over the tomatoes and let stand for twenty-four hours, then pour off, boil and pour over them again. Do this for three days, then seal in jars.

GREEN TOMATO SOY
Common Sense in the Household.

Two gallons green tomatoes—sliced without peeling; 12 good-sized onions—sliced; 2 quarts vinegar; 1 quart sugar; 1 tablespoon allspice; 1 tablespoon cloves; 2 tablespoons salt; 2 tablespoons ground mustard; 2 tablespoons black pepper.

Mix all together and stew until tender, stirring often—lest they should scorch. Put up in small glass jars.

This is a most useful and pleasant sauce for almost every kind of meat and fish.

GREEN TOMATO HIGDEN
Mrs. Hancock Johnston.

One peck green tomatoes; 12 large onions; ½ pound mustard; 1 ounce cloves; 1 ounce ground ginger; 1 ounce ground pepper; 1 ounce allspice; 1 bottle mixed mustard; 1 pound sugar; 2 soup ladles Howland's olive oil.

The tomatoes should be sliced thin, sprinkled with salt, and allowed to stand twenty-four hours. The onions should be cut very thin. Alternate layers of onion and tomato, with layers of spices. Cover with vinegar, and boil gently three hours.

OLIVE OIL PICKLES
Mrs. W. G. Worsham.

One hundred cucumber pickles, medium size, about as large round as a quarter of a dollar.

Cut in *thin* slices; sprinkle evenly through with salt, and let stand over night. Drain thoroughly, and if too salty, rinse and drain well. Take 1 large coffee cup Howland's olive oil; ¼ ℔ black mustard seed; ¼ ℔ white mustard seed; 1 tablespoon celery salt; 2 teaspoons sugar. Stir all well and mix. Pack closely in jar and cover with cold vinegar. Ready for use in ten days; and will keep without sealing in a cool, dry place.

OIL AND VINEGAR PICKLES
Mrs. M. G. Moore.

One hundred small cucumbers; 1 quart small onions; 8 tablespoons Howland's olive oil; 1 tablespoon celery seed; 1 tablespoon black pepper; salt; vinegar.

Quarter the cucumbers, slice the onions. Place in a colander in alternate layers, with a generous sprinkling of salt on each. Let them stand six hours, under a heavy weight. mix the spices and oil, put in the pickles, cover with cold vinegar and seal.

CUCUMBER PICKLES
Mrs. A. C. St. John.

Cucumbers; salt; vinegar.

Leave a small stem on each cucumber. Place them in a

brine, that will bear an egg, for twenty-four hours. Heat vinegar enough to cover the cucumbers. Heat them a few at a time in the vinegar, pack in a jar, and pour the boiling vinegar over them. These will keep for months.

RIPE CUCUMBER PICKLES, SWEET
Mrs. Hayward.

Ripe cucumbers; 1 pint vinegar; 1 cup sugar; 1 tablespoon ginger; 1 teaspoon mustard; 1 teaspoon cassia; ½ teaspoon mace and nutmeg.

Pare the cucumbers, quarter them lengthwise, remove the seeds, sprinkle with salt, let them stand over night, then drain them in a colander. Boil the sugar, vinegar and spices until clear, then put in the cucumbers and cook, taking out each piece carefully when done. There should be sufficient syrup to cover the cucumbers.

SPICED CUCUMBER PICKLES
Mrs. Kenyon Cox, Long Beach.

One hundred cucumbers; 3 large green peppers; 2 quarts vinegar; 1 tablespoon whole cloves; 1 tablespoon whole allspice; 1 tablespoon white mustard seed; slips of horseradish; alum—size of walnut; ½ cup salt.

Wash the cucumbers; rub them well, and put in a jar with the peppers, salt and alum. Add the spices to the vinegar. Heat to the boiling point and pour over the pickles Cover with cabbage leaves.

CUCUMBER MANGOES—A Kentucky Recipe
Mrs. G. Wiley Wells.

Large cucumbers; brine; cider vinegar; cloves; allspice; ginger root; red pepper; cinnamon; white mustard seed; celery seed; one cup of Howland's olive oil; alum.

Keep the cucumbers in brine that will float an egg, three or four weeks; then soak in water until the salt is well out. Green them in a brass kettle with alum. Cover them with grape leaves, then cover with vinegar. When green, throw them into water until cold. Wipe dry, and put them in vinegar, with oil and spices.

Stuffing for Mangoes.—Two dozen heads cabbage—chopped fine; 1 dozen onions—chopped fine; 1 pound celery seed; 1 pound black mustard seed; 1 pound white mustard seed.

Half pound stick cinnamon; 1 cup horseradish; ½ cup mace; white ginger root; a piece garlic;—all chopped fine and well mixed.

Three quarts chow chow—(Cross & Blackwell's); 1 cup mustard and tumeric—mixed; 1 bottle olive oil—the best.

Mix the spices with the oil. Chop the chow chow and mix it with the mustard and tumeric. Cut a slit in the cucumbers, stuff, tie, and put them in the prepared vinegar. If any stuffing is left, add that also.

CHILI SAUCE
Mrs. Geo. B. Dunham, Moreno

Half pint chopped onions; ½ pint chopped green peppers; ½ cup sugar; 2½ quarts ripe tomatoes, peeled and crushed; 1 tablespoon salt; 1 pt. vinegar.

The chopped onions and peppers should be cooked about one hour (in sufficient water to prevent burning) before adding the tomatoes, then cook till the tomatoes are thoroughly softened. Rub through a sieve, then add the salt and sugar, boil until about half cooked away, then add the vinegar and continue boiling till as thick as desired. This will keep indefinitely without sealing.

CHILI SAUCE
Mrs. W. J. Horner.

Twenty four large, ripe, tomatoes; 12 chili peppers; 2 large onions; 1 tablespoon salt; 1 dessert spoon cinnamon; 1 dessert spoon allspice; 1 dessert spoon ginger; ½ teaspoon cayenne; 1 cup sugar; 1 quart vinegar.

Boil slowly two hours, bottle while hot, and seal.

FRENCH MUSTARD
Alice L. Curtain.

One generous pint vinegar; 3 large onions, chopped fine; 1 teaspoon white pepper; 1 teaspoon salt; 1 tablespoon brown sugar; 3 tablespoons mustard; 1 tablespoon Howland's olive oil or butter.

Cover the chopped onions with the vinegar, let it stand three days, then strain through a coarse cloth, squeezing the onions dry. Mix the mustard smooth, in a little vinegar, add to it the other ingredients and cook until it thickens, stirring, to prevent burning, bottle. Will keep a long time.

AROMATIC MUSTARD

The same as French, with the addition of another tablespoon of sugar, and one teaspoon of ground cinnamon and cloves.

TOMATO CATSUP
Mrs. E. F. Spence.

Three gal. tomato juice; 3 pints vinegar; 9 tablespoons salt; 6 tablespoons black pepper; 1 tablespoon cayenne; 5 tablespoons cloves; 3 tablespoons allspice; 3 tablespoons cinnamon; 3 tablespoons mustard.

Boil until of the usual consistency of catsup.

TOMATO CATSUP
Mrs. John Beckwith.

One gallon peeled tomatoes; 2 tablespoons allspice; 3 tablespoons salt; 3 tablespoons ground mustard; 3 tablespoons black pepper; 6 pods red peppers; 1 quart vinegar.

Cook all the ingredients slowly in the vinegar for three hours, press through a sieve and then simmer down to one-half. Put in bottles and seal while hot.

CUCUMBER CATSUP
A. C. B.

Three doz. large, ripe cucumbers; 1 doz. onions; 1 tablespoon black pepper; 3 pods red peppers; 1 teaspoon ground cloves; mace; allspice; vinegar, salt.

Slice the cucumbers and onions, sprinkle with salt, and let drain over night. In the morning add the black pepper; red pepper, chopped; cloves; mace and allspice, put in jars, pour hot vinegar over, and seal.

PICALILLI
Mrs. Geo. B. Dunham, Moreno.

Three-fourths gallon chopped cabbage; 1½ tablespoons all-spice; 1 gallon chopped green tomatoes; 1½ tablespoons broken mace; 6 tablespoons mustard; 1½ tablespoons cinnamon; 3 tablespoons celery seed; 1 tablespoon cloves; 1 tablespoon black pepper, ground; ½ ℔ sugar; 3 quarts vinegar.

Sprinkle the cabbage and tomatoes with salt, let stand over night. In the morning squeeze lightly in a cheese cloth bag to free the mixture from excess of water.

Place in a granite ware pan, add spices, sugar, and vinegar. The allspice, mace, cinnamon, and cloves should be chopped, not ground. Boil fifteen minutes, stirring. In this climate I have found best to seal.

PICKLED WALNUTS
Mrs. Cameron Thom.

One quart vinegar; 1 ounce black pepper; 1 ounce ginger; 1 ounce eschalots; 1 ounce salt; 1 ounce pepper; 1 ounce mustard seed.

Secure the walnuts before they become woody. Steep them in brine one week, then put them in a kettle with new brine and allow them to simmer gently. Drain and put in a cool place until they become black, (about two days), then put them in the hot pickle of vinegar and spices.

MARTYNIA BEAN PICKLES
Mrs. M. G. Moore.

One gallon beans; 3 pounds brown sugar;

The beans should be tender enough to pierce with your nail. Scald with fresh, weak brine seven times, every other day. Cook them until tender, and proceed as with any other sweet pickle.

GREEN PEPPER PICKLES
Mrs. M. G. Moore.

Peppers; vinegar; cabbage; cucumbers; mace; cloves; cinnamon; mustard.

If the peppers are preferred less pungent, open the top of

each and remove half the seeds. Lay them in a brine of salt and water strong enough to bear an egg. Let them remain in this two weeks, being careful that the brine covers them and to remove the scum as it rises. If they are not yellow at the end of two weeks, let them remain a little longer. When yellow, take them from the brine, wash, and place in a kettle of cold water, cover with grape leaves, set near the fire where they will get hot, but not cooked. When they are greened, drain, pack in jars, and pour over them cold, spiced vinegar. If they are to be stuffed, chop cabbage and cucumbers very fine. Season highly with mace, cloves, cinnamon and mustard seed. Stuff each pepper with this preparation and tie it with a thread.

The bell pepper here is not too fiery for pickling.

PICKLED ONIONS
Mrs. John Beckwith.

Small, white onions; vinegar; unground black pepper; unground allspice.

Peel the onions and put them in dry bottles or jars. Pour over them enough cold vinegar to cover them. To each jar, add two teaspoons of allspice and the same of black pepper. Cover securely and put in a dry place; they will be ready for use in a fortnight.

This is a simple recipe, but very delicious, the onions being nice and crisp.

PICKLED CABBAGE
Mrs. M. G. Moore.

One cabbage; 1 spoonful cloves; 2 spoonfuls allspice; vinegar.

Quarter cabbage as for boiling. Steam until about three-fourths done. Remove from the fire. When cool enough, stick in the cloves. Put in a jar, cover with vinegar, add cinnamon and allspice.

SPICED ONIONS
Mrs. M. G. Moore.

One quart cider vinegar; 2 cups sugar; 1 teaspoon pepper; 1 teaspoon cloves; 1 teaspoon allspice; 1 teaspoon salt.

Slice the onions, pack them in a jar, sprinkling a little salt on each layer. Scald the vinegar with the spices, and pour it over the onions while hot. After twenty-four hours, repeat the scalding of the vinegar. The onions will be ready for use in three or four days.

CANDIES

Mrs. W. T. Carter

The materials used in the home manufacture of the finest quality of so called French candy are neither expensive nor difficult to obtain. Aside from sugar, the basis of all confections, these materials consist chiefly of flavors and colorings. These can be procured from your druggist or grocer. The basis of Cream Nuts, Chocolate Drops, Butter Cups, Cream Bars, Cocoanut Drops and many others is "fondant", or in other words, *granulated sugar creamed.*

TO MAKE FONDANT

Take of granulated sugar 4 pounds; water, 1 quart; cream tartar, ½ teaspoon. Mix the sugar and water together in a granite or porcelain kettle and put over a hot fire; when it comes to a boil, add the cream tartar. Let the syrup cook to the consistency of jelly, keeping the sides of the kettle wiped down with a cloth and cold water. Try the syrup by dropping into a cup of cold water; when it can be rolled into a ball, it is done and should be taken instantly from the fire and the kettle placed in a large vessel of cold water; now flavor with one tablespoon vanilla. While it is still warm—not hot—stir the mass briskly with a wooden spatula or paddle, always stirring in the same direction, until it is perfectly white and of a soft creamy texture. Let the stirring be brisk and uninterrupted in order that the syrup may not granulate. After the sugar *creams*, turn it out on to a sheet of tin, or a cake board and knead as you would dough or bread. When it is worked until perfectly smooth, the cream is ready for use, and should be put into an earthen jar and covered with a damp cotton cloth and closely covered. It will keep for weeks, and can be sliced like butter.

CREAM WALNUTS

Take from the fondant pieces the size wanted and roll them into little balls, then press upon them the half of a walnut kernel until flattened; set on edge to dry. Cream dates, cream figs, and cream almonds are all made in the same way.

CHOCOLATE CREAM DROPS

Balls the size and shape of small birds' eggs are made of the fondant, and when they are hardened (which will be in 10 or 12 hours), they may be dipped in chocolate which has been melted; the vessel containing the melted chocolate must be kept in pan of hot water to prevent hardening. Throw the drops into the melted chocolate, one at a time, and immediately dip them out with a bent wire or a table fork and set them on a slightly buttered paper to dry. When dry, they are ready to be eaten or put into boxes.

FRUIT DROPS of all kinds are made in the same way, except that the fondant must be flavored with the desired fruit flavor, and instead of the chocolate coating, use the fondant which should be colored to represent the fruit: as, red for the strawberry flavor, yellow for lemon or peach, etc. Melt the fondant to be used for a glacé, add the coloring and keep warm; but if it should become too stiff, add carefully a *few drops* of hot water.

WALNUT CREAM BAR

Have ready a quantity of walnuts finely chopped. Melt over a slow fire the desired quantity of fondant; add the walnuts and, if desired, finely sliced citron, chopped raisins, etc. Turn into a shallow pan lined with buttered paper; when cold, cut into bars.

COCOANUT BAR

Proceed in exactly the same manner, except you thicken the melted fondant with dessicated or grated cocoanut.

COCOANUT CAKES OR KISSES

Prepare as for cocoanut cream bars, and while the mixture is hot, spread on buttered paper or tins in cakes the desired

size; these can be varied by the use of different coloring
matter: making some pink, some yellow, some chocolate, etc.
This fondant, which is the basis of all the preceeding candies,
or "bon-bons", is also used to glaze cakes, biscuits, etc., and
is called "French glacé", "sugar icing", "Conservé", etc.
When used for covering cakes, it must be diluted and poured
over them. If for small cakes or biscuits, melt, color, or not,
as you fancy, and dip them in. I have confined my recipes
exclusively to French candies. To go into full details con-
cerning *all kinds* of candies would require too much space.
These I have very often and very successfully made.

TAFFY
Miss Mary Dickson, Petaluma.

Two cups sugar; 1 cup boiling water; ¼ teaspoon cream
tartar; butter the size of a walnut.

Drop into cold water to find when done. Pour into buttered pans and when cool pull until white.

NUT BARS
Mrs. A. W. O'Melveney.

Peanuts, almonds, English walnuts or pecans may be
used for this candy. Prepare the nuts by removing the
inner covering and chopping them. Grease the bottom and
sides of a broad, shallow tin or pan with fresh butter and put
the nuts into it, spreading evenly. Put a pound of granulated sugar, with half a teacup of water and a pinch of cream
tartar into a kettle and boil until thick, but not too brittle.
Pour the syrup over the nuts, and set aside to cool. When
slightly stiff, mark off into wide bars with a sharp knife and
let stand several days when it will become soft and delicious.

POPCORN CANDY
Mrs. A. W. O'Melveney.

Put two cups sugar, 2 tablespoons butter, and a cup of
water into a kettle to boil, until the syrup threads. Mix in
four quarts of popped corn, stir, take from the fire, and stir
until cool. Make into balls or flat cakes.

CREAM CANDY
Miss Mary Dicksou, Petaluma.

Two large coffee cups sugar; ½ cup boiling water; ¼ teaspoon cream tartar; 1 rounding tablespoon glucose.

Cook until, when lifted out, it will stay on the spoon like jelly, when it is done—this will not be long. Remove from the fire and stir until it creams; then mold with the hands. This is good cream for nuts.

HARD CREAM CANDY
Mrs. F. H. Pieper·

Three teacups granulated sugar; 1 cup weak vinegar; 2 teaspoons flavoring.

Boil until it hardens in water. Do not stir while boiling. Pull until white, and cut in sticks or kisses.

NUT TAFFY
Mrs. Vaughn.

Two pints maple syrup; ½ pint water.

Boil, until brittle in cold water. Before taking off, add a tablespoon of vinegar. Line buttered pans with nut kernels and pour taffy over them.

UNCOOKED FRENCH CANDIES
Miss Mary Dicksou, Petaluma

Break the whites of two eggs into a bowl, add three tablespoons cold water; beat just enough to mix the water and egg, and stir in powdered sugar until stiff enough to be molded into shape by the fingers; flavor with any essence you like. This is a very good foundation for walnut, date, fig, chocolate, pineapple or any kind of fruit or nut creams, or may be flavored or colored in any way.

CREAM CANDY
Mrs. A. W. O'Melveuey.

Put four cups granulated sugar with two of water and one of thick cream into a kettle; stir until the sugar dissolves; add a tablespoon butter and a pinch of soda. Let it boil until it is brittle; flavor with lemon or vanilla. Pour into buttered plates and cool quickly. Take up and pull rapidly and evenly until the mass becomes soft and smooth to the touch. Draw out into flat sticks and let stand in a dry place until creamy; then drop in wax or buttered papers, and put away in an air tight box.

OLD-FASHIONED BUTTER SCOTCH
Mrs. A. W. O'Melveney.

Put three pounds of yellow sugar in a kettle with three-fourths pound of butter. Set it over the fire to melt. Let boil until thick, stirring all the time to prevent scorching. Take from the fire, pour into buttered tins or trays; when stiff, mark off into squares; when cold, break apart and wrap in wax paper. Will keep for a long time and improve with age.

LEMON CARAMELS
Mrs. F. H. Pieper.

Two cups white sugar; 2 tablespoons glucose; $\frac{2}{3}$ cup boiling water.

Boil together, stirring all the time, till it snaps in cold water; then add one cup cream, one tablespoon butter, flavor with lemon. Pour out, cut into squares. Cocoanut may be used by sprinkling on before cutting.

NUT CARAMELS
Mrs. F H. Pieper.

Four cups sugar; 3 tablespoons glucose; 1 cup boiling water.

Boil, stirring constantly till it snaps; then add one-half cup butter and one cup cream; boil one minute, add two cups chopped nuts; pour on buttered tins. Can be flavored with vanilla, making vanilla caramels.

KISSES
Mrs. F. H. Pieper.

Whites of 2 eggs into which beat gradually 2 cups powdered sugar and 2 tablespoons corn starch.

Drop on well-buttered paper one teaspoonful to the kiss, (two inches apart), place paper on a tin and bake in a moderate oven, just long enough to turn a little yellow.

CHOCOLATE CARAMELS

Mrs. M. J. Danison.

One cup grated chocolate; 1 cup milk; 1 cup molasses; 1 cup sugar; butter the size of an egg; flavor with vanilla.

Boil until it will harden when dropped in cold water. Put into buttered pans and before it is cold, mark off into square blocks.

PEANUT CANDY

Mrs. H. W. Hayward, St. John, N. B.

Two cups molasses; 1 cup brown sugar; 1 tablespoon butter; 1 tablespoon vinegar.

Boil all together until brittle when dropped in cold water. Put the skinned peanut kernels into buttered pans and when the candy is done, pour over them. Mark into squares while warm.

NUT MACAROONS

One pound powdered sugar; 5 eggs, whites only, unbeaten; 1 pound nuts, chopped fine; 1 tablespoon flour; 2 small teaspoons Cleveland's baking powder.

Weigh the nuts before cracking. Mix the ingredients together and drop from a teaspoon upon buttered paper, on baking tins. Do not put them too near each other. Bake to a light brown in a moderate oven.

COCOANUT DROPS

Mrs. W. H. Hayward, St. John, N. B.

Whites of two eggs beaten to a froth; add gradually 1 small cup sugar; 1 cup cocoanut, and 1 spoonful of flour. Bake five minutes in a quick oven.

MOLASSES TAFFY

Mrs. W. H. Hayward, St. John, N. B.

One cup molasses; 1 cup sugar; piece of butter the size of an egg. Boil hard and test in cold water. When brittle, pour into buttered pans. As it cools, mark in squares with the back of a knife.

SUGAR CANDY
Mrs. Alice Curtain.

Six cups white sugar, 1 cup water; 1 tablespoon butter; 1 cup vinegar; 1 teaspoon soda in a little hot water; 2 teaspoons Watson's vanilla.

Put together the sugar, water, and vinegar, and boil without stirring; test by dropping into cold water; when it snaps in pieces when struck against the side of the cup, it is done. Before removing from the fire, add butter, soda and vanilla.

COCOANUT CANDY
Mrs. F. H. Pieper.

Two and a half cups powdered sugar; 4 cups water; 4 teaspoons vinegar; butter, size of an egg.

Boil all till thick, or about forty-five minutes. Just before removing from fire, stir in 1 cup grated cocoanut. Pour on buttered plates to cool.

SALTED ALMONDS
Miss K. R. Paxton.

Procure, if possible, the finest Jordan almonds, cover 1 quart of them with boiling water; put on stove, stir two or three times from the bottom that they may be blanched evenly. When the skins slip off easily, drain off the water and cover with cold water for about two minutes. Drain, rub off skins and spread on cloths in a warm place to dry, stirring occasionally. Leave in warmth till brittle. Put one scant teaspoon Howland's olive oil in a shallow pan, heat it, put in almonds and stir them until slightly oiled. Place in a moder-oven until a delicate brown, stirring often. Take from oven and sprinkle, while hot, with the finest powdered salt.

ORANGE DROPS
Mrs. W. H. Hayward, St. John, N. B.

Grate rind and squeeze the juice of one orange, add to this a pinch of Tartaric acid; then stir in confectioner's sugar until stiff enough to form into balls the size of small marbles. Substitute lemon for orange and you have delicious lemon drops.

MARSH MALLOWS
Mrs. A. W. O'Melveney.

Dissolve, by heating over a slow fire, eight ounces gum arabic in three gills water; stir and strain. Boil one ounce marsh mallow roots in a little water for half an hour low. Add the gum solution with a half pound of loaf or powdered sugar; let cook slowly and stir constantly until it becomes a thick paste which will roll between the fingers. Add the well beaten whites of two eggs, stir for a minute or two and pour into a pan to cool. Sheets of white paper should be placed in the bottom of the pan with the ends projecting in order to lift out the paste, when it may be cut into little blocks and rolled in powdered sugar.

FIG PASTE
Mrs. A. W. O'Melveney.

Chop into small pieces and boil, one ℔ figs; when soft, press through a sieve. Return to the water in which they were boiled, which should be reduced to one cupful. Stir in three ℔s granulated sugar and cook down slowly, until a thick paste is formed. Pour into pans lined with paper; let cool, take out on paper and cut into sections. Dust with powdered sugar.

PENOCHA CANDY
Mrs. Alice Curtain.

One cup sweet milk; 3 cups brown sugar; 2 ℔s walnuts or as many as you like.

Do not stir. This candy takes a long time to cook. Just before it is done, put in the nuts.

INVALID COOKERY

GRAHAM GEMS
Mrs. T. F. McCamant.

Mix a batter of graham flour and water. Let it stand until sour, the same as for old-fashioned buckwheat cakes. When of the proper consistency, add a little melted suet or butter and salt. While your gem tins are heating, stir in thoroughly ½ teaspoon soda. Bake in a hot oven. The quantity of soda must necessarily be regulated by the sourness of the batter, it is not always alike. "Practice makes perfect."

GRAHAM PANCAKES
Mrs. T. F. McCamant.

Mix the same as for gems, only thinner and leave out the shortening. Sour milk may be used instead of water. A little sugar put in the batter will make the cakes brown nicer. Use the soda of course.

EGG LEMONADE

Beat the white of one fresh egg; the juice of one lemon and a teaspoon of sugar into a glass of water. Pleasant and nourishing for invalids.

BAKED MILK

Put ½ gallon milk in a jar, and cover closely with writing paper, tie over the mouth. Let it stand in a moderate oven 8 or 10 hours. It will then be like cream, and is excellent for invalids; consumptives especially.

REFRESHING DRINK

One ℔ ground flax-seed and 2 lemons boiled together in 4 quarts of water. When cool, sweeten to taste. Good for persons with weak lungs.

CIDER PANADA

Pour ½ cup water over a slice of nice toast; sprinkle lightly with nutmeg and sugar. Then add 4 tablespoons cider. Any fruit cordial may be used if preferred.

QUICK BEEF TEA
Mrs. J. F. Conroy.

Take a round steak (always the best piece of meat for invalids), cut into pieces the size of your hand. Have ready a cup in hot water. Broil your steak quickly on both sides, turning quickly to retain the juice; broiling only enough to start the juice. Squeeze with a lemon squeezer the juice into the hot cup; add a little salt; and carry to the invalid with the cup still in hot water, to prevent coagulation.

STEAK
Mrs. J. F. Conroy.

Scrape from round steak sufficient meat to make a patty the size of a dollar or larger. Have ready a nicely browned piece of toast moistened with hot water. When you broil your patty, broil also pieces of steak, turning every minute. Put the patty on the toast, and squeeze the juice from the steak over it. Serve very hot.

BOILED RICE
Mrs. J. F. Conroy.

Thoroughly wash 1 cup rice; put into plenty of boiling water, and salt it; boil until tender enough to pierce with finger nail. Turn into a colander and hold under water faucet until the water runs through perfectly clear. Put into a clean saucepan, salt to taste. Set in a hot oven for five minutes, shaking occasionally. Grate a little loaf sugar over it and serve immediately. *Never stir rice with a spoon or fork* as it breaks the grains and spoils the flavor.

TO POACH AN EGG
Mrs. J. F. Conroy.

Take fresh, cold water and let it come to a good boil. Take from over the fire and drop an egg into it; from 8 to 10 minutes will be required to cook sufficiently. Never let the water boil after the egg is added as that make it indigestible.

CARAMEL COFFEE
Mrs. Jerome Curtin.

Six cups bran; 6 cups rolled oats; 1 large cup New Orleans molasses.

Rub the ingredients thoroughly with the hands. Brown in the oven very carefully, stirring often; no grinding is necessary. This recipe has been used very successfully in a Sanitorium. One tablespoonful to the person. If desired, clear with white of egg.

OAT MEAL GRUEL
Mrs. A. S. Baldwin.

One cup rolled oats; put in a pint of cold water. With the hands, squeeze the oats in the water three or four times. Then strain the water and boil from one-half to three-quarters of an hour, and you will have a delicious gruel. Add a little salt and sugar, if desired.

EGG RELISH
Mrs. A. S. Baldwin.

Break the egg separately, and beat each part one-half an hour; put together and beat one-quarter hour. Then add one teaspoon fruit cordial and fill the glass with milk.

BLACKBERRY SYRUP

One quart blackberry juice; 2 ℔s granulated sugar; 1 oz. ground cinnamon; ½ oz. ground mace; 3 teaspoons ground cloves.

Boil all together in a porcelain kettle for fifteen minutes; then strain, and seal in glass jars.

MULLED BUTTERMILK
Mrs. Wm. F. Marshall.

One quart buttermilk; 1 scant, rounded tablespoon flour.

Put the buttermilk in a bowl; place in a saucepan of cold water and put over the fire; stir slowly all the time. Mix the flour smooth with a little buttermilk or water; when the buttermilk is a little more than lukewarm, stir in the thickening. Now stir thoroughly, watching closely, and when it looks as if full of fine grains as it runs from the spoon, remove from the fire, take out of the hot water and keep stirring for five or ten minutes.   In order to make this successfully, the buttermilk *must* be fresh, and procured where churning is done frequently so that it shall be good and sweet.

MULLED BUTTERMILK
By an Invalid.

Make a thickening of 1 tablespoon flour and cold butter-milk.   Stir into a pint of boiling buttermilk; stir constantly after putting over the fire.   Add a little allspice and sweeten to taste.   Pour over slices of toast.

JELLY WATER FOR FEVERS
Mrs. J. F. Conroy.

Mix 1 teaspoon cherry or blackberry jelly in a glass of cool water; drink immediately.

ISLAND MOSS JELLY

Soak one handful of moss in water enough to cover, for one hour; then stir it in to a pint of boiling water and simmer until it is dissolved.   Remove from the fire, sweeten to taste and flavor with lemon juice, cinnamon stick or fruit cordial; strain and pour into molds; cool before using.

ISINGLASS JELLY

Put 1 oz. of isinglass and 1 oz. loaf sugar into a gill of cold water, and place over the fire until the isinglass dissolves. Remove the jelly from the fire; add 1 pint rich currant or blackberry cordial, and strain through a flannel jelly bag.

ARROWROOT JELLY
Mrs. J. F. Conroy.

One cup boiling water; 2 heaping teaspoons arrowroot; 2 teaspoons white sugar; 3 tablespoons blackberry cordial. Excellent for children with any bowel trouble.

WEIGHTS AND MEASURES

4 teaspoons of liquid......................... = 1 tablespoon
3   "   " dry material................. = 1   "
1 pt. of milk or water........................ = 1 pound
1 pt. of chopped meat packed solidly... = 1   "
9 large eggs or 10 medium ones............ = 1   "
1 round tablespoon butter.................... = 1 oz.
1 heaping   "   "   .... = 2 oz. or $\frac{1}{4}$ cup
Butter size of an egg........................... = 2 oz. or $\frac{1}{4}$ cup
2 round tablespoons flour, coffee or
    powdered sugar............. .... = 1 oz.
1 tablespoon liquid........... .... = $\frac{1}{2}$ oz.

TABLE OF PROPORTIONS

1 even teaspoon soda and 2 full ones of cream tartar to 1 qt. flour.

3 heaping or 4 even teaspoons baking powder to 1 qt flour.

1 teaspoon soda to one pint of sour milk.

1 teaspoon soda to 1 cup molasses.

1 saltspoon salt to 1 qt. milk for custard.

A pinch of salt or spice is about a saltspoonful.

LIST OF UTENSILS

Needed in Every Well-to-do Family of Six Persons or More.

MISS IDA G. MAYNARD.

EARTHENWARE

1, 2 qt. pitcher.
1, 1 qt. pitcher.
1, 1 pt. pitcher.
2, 6 qt. bowls.
2, 2 qt. bowls.
2, 1 qt. bowls.
2, 1 pt. bowls.
12 cups for popovers.
2 round baking dishes.
2 medium oval platters.
1 blanc mange mold.
2 stone jugs, one each for molasses and vinegar.
1 bean pot.
Glass jars for groceries.
4 plates.
2 stone jars.

IRONWARE

1 frying-pan.
1 griddle.
1, 6 qt. pot.
1 dripping-pan for meat.
1 dripping-pan for fish.
1 meat rack.
1 lemon squeezer.
1 French frying-pan.
1 Scotch bowl.
2 sets gem pans.
1 waffle iron.

1 salamander.
1 pair scales.
6 kitchen knives.
6 kitchen forks.
2 vegetable knives.
1 carving knife.
1 bread knife.
1 palette knife.
1 French vegetable scoop.
1 meat fork.
1 pie fork.
2 mixing spoons.
2 ivory salt spoons.
6 tablespoons.
6 teaspoons.
1 set skewers.
1 set larding needles.
1 pastry wheel.
1 cake turner.
2 cake pans, Russian iron.
3 bread pans, Russian iron.
1 roll pan, Russian iron.
1 chopping knife.

AGATE WARE.

1, 2 qt. double boiler.
1, 4 qt. covered kettle.
1, 2 qt.   "   stewpan.
1, 3 pt.   "   "
1, 3 pt. saucepan.
1, 1 pt.   "

1, 1 qt. saucepan
1 preserve kettle.
1, 2 qt. round pan.
1, 3 qt.   "   "
1 soup kettle.
1 teapot.
1 coffee pot.
2 shallow pie plates.
2 deep pie plates.
1 egg poacher.

WOODENWARE

1 large bread board.
1 small bread board.
1 meat board.
1 large chopping tray.
1 small chopping tray.
1 potato masher.
1 mortar and pestle.
1 potato slicer.
1 gal. ice cream freezer.
1 ice pick.
1 wooden mallet.
2 butter paddles.
1 rolling pin.
Wooden buckets for sugar and meal.

TINWARE

1 large grater.
1 nutmeg grater.
1 apple corer.
1 flour dredge.
1 sugar dredge.
1 salt dredge.
1 pepper box.
1 spice box.
1 grocers' funnel.
1 funnel for liquids.

1 wire broiler for steak.
1 wire broiler for fish.
1 wire broiler for toast.
1 wire potato masher.
1 wire frying-basket.
1 large Dover egg beater.
1 small Dover egg beater.
1 fine wire strainer.
1 flour sifter.
1 soup strainer.
1 colander.
1 wire dish cloth.
2 large dish pans.
1 small dish pan for flour.
1, 4 qt. milk pan.
1, 1 pt. measure.
4, ½ pt. measuring cups.
1 brown bread mold.
1 oval mold.
1 pudding mold.
1 melon mold.
1 jelly mold.
1 doz. small corn cake tins.
1 doz. scalloped tins for cakes.
1 doz. muffin rings.
1 whip churn.
1 large biscuit cutter.
1 small biscuit cutter.
6 vegetable cutters.
2 pattie cutters.
1 ladle.
1 doughnut cutter.
1 long handled skimmer.
1 long-handled dipper.
2 shallow jelly cake pans.
2 deep jelly cake pans.
1 canister for tea.

1 canister for coffee.
1 cake box.
1 bread box.

1 streamer to fit over kettle.
1 fish sheet.
1 ginger-bread sheet.

HINTS

Cold tea is excellent for cleaning grained wood.

The ashes of wheat straw make an excellent silver polish. Apply with soft leather or chamois.

Little bags of unground pepper pinned to hangings and among clothes in wardrobes will keep away moths. Ground black pepper sprinkled plentifully into fur will preserve effectually from moths.

Sprinkle fine meal on grease spots in your carpet. Let it remain several hours and it will have absorbed the grease.

Tar on cotton goods can be removed by spreading clean lard on the part stained, and allowing it to remain for some little time.

Rub ink stains on linen with clean tallow before washing and boiling.

To remove grease from silk goods, wash with ether.

Mrs. W. B. A.

To *set* the color in any cotton or linen goods, dissolve one tablespoon of sugar of lead in a pail of very hot water. This will be sufficient for 10 or 12 yards of goods. Dip thoroughly, seeing that every part is evenly wet. Keep in the water from 20 to 30 minutes. This will not injure the most delicate color, but *fix* it indelibly. If you feel at all doubtful, try a small piece of your goods—dry, then wash in the ordinary way.

Lemon juice and salt will usually remove rust.

To take stains from silk, use 1 part essence of lemon and 5 parts spirits of turpentine. Apply with a linen cloth.

EVENING SUPPERS

Mrs. J. J. Ayers.

One gallon of ice-cream for every twenty guests; one hundred and fifty sandwiches for every hundred people; five chickens and one dozen heads celery to fifty persons; twenty cakes for every hundred persons.

TO PURIFY WATER
Mrs. George Bixby.

Pare a cactus, slice, and lay in bottom of water pitcher.

A little kerosene oil, stirred into starch, will prevent flatirons from sticking.

Kerosene will remove the smoke of coal oil stoves from tins.

Red Seal, Granulated 98 per Cent. Lye or Potash.
P. C. Thomson, 955 Otsego Street, Phil.

For making 10 pounds of hard soap without boiling. Take 5½ pounds of clean grease, free from salt, melt in ordinary pan or kettle, and set aside to cool until lukewarm. While the grease is cooling, take one can of Thomson's Red Seal Lye or Potash, and dissolve the contents in 3½ pints cold water, in an earthen or iron vessel or pan. When the lye or potash is about summer heat, pour it slowly into the grease—not the grease into the lye. Stir until the lye and grease are thoroughly combined and become thick, when the stirring should cease. Set in a cool place till the soap becomes hard.

INDEX

FOOD COMBINATIONS

MENUS AND DECORATIONS

SALADS

SOUPS

EGGS AND CHEESE

BREAD

PUDDINGS AND THEIR SAUCES

PIES

CREAMS AND CUSTARDS

BEVERAGES

SPANISH DEPARTMENT

GERMAN DEPARTMENT

Even a competitor calls Marion Harland's letter April 5, 1893, commending Cleveland's Baking Powder,

A Handsome Tribute.

He tries, however, by inserting old quotations in his advertisement, to make the public believe that this letter of Marion Harland's applied to his own baking powder and not to Cleveland's, as it actually does.

Some people think such advertising is " smart "; others believe it is dishonest.   One thing is sure ; "smart", tricky and deceptive advertising is a poor way to regain lost confidence or lost trade.

Here is Marion Harland's letter in full, with date and signature :

April 5th, 1893.

I wish to say that I use and recommend one and only one baking powder, and that is Cleveland's.

Years ago I did use others and spoke favorably of them at the time.   In preparing the new edition of "Common Sense in the Household," however, I thought it best to substitute baking powder in the recipes instead of cream-of-tartar and soda, and made a careful investigation of the baking powder question.

Finding Cleveland's Baking Powder to be really the best, I recommended it in "Common Sense in the Household," and now use it exclusively.

Brooklyn, N. Y.   *Marion Harland*

1

Jelly, Peach 325
" Pineapple . . . 326
" Plum 326
" Raspberry . . . 323
" " and Currant 323
" Strawberry . . . 323
Jelly, " . . . 323
Marmalade, Orange . . 316
" " . . . 317
" " . . . 318
" " English . 317
Pickled Apricots, sweet . . 329
" Crab Apple . . . 329
" Figs 329
" Limes 330
" Pears, sweet . . 330
Preserved Almonds, Green . 322
" Blackberries . . 318

Preserved Citron . . . 322
" Figs . . . 320
" " . . . 320
" " . . . 321
" Grapes . . 320
" Loquats . . . 321
" Oranges . . . 321
" Orange Peel . . 321
" Peaches . . . 319
" Pears . . . 319
" Quinces . . . 320
" Strawberries . . 319
Spiced Currants . . . 328
" Gooseberries . . 328
" Grapes. . . . 328
" Peaches . . . 328
Stewed Cranberries . . 312
Syrup, Orange Flower . . 318

PICKLES

Olive Culture in California . 332
Olives, Kind to Plant . . 334
" Location for Growing 334
Olive Oil, Used as Food . . 334
Pickles 336
Catsup, Cucumber . . . 343
" Tomato . . . 243
" " . . . 343
Chowder 338
Chow-Chow 338
" 338
" Tomato . . 339
Higden Green Tomato . . 340
Mangoes Cucumbers . . 341
Mustard Aromatic . . . 343
" French . . . 342
Pickles, Cabbage . . ' 345
" Cucumber, ripe, sweet 341
" " spiced . 341

Pickles, Cucumber . . . 340
" Green Pepper . . 344
" Martynia Bean . . 344
" Oil and Vinegar . . 340
" Olive 336
" " 336
" " 337
" " 337
" " 337
" Olive Oil . . . 340
" Onion 345
Picalilli 344
Pickled Tomato . . . 339
" Walnuts . . . 344
Sauce, Chili 342
" " 342
Soy Green Tomato . . . 339
Spiced Onions . . , . 346

CANDIES

Almonds, Salted . . . 353
Bar, Cocoanut 348
" Nut 349

Bar, Walnut Cream . . 348
Butter-Scotch, old-fashioned . 351
Cakes or Kisses, Cocoanut . 348

www.ingramcontent.com/pod-product-compliance
Lightning Source LLC
Chambersburg PA
CBHW030904270326
41929CB00008B/573